Tools for Education Policy Analysis

Alain Mingat
Jee-Peng Tan

with

Shobhana Sosale

THE WORLD BANK

0-8213-5183-4

Library of Congress cataloging-in-publication data has been requested.

Cover design by Drew Fasick
Typesetting by Precision Graphics
POD by LSI

Contents

Tables

Chapter 6

Chapter 9

Chapter 10

Figures

Foreword

For more than 40 years the World Bank has partnered with other donors to support educational development throughout the developing world. Progress has been notable everywhere, including Africa. Yet far too many children do not have the chance to go to school, and far fewer complete the bare minimum of schooling needed to become permanently literate and numerate. The unacceptability of this state of affairs has galvanized governments and the international development community to push for better progress in the coming decades. Thus in 2000 the member states of the United Nations unanimously adopted the Millennium Declaration and agreed to operationalize it by defining eight explicit goals, known collectively as the Millennium Development Goals (MDGs). Two of these goals pertain directly to education: that by 2015 all children will complete a full course of primary schooling and that gender disparities in primary and secondary education will be eliminated, preferably by 2005, and in all levels of education no later than 2015. Progress in education is crucial for achieving the other MDGs, including lower child mortality, better maternal health, more effective control of infectious diseases, and improved management of the environment.

Reaching the MDGs will require rich and poor countries to act together. Rich countries must, among other measures, boost aid to poor countries, while poor countries must pursue the right policies and strengthen governance structures to ensure that all available resources, whether generated domestically or received through foreign aid or debt relief, are used effectively. That schooling outcomes vary enormously for given levels of spending across countries (and across schools) points to the need for better analysis of the sources of differences in performance and the potential direction of more effective policies.

In light of this evolving context, I am very pleased that this volume on analytical tools is now being published. Originally developed by the authors while they were working in the anchor unit of the World Bank's Human Development Network, the concepts and techniques they discuss cover a broad range of issues relevant for policy analysis in education—especially at the primary and secondary levels—in low-income countries. The topics include student flow patterns, unit costs, cost-effectiveness of school inputs, teacher management in terms of policies for recruitment and deployment as well as classroom effectiveness, disparities in educational access and performance, educational technology, and comparative policy analysis. Noteworthy is the authors' highly pedagogical approach in explaining concepts and their application, as exemplified by the many detailed hands-on exercises included in this volume.

I am happy to note too that the methods have been applied in the analytical work currently being done in the World Bank's Africa Region and, to some extent, in other regions of the institution. Collaboration between World Bank staff and counterparts in several African countries has resulted in a growing body of findings that are collected in education status reports for countries such as Benin, Guinea, Madagascar, Mauritania, Niger, and Rwanda.

My hope is that the publication of this volume will encourage more education policy analysts to apply the concepts and methods it contains. If the result is to deepen the knowledge base on which policies are designed, the book will significantly contribute to enhancement of the partnership between rich countries and poor countries in the quest to attain the MDGs.

Birger Fredriksen
Senior Education Advisor
Human Development Department
Africa Region
The World Bank

Acknowledgments

This publication would not have been possible without the input and assistance of many colleagues and friends. We are especially grateful to Shobhana Sosale for encouraging us to publish the learning modules and for shepherding the publication through production. We would also like to thank her, along with Jean-Pierre Jarousse, Esin Sile, and Stella Tamayo, for collaborating on the preparation of the modules. In addition, we thank Robert Prouty and Carolyn Winter, respectively, for their help in refining the modules presented in the chapters "Assessing Policy Options for Teacher Training and Pay" and "Addressing Policy Issues in Girls' Schooling."

Many colleagues at the World Bank—too many to name individually—did us a great service by testing the modules during training courses. In particular, we would like to acknowledge the contribution of various education ministry officials whose participation in the courses allowed us to evaluate the relevance of the modules for policy development. Finally, thanks are due to Anahit Poghosyan and Ruth Utz for the excellent logistical support they provided during the courses.

In the World Bank Office of the Publisher, assistance was provided by Melissa Edeburn and Ilma Kramer.

Introduction

Policymakers in education are responsible for developing a vision and strategy for educational development, and mobilizing support and cooperation for implementing the vision and strategy from a wide range of constituencies. The key parties include government ministries in other sectors and nongovernment providers of services who have influence over the amount of resources available to the sector; teachers and school administrators who do the work of delivering education services; students and their families who are the immediate beneficiaries of the services provided; and employers and the public at large who look to the education system to supply skilled labor and future adults who can contribute to nation building and enrich the country's social and cultural life. Given the diversity of constituencies, conflict of interests among them is inevitable, so it is hard to identify policy choices that best serve the whole country. The way forward typically will involve tradeoffs among competing ends. Managing these tradeoffs well is therefore a key mission for decisionmakers in the education sector.

This learning manual contains a set of analytical tools that can assist in that task. The material does not pretend to address the gamut of issues that are relevant in this regard. Instead, its main focus is on some economic and financial aspects of the education sector, as well as selected features in the arrangements for service delivery. The objective is to show how simple methods can be applied to readily available data to analyze a variety of important policy issues in education. Such quantitative analytical work is feasible and the results can make a significant contribution to policy discussion. Improving factual knowledge about the education system and the constraints on its performance minimizes a potential source of flaws in policy development. Such knowledge also

1

provides a basis for building consensus, thereby attenuating an inherent difficulty in policy implementation. In the education sector, developing a shared understanding of the problems and a strategy to address them is critical for achieving results on the ground because such consensus is a key ingredient for encouraging cooperative and synergistic action by the many parties who typically play a part in implementing policies in education.

To illustrate the difficulty of building consensus in the absence of good analytical work, we need only note that most participants in policy debates have certain a priori views on the strengths and weaknesses of the education system and how best to improve its performance. Those views are necessarily conditioned by each group's vested interests and by the particular circumstances of its contact and experience with the system. As a result it is not surprising to find policy debates at an impasse because the pros and cons of the choices are hard to assess on the basis of purely theoretical arguments. For example, one can argue that multi-grade teaching is a poor pedagogical arrangement that compromises student learning because a child receives only part of a teacher's attention during the school day; but one can argue equally that the arrangement is highly effective because it allows more time for independent work by each student and makes explicit demands on teachers to teach to the diversity of students' learning styles. Without empirical evidence to compare learning outcomes under alternative teaching arrangements, it would be impossible to make much headway in evaluating the validity of either assertion about the effectiveness of multigrade teaching. Admittedly, analytical work alone cannot settle the debate, but it can help reduce the scope given to opinions in reaching a conclusion.

The need for policy-relevant work is not new, but the demand for it has been growing in recent years. This trend coincides with a shift in focus in policy debates, in the education sector as in other sectors, from inputs alone to policy outcomes. Attending to outcomes is consistent with everyone's concern about the ultimate objective of investing in education—to produce literate and numerate citizens and skilled labor in a volume and mix that match demand in the labor market. More accurately, two things should matter: schooling outcomes and the efficiency with which resources are used to produce them.

In line with these concerns, the material in this manual shows how various topics under these rubrics can be analyzed and made relevant to policy discussions. On outcomes, for example, the first module (which is on diagnosing structural weaknesses in education) shows how important it is to go beyond the usual definition of gross or net enrollment ratios, to evaluate progress toward ensuring that all children complete a full course of primary schooling (that being one of the eight Millennium

Development Goals [MDGs] cited in the 2000 United Nations Millennium Declaration). Reaching this goal as well as the other education-related MDGs (such as parity between boys and girls in secondary school enrollments) will require substantial investment of resources. But resources are limited and there are competing demands for their use, so we can expect issues of costs (of which teacher costs are the most important item), cost-effectiveness in service delivery, and management of teachers and classroom pedagogical processes to take on increasing importance. Aspects of these issues are addressed in chapters 2 to 6. In line with the thrust of the MDGs and with countries' expressed interest in reducing poverty, there is growing concern about equity in education, including the chances for girls to go to school. Techniques for analyzing such issues in a policy-relevant manner can be found in chapters 7 and 8. In recognition of the growing incorporation of new pedagogical technology into classroom settings, the authors have included chapter 9 to illustrate the kinds of analyses that might be performed in pursuit of informed policy decisions. Finally, chapter 10 completes the manual by demonstrating techniques for comparative policy analysis, which is especially useful for showing the scope of policy reform based on other countries' experience in managing tradeoffs in the sector.

Originally offered as a series of training workshops for World Bank staff and clients in the education sector, the modules are offered here as a self-contained set, complete with answer sheets to the exercises collected on a CD-ROM, to promote wider sharing of the resource. Where appropriate, the answer sheets provide detailed explanations to justify the numerical results. In most other cases the explanations to the numerical answers are left open to allow space for debate and interpretation from the learner's perspective. A broad cross-section of users, including policymakers, practitioners, researchers, and students, may find this publication useful for their work. Of course, not everyone will use it in the same way. Those who choose to read the materials without performing the exercises will be exposed to ideas on how analytical work on education, particularly analyses relating to cost, finance, and efficiency and equity in resource use, might be structured to inform policy discussion. Such information can help in defining an agenda for analysis to support policy development. Those who read only the completed exercises will improve their understanding of how data and analytical results on the topics addressed can be interpreted in a policy-relevant manner. The greatest benefits are likely to accrue to those who work through the examples systematically before looking up the answers. They will acquire skills to implement similar analysis using country-specific data that are available to them, thereby making a direct and concrete contribution to well-informed policy discussions.

1

Chapter 2: Diagnosing Structural Weaknesses in Education—Implications for Project Selection

Policymakers face two main types of problems in formulating policies in education: setting priorities in the placement of intervention, and choosing the right instruments for intervention. This module contains two problem sets to illustrate how one might approach the first type of problem.

Chapter 3: Analyzing Costs in Education

Cost analysis is a basic ingredient of sector and project work in education. There are many ways to conduct the analysis depending on the specific purpose at hand: for example, focusing on foregone costs and private out-of-pocket schooling expenses is relevant for understanding the demand for schooling; and focusing on institutional cost functions is useful for assessing the cost implications of alternative delivery mechanisms for expanding enrollments. Because the government typically plays a predominant role in education, the cost of public education warrants close scrutiny. This module examines analysis of the recurrent cost of schooling financed by government; it does not deal with issues relating to capital costs, opportunity costs, and direct private costs. In three parts, the module (a) elaborates on the basic concepts and shows how simple manipulations of data that are typically collected by ministries of education and other government agencies can improve knowledge about education costs and the underlying sources of variation; (b) goes beyond the average pattern of costs to consider its variation across schools, with exercises that show how cost data can be linked to schooling outcomes to diagnose possible misallocation of public funds across schools; and (c) offers the opportunity to apply to actual data the techniques and concepts from the first two parts. As in most situations, the available data do not match the theory precisely, and learners are expected to adapt their analyses as appropriate.

Chapter 4: Conducting Cost-Effectiveness Analysis in Education

Among educators and policy analysts alike, opinions vary on the best way to improve schooling outcomes. Because opinions, even those of experts, often are contradictory and inevitably subjective, they offer an unsatisfactory basis for policy or project development. Needed instead are hard facts about the impact of alternative options and their costs. Not only do facts reduce the influence of personal perspectives in policy formulation but they also shift the focus away from inputs and processes

1

alone, toward a focus in which outcomes also matter centrally. The overall purpose of this module is to illustrate the evaluation of costs and their impact through cost-effectiveness analysis. The module is intended to enhance learners' skills in (a) appreciating the policy context for cost-effectiveness; (b) understanding the steps involved in the analysis, including the specification of education production functions and cost analysis; (c) drawing policy conclusions from the results of cost-effectiveness analysis; and (d) applying the concepts of cost-effectiveness in policy or project design.

Chapter 5: Managing Teacher Deployment and Classroom Processes

Education is a complex social undertaking. Although there is no easy way to analyze the many dimensions of policy involved, it is useful to adopt a simple characterization of education as a process involving the allocation and use of available resources to achieve certain educational, social, or economic objectives. This module focuses on policy choices—allocations within each level of education—that affect the operational arrangements in schools and classrooms, taking as a given the macroeconomic pattern of resource allocation across levels of education. Within this context, the management of overall spending at a given level of education or a focus on specific components of spending can be analyzed. This is especially useful in analyzing the cost of teachers, which can make up as much as 95 percent of total spending at the lower levels of education in poor countries; even in rich countries, where spending on other schooling inputs is generally larger, teacher costs seldom fall below 80 percent of total spending.

In most education systems the better-endowed schools tend to produce better results, as measured by such indicators as student achievement and schooling careers, but the pattern is not necessarily a tight one. Some teachers simply are more skillful than others, so they achieve better outcomes despite having fewer resources than other teachers. This result underlines the fact that, although tangible resources may affect schooling outcomes through their impact on the quality of the classroom environment, the interaction between the teacher and his or her pupils also plays an important role. For the policymaker, the management of teachers therefore requires attention to two types of problems: efficiency in the deployment of teachers across schools (or classrooms), and efficiency in teachers' management of the pedagogical process within the classroom. This module addresses the two types of problems. The focus is on illustrating methods for evaluating options to improve management of the system.

1

Chapter 6: Assessing Policy Options for Teacher Training and Pay

Teacher issues undoubtedly are central in educational policy because teacher salaries represent nearly 80 percent of total spending on education and because teachers constitute a crucial input in the quality of education. The importance of teacher-related issues suggests that it is necessary to conduct specific studies to assess relevant policies pertaining to teacher training and pay. It is worthwhile to analyze, separately or in turn, teacher training and teacher pay policies even though some interrelationships exist between the two domains. The purpose of this module is to illustrate the principles, concepts, and methodology and techniques to accomplish the analyses. Techniques include (a) estimating the impact of teacher education and training on student outcomes, (b) estimating the costs associated with changes in inputs, (c) analyzing cost-effectiveness, and (d) assessing the economics of teacher pay.

Chapter 7: Analyzing Equity in Education

Equity in education attracts interest in the realm of public policy for several reasons. In most countries the government subsidizes education, so access to education determines who benefits from the subsidies. Because spending on education represents a substantial share of government budgets, in both industrial and developing countries, the education system is effectively a major conduit for the distribution of public subsidies. Furthermore, education affects people's life chances as adults, in terms of earning capacity as well as social mobility, so equity in educational opportunity influences the future distribution of income, wealth, and status in society. Beyond its economic significance, education is widely viewed as a good in itself, and indeed a basic human right with regard to the lower levels of education. For this reason too, equity in education often is a focus of public policy debate. This module offers some methods for analyzing equity in education. The focus is on four broad approaches: (a) comparison of differences in access to a specific level or type of education across population groups, using such indicators as relative rates of entry, transition, and completion; (b) comparison of benefits from education received by various population groups—public subsidies received as a student and increased earnings (or income) and upward social mobility after the student exits the education system; (c) comparison of who pays for and who benefits from education—distributional implications of financing arrangements in education; and (d) comparison of differences in achievement or learning across students—analysis concerning the education process itself, the influences of pedagogical methods rather than access to education or financial arrangements.

Chapter 8: Addressing Policy Issues in Girls' Schooling

In many developing countries girls have fewer opportunities for schooling than boys do; and where education systems are poorly developed only a tiny proportion of girls receive any schooling at all. These patterns are both inequitable and inefficient. Wide gaps in the opportunities for schooling mean that most girls will grow up without the personal human-capital advantage that most boys will have. They also imply efficiency losses to the extent that poorly educated girls will be less effective than other girls in their future roles as caregivers and managers at home and as workers in the labor force. As a response to these problems, two extreme positions are surprisingly common in the education sector: (a) the do-nothing-specific position and (b) the do-everything-possible position. This module offers some methods for reaching a more rational perspective on girls' schooling. It focuses on three specific analytical issues: (a) diagnosis of the problem, including its locus in the education system; (b) assessment of potential options to address it; and (c) translation of the analysis into a well-justified and locally appropriate implementation strategy. The objective is to demonstrate how relatively simple approaches can yield reasonably persuasive inputs for policy design.

Chapter 9: Performing Economic Analysis of Educational Technology

Educators and others have long recognized the potential of computers and other advanced technology to transform education. Most education systems currently rely on labor-intensive pedagogical processes, typically involving teachers in face-to-face interaction with their students in classroom settings. The process may include textbooks, workbooks, chalk, blackboards, and other pedagogical materials as additional inputs, but the classroom teacher invariably plays a central role. What students learn depends to a large extent on the teacher's personal knowledge of the subject matter, expository technique, and skill in arranging the lessons and exercises.

Electronic media create opportunities for reshaping education in important ways. At their most passive they make it possible to expand the sheer volume of intellectual resources readily available to students in the classroom or at home. But the technology also allows for more focused learning, for example, through educational radio or television broadcasts and computer software, which opens the way for students to receive lessons from off-site expert teachers. As a conduit for information flow, the new educational technology is akin to the printing press in an earlier era. But it can pack far more content into the same space as

1

printed matter, and transmit the material faster and in forms that can be customized to each student's learning needs. The new educational technology entails logistical arrangements that distinguish it from traditional classroom teaching, with important cost implications. The purpose of this module is to illustrate methods for addressing the question: Are the costs of educational technology, including both the initial investment and subsequent recurrent costs, worth the benefits in education outcomes? Two applications of new educational technology are considered: computer-assisted instruction in primary and secondary education, and distance learning in higher education. The exercises rely on hypothetical data because such data allow a sharper focus on the overall analytical concepts. In actual project- or country-specific contexts the analysis would obviously need to be adapted to the explicit policy choices involved as well as to the scope of the available data.

Chapter 10: Conducting Comparative Policy Analysis in Education

Comparative policy analysis offers a simple yet surprisingly insightful approach for gauging the performance of education systems across countries as well as across regions within a country. Although data problems do place limitations on the analysis, the results often remain relevant for policy development. The purpose of this module is to illustrate some approaches for accomplishing the analysis. The module is designed to commence with simple comparisons of education indicators, moving on to adjust the comparisons for differences in economic context across comparators; to incorporate structural aspects of education in the comparisons; and to consider the use of comparative analysis in assessing the relationship between education resources and outcomes. The module culminates with the consolidation of the various pieces of analysis to form an overall assessment of education in the country or region of interest.

Diagnosing Structural Weaknesses in Education—Implications for Project Selection

A Two-Part Module

Alain Mingat and Jee-Peng Tan

Policymakers face two main types of problems in formulating policies in education: setting priorities in the placement of intervention and choosing the right instruments for intervention. This module contains two exercises to illustrate how one might approach the first type of problem.

Part A: Concepts for Analyzing Structural Weaknesses

Exercise 1

This exercise conveys basic concepts for analyzing structural weaknesses in education using student flow profiles (that is, the grade-to-grade percentage of the population enrolled) as a quantitative indicator of the weaknesses. The hypothetical data illustrate both the calculations involved and the implication of the results for project selection.

Basic Data for Country A

Suppose country A has requested international assistance to finance a school construction project to expand opportunities for secondary schooling in rural areas, especially for girls. To see whether the proposal is justified, a first step is to assess the extent to which students in rural areas in fact have lower rates of transition between primary and

Table 2.A.1.1: Gross Enrollment Ratios by Population Group in Country A

Population group		Gross enrollment ratio (%)		Apparent transition rate (%)
		Primary	Secondary	
All groups		75	54	
Girls	Urban	104	85	
	Rural	33	14	
Boys	Urban	108	90	
	Rural	62	30	

secondary education. Consider, therefore, the data in table 2.A.1.1 on gross enrollment ratios by level of education for the population groups in the country. Use the data to compute the apparent transition rates for the various population groups (by dividing the gross enrollment ratios for secondary education by the corresponding ratios for primary education) and enter your results in the last column of the table.

The estimated transition rates may be criticized as being overly crude. One way to improve them is to use the actual numbers of students enrolled in the last grade of primary school and the first grade of lower secondary school. Using the data in table 2.A.1.2, compute the transition rates for each population group, again entering the results in the last column.

What conclusions can you draw from the above calculations? To what extent are they helpful in justifying the proposed project?

Additional Data and Further Analysis

That substantial social disparities exist in country A is clear from the data presented so far. Less clear, however, is that secondary education is the most appropriate locus for addressing the disparities. It is possible that

Table 2.A.1.2: Enrollments in the Last Grade of Primary Education and First Grade of Secondary Education by Population Group in Country A

Population group		Number of students		Apparent transition rate (%)
		Last grade of primary	First grade of secondary	
All groups		93,000	70,000	
Girls	Urban	32,000	28,000	
	Rural	7,000	3,000	
Boys	Urban	35,000	31,000	
	Rural	19,000	8,000	

interventions at earlier points in the system—in preschool or primary education—may be more effective in expanding educational opportunities in rural areas. To make a judgment the analyst must go beyond the data on enrollment ratios and analyze the grade-to-grade pattern of student flow for each social group.

Unlike enrollment ratios the requisite data are not normally found in ready-to-use form; they must be constructed from raw data. Because the data are likely to be available in different formats across countries, there are no hard-and-fast rules for handling them. As an example, suppose the available data permit us to arrange them as in tables 2.A.1.3 to 2.A.1.5. The tables show the total number of students by repetition status and grade (table 2.A.1.3), the age distribution of students at each grade in primary school and the first year of secondary school (table 2.A.1.4), and the population by single years of age over the age range represented by the student population in primary and lower secondary school (table 2.A.1.5).

The data in tables 2.A.1.3 to 2.A.1.5 can be used to construct student flow profiles for boys and girls in urban and rural areas. We proceed by computing in Practice Examples 2.A.1.5.1a to 2.A.1.5.2b (see the CD-ROM that accompanies this book) the enrollment rate at each grade, defined as the number of nonrepeaters at each grade as a percentage of the population in the corresponding age groups. For urban boys in the first grade of primary school, the number of nonrepeaters is

Table 2.A.1.3: Number of Students by Repetition Status and Grade

Population group		Primary 1	Primary 2	Primary 3	Primary 4	Primary 5	Secondary 1
Urban boys	Total	42,000	38,500	36,500	37,000	35,000	31,000
	Nonrepeaters	35,900	35,100	33,800	33,100	32,000	30,000
	Repeaters	6,100	3,400	2,700	3,900	3,000	1,000
Urban girls	Total	37,000	34,800	33,400	32,400	32,000	28,000
	Nonrepeaters	32,900	31,800	31,100	30,000	29,000	27,000
	Repeaters	4,100	3,000	2,300	2,400	3,000	1,000
Rural boys	Total	31,600	25,800	22,500	19,500	19,000	8,000
	Nonrepeaters	28,100	23,600	20,700	18,000	16,500	7,300
	Repeaters	3,500	2,200	1,800	1,500	2,500	700
Rural girls	Total	17,100	14,300	12,000	8,300	7,000	3,000
	Nonrepeaters	15,100	12,900	10,800	7,700	6,200	2,700
	Repeaters	2,000	1,400	1,200	600	800	300
All groups	Total	127,700	113,400	104,400	97,200	93,000	70,000
	Nonrepeaters	112,000	103,400	96,400	88,800	83,700	67,000
	Repeaters	15,700	10,000	8,000	8,400	9,300	3,000

Table 2.A.1.4: Age Distribution of Students and Nonrepeaters by Grade (percentage)

Age (years)	Primary 1		Primary 2		Primary 3		Primary 4		Primary 5		Secondary 1	
	All	NR	All	NR	All	NR	All	NR	All	NR	All	NR
5	5	6										
6	80	91	5	6								
7	10	3	75	84	4	4						
8	5		15	10	65	71	3	3				
9			5		20	20	60	66	2	2		
10					8	5	25	25	53	58		
11					3		10	6	25	26	1	1
12							2		15	14	54	56
13									5		25	24
											20	19

NR Nonrepeaters.

35,900, and the corresponding population is estimated to be 36,630 (= 37,500 × 0.06 + 36,600 × 0.91 + 35,800 × 0.03); thus, the enrollment rate for them is 98 percent. Repeat the procedure at each grade for the four population groups in the table and enter your results in table 2.A.1.6. Try out the calculations manually for a few entries and complete the rest of the computations using the file prepared in Excel software on the CD-ROM. Use your results to plot the estimated enrollment rates against the corresponding grades.

Table 2.A.1.7 is another revealing way to summarize your results. The upper block refers to the absolute difference in enrollment rates for rural girls and boys relative to urban boys at three points in the education

Table 2.A.1.5: School-age Population by Single Years of Age

Age (years)	Urban boys	Urban girls	Rural boys	Rural girls
5	37,500	35,100	41,200	38,700
6	36,600	34,300	40,200	37,800
7	35,800	33,500	39,300	36,900
8	34,900	32,700	38,400	36,100
9	34,100	31,900	37,500	35,200
10	33,300	31,200	36,600	34,400
11	32,500	30,500	35,800	33,600
12	31,700	29,800	35,000	32,800
13	31,100	29,100	34,100	32,000

Table 2.A.1.6: Population, Nonrepeaters, and Enrollment by Grade

Population group		Primary 1	Primary 2	Primary 3	Primary 4	Primary 5	Secondary 1
Urban boys	Nonrepeaters	35,900	35,100	33,800	33,100	32,000	30,000
	Population	36,630					
	Percent enrolled	98					
Urban girls	Nonrepeaters	32,900	31,800	31,100	30,000	29,000	27,000
	Population						
	Percent enrolled						
Rural boys	Nonrepeaters	28,100	23,600	20,700	18,000	16,500	7,300
	Population						
	Percent enrolled						
Rural girls	Nonrepeaters	15,100	12,900	10,800	7,700	6,200	2,700
	Population						
	Percent enrolled						
All groups	Nonrepeaters	112,000	103,400	96,400	88,800	83,700	67,000
	Population						
	Percent enrolled						

system: entry to primary 1, survival to the end of primary schooling, and selection into the first year of secondary school. The absolute gap in enrollment rates in primary 1 would be 58 (= 98 – 40) percentage points for rural girls. Repeat the calculation to complete the rest of the entries in the upper block of the table.

The lower block of table 2.A.1.7 shows the percentage of the contribution to disparities in enrollment rates in secondary 1 arising at various points in the education cycle. Using the procedure described above, you should have calculated that rural girls lag behind urban boys by 86 percentage points in their enrollment rate in secondary 1. Of this gap, 58 percentage points originated in the entry to grade 1,

Table 2.A.1.7: Social Disparities in Enrollment Rates and Their Point of Origin in the Education System

Disparity	Rural girls	Rural boys
Difference in enrollment rates at selected points in the education cycle (relative to urban boys)	58	
Entry to primary 1		
End of primary cycle		
Entry to secondary 1		
Percentage contribution to differences in enrollment rates in secondary 1 (relative to urban boys)	67	
Entry to primary 1		
During primary schooling		
Transition between primary and secondary school		

therefore accounting for 68 percent [= (58/86) × 100] of the total. By the end of primary schooling, the absolute gap between urban boys and rural girls rises to 79 percentage points, implying that 21 percentage points were added during the course of primary schooling. Thus, of the 86-point gap in enrollment ratio in secondary 1, 24 percent [= (21/86) × 100] arose during primary schooling. Follow the same procedure to complete the other entries in the lower block of table 2.A.1.7.

Discuss the implications of your results regarding priorities in the placement of policies to improve educational opportunities in rural areas of country A. How would you use your results in policy dialogue with your counterparts in country A? How would the results influence discussions for future analytical work on education in the country?

Discuss the availability of data to construct student flow profiles in the country you are currently working on and potential data problems that you might encounter in constructing the profiles.

Part B: Extensions of the Basic Concepts

Exercise 2

This exercise builds on the basic concepts of student flow profiles introduced in exercise A, and adds student learning as a further dimension in project selection.

Basic Data for Country B

The education system in country B has the following main features:
- The gross enrollment ratio is estimated at 90 percent at the primary level and 45 percent at the lower secondary level.
- In primary education almost all schools are publicly financed but, as in other countries, schools differ across locations.
- In lower secondary education there are three types of schools: national schools, private schools, and community schools. Most national schools are located in cities and tend to serve better-off communities. These schools charge fees, but the amount is relatively small. Private schools are found in both urban and rural areas but the majority operate in urban areas; they charge higher fees than national schools and tend to cater to students from relatively well-off families who would have attended a national school if they had been admitted. Community schools usually are found in rural areas. As the name suggests, they are the result of communities' own efforts to expand educational opportunities in areas where national schools are too few

Table 2.B.2.8: Selected Characteristics of National, Private, and Community Secondary Schools in Country B

Characteristic	All schools	National	Private	Community
Number of students	400,000	45,000	145,000	210,000
Mean family income (US$)	12,300	17,700	15,500	9,000
Operating cost per student-year (US$)	825	1,400	900	650
Fees per student-year (US$)	584	120	850	500
Pupil-teacher ratio	23	14	22	26
Percentage of teachers with formal certification	65	90	80	50
Average score at national end-of-cycle examination	51.2	60.2	57.1	45.2

2

to meet the demand for secondary education and where the cost of attending a private school is unaffordable for most families. Some data on the three types of schools appear in table 2.B.2.8.

Based on the foregoing data, what is your initial assessment of potential educational priorities in the country? What is your response to the government's request for international assistance to upgrade community schools to a par with national schools and to reduce the private cost of lower secondary education, particularly for children from poor families? In your assessment you may wish to consider such issues as equity in the financing of secondary education, differences in the level and mix of school inputs across types of secondary schools, and student performance. It may be helpful to present your manipulations of the data in a summary table or graph highlighting the differences across types of schools. (The data in the foregoing table are in sheet "Items 1–3" in the Excel file "Str_Weaknesses_Ex2.")

Additional Data and Further Analysis

It is clear from the data provided thus far that community schools lag behind the other two types of secondary schools. We need to ascertain, however, that lower secondary education is the appropriate locus of intervention. To this end, document the grade-to-grade student flow profile using the data in tables 2.B.2.9 to 2.B.2.12 (also in sheet "Item 4" in the Excel file "Str_Weaknesses_Ex2"), and following the same procedure as in "Str_Weaknesses_Ex1." Enter your answers in table 2.B.2.13. For primary schooling, the profiles should be disaggregated by income group. Plot your results and discuss their implications with regard to the placement of intervention to improve secondary outcomes in country B.

Table 2.B.2.9: School-age Population by Single Years of Age and Income Groups (thousands)

Age (years)	All income groups	Income group		
		< 5	5–15	> 15
5	334	67	200	67
6	328	66	196	66
7	322	64	194	64
8	317	63	191	63
9	311	62	187	62
10	306	61	184	61
11	300	60	180	60
12	295	59	177	59
13	290	58	174	58
14	285	57	171	57
15	280	56	168	56
16	275	55	165	55

Incorporating Considerations of Student Learning

Recall from the basic data provided in table 2.B.2.8 that community schools cost only $650 a pupil-year, compared with $1,400 in national schools and $825 in private schools. On average, however, community school students obtain the lowest scores on the national examination at the end of lower secondary school: 45.2, compared with 60.2 in national schools and 51.2 in private schools. If the objective is to improve student

Table 2.B.2.10: Age Distribution of Students by Grade (percentage)

Age (years)	Grade 1	Grade 2	Grade 3	Grade 4	Grade 5	Form 1	Form 2	Form 3
5	5							
6	85	4						
7	10	80	2					
8		10	70	2				
9		6	15	60	1			
10			10	18	50	1		
11			3	12	25	50	1	
12				8	14	28	45	
13					10	12	30	40
14						9	16	35
15							8	20
16								5

Table 2.B.2.11: Number of Students and Repeaters by Grade and Income Group in Primary Education (thousands)

Population group		Grade 1	Grade 2	Grade 3	Grade 4	Grade 5
All income groups	Total	348	317	284	253	229
	Repeaters	30	31	26	22	30
Income < 5	Total	66	54	41	32	26
	Repeaters	7	6	4	4	5
Income 5–15	Total	211	196	176	157	137
	Repeaters	19	21	17	15	19
Income >15	Total	71	67	67	64	66
	Repeaters	4	4	5	3	6

Table 2.B.2.12: Number of Students and Repeaters by Grade and Type of School in Secondary Education (thousands)

Type of school		Form 1	Form 2	Form 3
All types	Total	152	129	119
	Repeaters	16	9	16
National	Total	16	15	14
	Repeaters	1	1	2
Private	Total	52	48	46
	Repeaters	5	3	6
Community	Total	84	66	59
	Repeaters	10	5	8

Table 2.B.2.13: Population, Nonrepeaters, and Enrollment by Grade and Income Group in Primary and Secondary Education (thousands)

Income group	Grade 1	Grade 2	Grade 3	Grade 4	Grade 5	Form 1	Form 2	Form 3
All groups								
Population	328					296		
Nonrepeaters	318					136		
Percent enrolled	97					46		
< 5								
Population	66							
Nonrepeaters	59							
Percent enrolled	90							
5–15								
Population	196							
Nonrepeaters	192							
Percent enrolled	98							
>15								
Population	66							
Nonrepeaters	67							
Percent enrolled	102							

Table 2.B.2.14: Sample Means of Student Performance and Parental Income by School Type

Type of school	Cycle-end score	Incoming score	Parental income
National	57.4	52.0	17.7
Private	57.9	45.4	15.5
Community	45.7	39.4	9.0

learning, it would seem a good idea for the government to channel more resources to community schools. But the data in table 2.B.2.14, which summarizes a data set for 119 schools, suggest that the picture may be more complicated. (The full data set is found in sheet "Item 5–6" in the Excel file "Str_Weaknesses_Ex2.")

Use regression analysis to estimate the relationship between cycle-end score and incoming score, parental income, and type of school. Base your estimate on school-level data for the 119 sample schools in the data set found in worksheet "Item 5–6" in the Excel file "Str_Weaknesses_Ex2." What do your results suggest regarding the appropriate placement of intervention to improve learning outcomes in community schools?

Analyzing Costs in Education

A Three-Part Module

Jean-Pierre Jarousse, Alain Mingat, Stella Tamayo, and Jee-Peng Tan

Analyzing costs is a basic ingredient of sector and project work in education. There are many ways to conduct the analysis, depending on the specific purpose at hand. For example, focusing on foregone costs and private out-of-pocket schooling expenses is relevant for understanding the demand for schooling; and focusing on institutional cost functions is useful for assessing the cost implications of alternative delivery mechanisms for expanding enrollments. Because the government typically plays a predominant role in education, the cost of public education warrants close scrutiny. This module examines analysis of the recurrent cost of schooling financed by the government; it does not deal with issues relating to capital costs, opportunity costs, and direct private costs.

The module has three parts. Part A elaborates on the basic concepts and shows how simple manipulations of data that are typically collected by ministries of education and other government agencies can improve knowledge about education costs and the underlying sources of variation. The problems in part A can be done using a handheld calculator or a computer spreadsheet. If you choose the former option, simply ignore the spreadsheet-related instructions. Part B goes beyond the average pattern of costs to consider its variation across schools. The exercises show how the cost data can be linked to schooling outcomes to diagnose possible misallocation of public funds across schools. The exercise in this part of the module requires the use of a computer. It has been prepared in Excel but you may perform the calculations using another software package. Part C offers an opportunity to apply to actual data the techniques and concepts from the first two parts. As in most situations, the available data do not match theory precisely, and learners are expected to adapt their analysis as appropriate.

The three parts are self-contained in that the exercises can be attempted separately. However, doing them in sequence will yield a more complete understanding of cost analysis. In particular, understanding the underlying sources of cost variation across schools can help in the assessment of potential options for reducing the misallocations of public funds.

This module contains three exercises on the CD-ROM: "Cost_Analysis_Ex1," "Cost_Analysis_Ex2," and "Cost_Analysis_School_Survey."

Part A: Unit Costs Estimation and Analysis

Comparisons of aggregate public spending on education are commonplace. They give us an initial impression of the overall fiscal effort in education. The information is limited, however, and needs to be supplemented with analysis of spending per student (that is, unit costs).

There are basically two ways to compute unit costs, and both should yield consistent results. In one approach, we calculate unit costs simply by dividing aggregate spending, such as that reported in budget documents, by the number of students. Although easy to implement, the method is not without problems. First, the aggregate data may be organized under rubrics that prevent clear-cut attribution of spending by level or type of education. For example, administrative expenditures may appear as one entry, with no distinction by level of education. A second problem is that the aggregate data may be organized according to source of funds or to the structure of the government bureaucracy so that expenditure for a given level of education may appear in several places in the budget, possibly without any detail regarding functional categories. For example, in some countries the budget documents show spending supported by external donors separately, even though for analytical purposes the expenditure may belong in the same category as the government's own spending. In addition, the data may not distinguish between capital investments and recurrent spending, making it difficult to compute meaningful indicators of costs.

Given the potential shortcomings and incompleteness of the foregoing approach, it is useful to check the estimates against those obtained by another approach, namely, by building up from the constituent parts of costs. In this approach the cost components are identified, evaluated, and then aggregated to obtain the desired estimates. In primary education, for example, teachers and pedagogical materials are two of the main components of costs. Thus, we would calculate the unit cost of these components separately, and then add the results together to obtain an estimate of the overall unit cost of primary education. Furthermore, instead of dividing aggregate spending on each component by the number of students, we would use other data to make the estimates. For example, to obtain the unit cost of teacher inputs, we would use data on teacher salaries and pupil–teacher ratios. This approach yields more detailed analysis of education costs and provides a basis for simulating the cost implications of alternative choices in the delivery of education services.

Estimating Unit Costs from Aggregate Data

Definition

We begin by defining unit costs (UC) at each level of education simply as follows:

$$(1) \qquad UC = \frac{B}{N} = \frac{(P + G + W + A)}{N} = \frac{P}{N} + \frac{G}{N} + \frac{W}{N} + \frac{A}{N}$$

where B is aggregate public budget or spending at the indicated level, N is the total number of students, P is the spending on staff remuneration, G is the spending on goods and nonstaff services, W is the spending on student welfare services, and A is the spending on administrative overheads.

Problem 1 From the CD-ROM retrieve the Excel file titled "Cost_Analysis_Ex1" and make sure you are in worksheet 1. Then consider the data in table 3.A.1.1. They have been extracted from budget documents and other statistical reports for a hypothetical country whose per capita income is currently estimated at US$8,900. As is common in the budget documents of most countries, expenditures on administrative overheads are not reported by level of education. The analyst would have to make the breakdown using some reasonable assumption—for example, that the aggregate amount is distributed in proportion to

Table 3.A.1.1: Selected Data on Enrollments and Aggregate Public Spending on Education in a Hypothetical Country

	Primary education	Secondary education	Higher education	Administrative overhead	Aggregate spending
Number of students (millions)	3,206	299	205	n.a.	3,710.0
Recurrent public spending: (million US$)					
Staff remuneration	6,227.2	1,853.9	917.4	680.2	9,678.7
Goods and nonstaff services	185.0	40.0	130.0	225.7	580.7
Student welfare services	40.0	44.0	600.0	0.0	684.0
Total	6,452.2	1,937.9	1,647.4	905.9	10,943.4

n.a. Not applicable.

Table 3.A.1.2: Unit Cost Estimates by Component and Level of Education

Component	Primary education	Secondary education	Higher education
Staff component (US$)			
Goods and nonstaff services component (US$)			
Welfare component (US$)			
Administrative component (US$)			
Overall unit costs (US$)			
As a multiple of unit cost of primary education			
As a percentage of per capita income			
Relative cost index			

Note: The per capita income of the hypothetical country in this example is assumed to be US$8,900.

enrollments (which would imply that administrative costs per student are uniform at all levels), or in proportion to the aggregate salary bill (which would imply that the administrative costs per student are more or less proportional to the recurrent unit cost at each level of education). Go to the next paragraph for further instructions.

Apply equation (1) to the data in table 3.A.1.1 to compute overall unit costs, as well as the unit cost for each component by level of education. For the administrative component, assume that the aggregate amount is distributed across the three levels of education in the same proportion as their salary bills. Enter your results in table 3.A.1.2. Use the third and second rows from the bottom, respectively, to show the unit costs relative to those for primary education and to the country's per capita income. In the last row compute the relative cost index for each level of education. The index is defined as unit costs in the hypothetical country, expressed in terms of per capita income, relative to the average of the corresponding unit costs in comparable countries.[1] Comment briefly on the pattern of unit costs in the country.

Comment on results: _____

_____

_____

_____

_____

Estimating Unit Costs by Adding Up Their Constituent Parts

Definition

The main idea in this approach is that the relationship in equation (1) can be disaggregated into its component parts, as follows:

(2) $$UC_i = \frac{P}{N} + \frac{G}{N} + \frac{W}{N} + \frac{A}{N} = UC_p + UC_g + UC_w + UC_a$$

where UC_i is the cost per student for component i; here the components are for personnel (P), goods and nonstaff services (G), student welfare (W), and administration (A). Conceivably it is possible to identify more categories, but for our purposes, we assume that these are the four main ones.

Each of the four components can be disaggregated further. For example, consider UC_p, which can be expressed as:

(3) $$UC_p = \frac{(ST \bullet NT) + (SNT \bullet NNT)}{N} = UC_{pt} + UC_{pnt}$$

where ST and SNT are, respectively, the average annual salaries (including benefits) of teachers and nonteachers; NT and NNT are, respectively, the number of teachers and nonteachers; and UC_{pt} and UC_{pnt} are, respectively, the cost per student in salaries for teachers and nonteachers.

We can disaggregate UC_{pt} further as follows:

(4) $$UC_{pt} = \frac{(ST \bullet NT)}{N} = ST \bullet \frac{NT}{N} = \frac{ST}{PTR}$$

where PTR is the pupil–teacher ratio. Equation (4) says that the cost per student in terms of teacher inputs can be estimated directly from information about average teacher salaries and the number of students per teacher. Similarly, the unit cost in terms of nonteacher staff inputs can be calculated using data on the average salaries of nonteaching staff and the ratio of students to nonteaching staff.

It is sometimes useful to express UC_{pt} in terms of class size rather than pupil–teacher ratios. We begin with an identity:

(5) $$C = \frac{NT \bullet TH}{PH}$$

where C is the number of classes, NT is the number of teachers, and TH and PH are, respectively, the average weekly hours of instruction given by teachers and received by pupils. At the lower grades of schooling, TH and PH tend to be the same, so the number of classes is typically equal to the number of teachers. At higher grades, however, most education systems begin shifting to subject teaching, with each teacher teaching only certain subjects. Under this arrangement, teachers generally average fewer hours of classroom teaching than the number of hours of instruction received by students. Correspondingly, the number of teachers would exceed the number of classes of students, as equation (5) indicates.

Class size (CS), or the number of students per class, is simply the ratio of the number of students to the number of classes. Using equation (5), we can write it as follows:

(6)
$$CS = \frac{N}{C} = \frac{N}{NT} \bullet \frac{PH}{TH} = PTR \bullet \frac{PH}{TH}$$

(7)
$$UC_{pt} = \frac{ST}{PTR} = \frac{ST}{CS} \bullet \frac{PH}{TH}$$

By combining equations (3) and (6) we obtain another expression that is often very useful in cost analysis. In particular, we express spending per student in terms of teacher salaries, class size, and average number of hours of classroom instruction given by teachers and received by students.

In some settings, the relationships in equations (6) and (7) may not hold exactly because some teachers on the payroll may be on leave and actual teaching workloads may differ from official hours. To allow for these possibilities, we adjust NT by a factor corresponding to the ratio of active teachers on the payroll (a), and TH by a factor corresponding to the ratio of the official workload that teachers effectively carry (e). Using subscripts A and O to denote the actual and official indicators, we can modify equations (5) through (7) as follows:

(5')
$$C_A = \frac{NT \bullet TH_O \bullet a \bullet e}{PH}$$

(6')
$$CS_A = PTR \bullet \frac{PH}{TH_O} \bullet \frac{1}{a \bullet e}$$

(7')
$$UC_{pt} = \frac{ST}{CS_A} \bullet \frac{PH}{TH_O} \bullet \frac{1}{a \bullet e}$$

Problem 2 Go now to worksheet 2 and read the following information carefully. Suppose the data for primary education in table 3.A.1.1 above actually refer to basic education, which is made up of two cycles in this particular country. The first cycle corresponds to what would normally be primary schooling in most other countries, covering grades one through five, whereas the second cycle corre-

Table 3.A.2.3: Number of Students and Teachers in Basic Education in a Hypothetical Country

	Cycle 1	Cycle 2	Both cycles
Number of pupils	2,400,000	806,000	3,206,000
Number of teachers	89,000	50,400	139,400

sponds to lower secondary schooling, covering grades six through eight. The number of students and teachers in the two cycles of education appears in table 3.A.2.3.

The budget documents do not show separate data for primary and lower secondary education. Thus, to obtain estimates of spending and unit costs in the two cycles of education, we would need other information. Consider first the data in table 3.A.2.4, showing teachers' average annual salaries (including benefits and pensions) and their distribution in the two cycles of schooling by qualification. In most public education systems, a teacher's formal qualification, along with years of services, is the main determinant of his or her salary grade. The distribution of teachers by qualification is therefore closely tied to their distribution by salary grade.

Suppose that in addition to data on aggregate spending (table 3.A.1.1), we know the following about spending in cycle 1: (a) aggregate spending on staff remuneration amounts to a total of US$3,435.4 million; (b) transfer payments average US$300 a year per pupil, and 3,200 beneficiaries receive them annually; (c) per-pupil spending on goods and non-staff services is half as high as that in cycle 2 (this detail being obtained through survey data for a sample of schools).

Using the foregoing information, estimate the aggregate and unit cost of each component of input, doing the calculations separately for primary and lower secondary schooling. You may ignore administrative

Table 3.A.2.4: Teacher Salaries and Distribution of Teachers by Qualification in a Hypothetical Country

Qualification	Annual salary (US$)	Percentage distribution of teachers		
		Cycle 1	Cycle 2	Both cycles
A	40,000	23.0	60.0	36.4
B	35,000	45.0	30.0	39.6
C	25,200	32.0	10.0	24.0
All groups	n.a.	100.0	100.0	100.0

n.a. Not applicable.

Table 3.A.2.5: Estimates of Aggregate and Unit Costs in Cycles 1 and 2 of Basic Education in a Hypothetical Country

	Aggregate costs			Unit costs		
Input	Cycle 1	Cycle 2	Total for both cycles	Cycle 1	Cycle 2	Average for both cycles
Teachers						
Nonteachers						
Goods and nonstaff services						
Student welfare services						
All inputs						

overheads in this calculation. Enter your results in table 3.A.2.5 and comment on them.

Comment: _____

_____

_____

_____

_____

_____

Problem 3 Go now to worksheet 3 and read the instructions there. Continuing with the foregoing data, suppose also that pupils in primary education 1 receive 27 hours of classroom instruction weekly, and that all teachers, regardless of salary grade, give 27 hours of classroom instruction weekly. If all of the 89,000 primary school teachers are on active teaching duty, the average class size would be exactly equal to the pupil–teacher ratio, which in this case is 26.97. Because some of the teachers are on leave at one time or another, however, the average class size is somewhat higher—28.35. Estimate the percentage of teachers on the payroll who are on active teaching duty:

(*a*) Percentage of teachers on active teaching duty: _____ percent

In lower secondary education, students also receive 27 hours of classroom instruction weekly, but the official teaching workload of teachers varies according to the following schedule: 14 hours for those in salary grade A; 18 hours for those in salary grade B; and 27 hours for those in salary grade C. On average, the actual class size in cycle 2 is 34. Estimate the official average weekly teaching workload of teachers in this cycle of schooling. If the proportion of inactive teachers is the same as in primary education, estimate the actual average weekly teaching workload of teachers, and express it as a percentage of the official workload:

(b) Official average teaching workload = _____ hours per week

(c) Actual average teaching workload = _____ hours per week

(d) Actual workload as percentage of
official workload = _____ percent

Discuss why official and actual teaching workloads might differ, and suggest options that might lead to a better use of staff resources in lower secondary education:

Comment: _____

_____

_____

_____

_____

3

Problem 4   Go now to worksheet 4 and read the instructions there. To understand the sources of difference in unit costs between primary and lower secondary education, it is useful to express the relationship between them in terms of the key components of costs. Because teachers are the main item of cost, we focus on this component in the problem here. Below, you are asked to express the cost (and its components) of teacher salaries per student in lower secondary education as a multiple of the corresponding items in primary education.

(i)   Referring to your results from table 3.A.2.5, write down the overall unit cost of teacher inputs for lower secondary education (UC_{t2}) as a multiple of the overall unit cost of this input in primary education (UC_{t1}):

(e) $$UC_{t2} = \underline{\hspace{2cm}} \times UC_{t1}$$

(ii) Referring to equation (4) above, decompose your answer in (a) as the product of two components: relative average annual salaries of teachers and the relative pupil–teacher ratios in the two cycles of education. Enter your answers in the following blanks:

(f) $$UC_{t2} = \underline{\hspace{2cm}} \times \underline{\hspace{2cm}} \times UC_{t1}$$

(iii) Referring to equation (6) above, decompose the relative pupil–teacher ratio into three components: relative class sizes, relative average weekly hours of classroom instruction received by students, and relative average weekly hours of classroom instruction actually given by teachers. Enter your answer in the following blanks:

(g) $$UC_{t2} = \underline{\qquad} \times \underline{\qquad} \times \underline{\qquad} \times \underline{\qquad} \times UC_{t1}$$

(iv) Referring to equation (7'), decompose the unit cost of cycle 2 relative to that of cycle 1 into six components: the relative average annual salaries of teachers, the relative class sizes, the relative average weekly hours of classroom instruction received by students, the relative average hours of instruction that teachers are officially supposed to give, the relative share of teachers on active teaching duty, and the relative share of the official workload that teachers actually perform. Enter your results below:

(h) $$UC_{t2} = \underline{\qquad} \times \underline{\qquad} \times \underline{\qquad} \times \underline{\qquad} \times \underline{\qquad} \times \underline{\qquad} \times UC_{t1}$$

From your results in parts (e) to (h) above, comment on the main sources of differences in the unit cost of teacher inputs in the two cycles of education.

Comment: _____

_____

_____

_____

_____

_____

Problem 5 Go to worksheet 5 and read the instructions there. Decomposing unit costs into their components provides a useful basis for making quick simulations of the cost implication of policy changes in education. Below you are asked to perform some of these simulations relating to education in primary education.

(i) Using the data in table 3.A.2.5, and assuming no change in spending per pupil on all nonteacher inputs, calculate the unit cost in cycle 1 if all of the teachers with Qualification C (see table 3.A.2.4) were eligible for an upgrade to Qualification B (for example, they all received in-service training and the paper qualification needed for the upgrade).

(*i*)   Current unit cost   =

         New unit cost   =

         Percentage change in unit cost   =

(ii)   Suppose the government's budget for teacher salaries is fixed. Cal-culate the pupil–teacher ratio that would make it possible to accommodate the foregoing upgrade in teacher qualification within the budget constraint. What practical arrangements might be needed for the indicated change in the pupil–teacher ratio to materialize?

3

(*j*)   Current pupil–teacher ratio   =

         New pupil–teacher ratio   =

(iii) Suppose policymakers would like to know how unit costs differ between urban and rural areas in primary education. The only information available about schooling in urban and rural areas relates to the pupil–teacher ratio: it averages 34.52 in urban areas, and 20.21 in rural areas. Based on this information as well as what you know from previous steps about the composition of education costs and teacher salaries, make a rough estimate of the unit costs in cycle 1 in urban and rural areas. Indicate the assumptions you used and discuss their validity.

(*k*)   Urban unit cost   =

         Rural unit cost   =

(iv)   The average pupil–teacher ratio is currently 26.97, compared with 37.00 ten years ago. If the ratio had been maintained at 37.00, what would have been the aggregate savings in the cost of teachers? (Note that the savings can be interpreted as the implicit cost of the decline in the pupil–teacher ratio.)

(*l*)   Implicit cost of the decline in pupil–teacher ratio: US$_____ million

(v)   To make the above result more meaningful to policymakers it may be useful to express the savings in terms of the loss in enrollment coverage of the system. Assuming that lack of school facilities rather than a weak demand for schooling is the operative constraint on schooling in this context, compute what the enrollment ratio would have been had the pupil–teacher ratio been maintained at 37.00

instead of declining to 26.97. Assume that the current enrollment ratio is 42 percent.

(*m*) Simulated enrollment ratio: _____ percent

Summary and Potential Applications

The foregoing exercises showed two ways of estimating costs, using aggregate budget data as well as data on the components of costs. They reveal how the operational costs of schools depend on policy choices on underlying parameters relating, for example, to class size, teachers' teaching workloads, and salary structures. Comment briefly on how you might apply similar analysis to problems in another country with different circumstances, elaborating on specific topics of interest.

Comment: _____

_____

_____

_____

Part B: Cost Analysis at the School Level

In all education systems the average pattern of costs (which we analyzed in part A of this module) masks disparities across schools. Here we look more closely at these disparities and use the information to assess the efficiency of resource allocation in the education system. The analysis is particularly relevant at the primary and secondary levels where school outputs can be defined simply in terms of student achievement, and schooling careers are reflected in patterns of dropping out, grade repetition, and grade-to-grade survival. To focus attention on the main ideas, we will work with a relatively small hypothetical data set in the exercises below. In the context here, we use the terms "costs" and "resource allocation" interchangeably.

Cost Variation across Schools

We assume that the operational costs of education at individual schools consist of a fixed and a variable component. By definition, the fixed component—for example, the costs a school incurs to maintain a minimal administrative staff and a core teaching staff—does not vary with the size of enrollments. In contrast, the variable component depends on the size of enrollments. To a large extent, teacher salaries belong in the latter category because, as a school enrolls more students, it generally also hires more teachers. We can therefore conceptualize the relationship between a school's total costs (*TC*) and the other parameters—total fixed costs (*TFC*), unit variable costs (*UVC*), and enrollments (*N*)—as follows:

(8) $$TC = TFC + UVC \cdot N$$

When fixed costs are sizable, the overall costs per student tend to be substantially lower in large schools than in small schools. Where the fixed component is modest, however, overall unit costs are more or less constant (and almost the same as *UVC*). The existence of economies of scale in education is therefore an important source of variation in costs across schools.

From a cost perspective, the magnitude of scale economies has implications for optimal school sizes and is an important consideration in decisions to open new schools or consolidate existing ones. In some rural areas, for example, opening a primary school in every village may be too expensive because fixed costs are high, the population base is modest, and enrollments are likely to be low even if all the eligible children in the area attend. In other areas, enrollments are high, fixed costs are modest, and there may be no further cost advantage to expanding beyond current enrollments. In this situation, opening a second school in the same neighborhood may well be justified, in part because excessively large schools may be difficult to manage and may weaken students' sense of belonging—all of which are likely to create conditions detrimental to student learning.

In addition to economies of scale, observed differences in costs across schools also may stem from deliberate government action. For example, the government may pursue a policy of "positive discrimination" whereby extra resources are granted to schools that fulfill certain criteria relating, for example, to geographic location or socioeconomic profile of the student population. The policy may be implicit in the funding decisions, but it is nonetheless useful to examine the link, if any, between a school's endowment of public resources and its characteristics. Furthermore, if information is available on students' incoming and outgoing academic performances, the analysis can be extended to look at the relationship between a school's endowments—in financial resources, staffing profile, and size—and its performance in terms of schooling outcomes.

To form a well-articulated evaluation of the current allocation of resources across schools and to justify a strategy for improvement, we need to take account of both costs and outcomes. The exercise below aims at showing how these two dimensions can be addressed.

Application to Hypothetical Data

Consider the data in table 3.B.1.6 for 16 secondary schools on which we have information for one year on the following variables: total operational costs (*TC*), number of students (*N*), percentage of students from disadvantaged family backgrounds (*DISADV*), and the average scores of students on the national primary school–leaving examination (*PSLE*) and the national secondary school–leaving examination (*SSLE*). Although the data are not ideal—in that the examination results, for example, refer to a cross-section rather than a cohort of students—they correspond to what is often the best that can be found at hand in the context of analyzing the education sector in a country. In the following exercise, you are asked to accomplish the analysis following the steps below.

Table 3.B.1.6: Hypothetical Data Relating to Costs and Performance in 16 Schools

School number	Total operational costs (TC)	Number of students (N)	Percentage of students from disadvantaged families (DISADV)	Average scores of students on national examinations	
				PSLE	SSLE
1	334,000	165	34	53	57
2	1,126,000	927	31	59	66
3	622,000	420	24	56	71
4	421,000	350	26	51	63
5	203,000	112	51	54	59
6	1,018,000	665	23	64	77
7	920,000	845	48	55	69
8	1,290,000	1,050	52	58	75
9	420,000	326	47	54	68
10	182,000	140	34	56	61
11	723,000	510	29	62	78
12	440,000	224	31	57	64
13	912,000	713	29	60	75
14	524,000	532	47	52	57
15	362,000	147	43	59	68
16	368,000	228	39	57	69

PSLE Primary school–leaving examination.

SSLE Secondary school–leaving examination.

Step 1

Retrieve the Excel file named "Cost_Analysis_Ex2" and check that you are in worksheet 1. Use the data in table 3.B.1.6 to plot the relationship between *TC* and *N*, using the space designated as box 1 on the worksheet. If your computer is hooked up to a printer, you may wish to print the graph at this point.

Comment on the graph:

_____

_____

_____

_____

Step 2

Go to worksheet 2 and, using data in table 3.B.2.7, invoke Excel's regression function to estimate the relationship between TC and N. Examine the results on the worksheet and write them down here:

(*a*) $TC =$ _____ + _____ $\times N$

Comment on the results:

_____

_____

_____

_____

_____

Step 3

Go to worksheet 3. Using the above equation, simulate the total cost and unit costs for schools ranging in size from 100 students to 1,100 students, reporting your results in table 3.B.3.8 of the worksheet. Next, plot the estimated relationship between unit costs and size of school in the space designated as box 2 in the worksheet. Again, if your computer is hooked up to a printer, print a copy of the graph here. From your results, can you identify an optimal school size if you are concerned only about costs? Is it reasonable for policy choices regarding school size to be made on this basis alone?

Optimal school size: _____

Comment on the results:

_____

_____

_____

_____

_____

Step 4

Go to worksheet 4. For each of the 16 sample schools shown in table 3.B.4.9, simulate the total operational costs using equation (a) in worksheet 2. For each school, the simulated costs, denoted TC_e in the table, may be interpreted as the cost consistent with the average for a school of the same size. In the same table, compute the difference between TC and TC_e for each sample school, and express the difference as a percentage of TC_e. Plot this percentage against school size in box 3. Briefly comment on the result.

Comment on the graph:

_____

_____

_____

_____

Step 5

Go to worksheet 5. Apply regression analysis to the data in table 3.B.4.9 to assess the relationship between a school's resource endowment and its characteristics. For example, you may wish to examine how the percentage deviation of actual costs from the estimated costs (_DEVIATION_) relates to such variables as the share of disadvantaged students (_DISADV_) and the quality of incoming students (_PSLE_). Review the relationships that you have estimated in table 3.B.5.10 and comment on them:

DEVIATION =

DEVIATION =

DEVIATION =

Comment on the results:

_____

_____

_____

_____

_____

Step 6

Go to worksheet 6. The data in the table are repeated from previous worksheets to facilitate your analysis. Apply regression analysis to the data in table 3.B.6.11 to examine the relationship between the schools' resource endowment and the performance of their students on the secondary school–leaving examination. As before, write down the relationships that you have estimated:

$SSLE =$

$SSLE =$

$SSLE =$

Briefly comment on the results, focusing on their policy implications:

_____

_____

_____

_____

Part C: Application to Actual Data

Using the techniques described in the first two parts of this module, analyze actual data relating to lower secondary schooling in a country where this cycle of schooling lasts three years. For this country, the data came from a survey of schools. Similar data probably can be found in other countries because the survey is typical of those used by ministries of education to collect data when preparing their statistical yearbooks. Often, however, only the aggregated data are published. Access to the school-level data may require a specific request, and special arrangements to code the data may have to be made.

You may proceed in two ways. For those wishing to explore the analysis with minimum help, simply read the sections relating to the data and overview of the problem and then report your results at the end of your work. For those who wish to have more guidance, read these sections, then follow the more detailed instructions. Learners are encouraged to work in groups of two or three to benefit from each other's expertise.

The data for this part of the module have been prepared in Excel, and the analysis can be accomplished using that software. You may do the analysis using another package by first transferring the data from Excel.

Table 3.C.1.12: Names and Definitions of Variables

Variable name	Definition
dcode	Code to indicate province and district of the school
schcode	Unique identification code for each school
students	Number of students
repeatrs	Number of repeaters
form3	Number of students in form 3 (the last year of the lower secondary cycle) in 1993–94
passes3	Number of students who passed the national lower secondary school examination in 1993–94

Qualified teachers[a]

qteach0	Number with less than 8 years of general education + 3 years of TTC training
qteach1	Number with 8 years of general education + 3 years of TTC training
qteach2	Number with 11 years of general education + 1 year of TTC training
qteach3	Number with more than 11 years of general education + 1 year of TTC training

Unqualified teachers[a]

uqteach0	Number with incomplete lower secondary schooling
uqteach1	Number with complete lower secondary schooling
uqteach2	Number with incomplete upper secondary schooling
uqteach3	Number with complete upper secondary schooling
uqteach4	Number with university education
nonteach	Number of nonteaching staff

Region	**Dummy variables with the following values:**
north	1 if school is in the indicated region
south	0 if school is not in the indicated region
east	
west	

a. Qualified teachers are those who have received training in a teachers' training college (TTC); unqualified teachers are those who have not received such training.

The data can be found in the Excel file titled "Cost_Analysis_School_Survey." They refer to school-level information for the population of 329 schools in the system. The variables in the data set and their definitions appear in table 3.C.1.12 here.

In addition to the data on individual schools, there are data on teacher salaries by qualification, as shown in table 3.C.1.13. No data are available on nonpersonnel costs, however. The data gap means that the analysis will concern only the staff costs of lower secondary schooling. In this particular country, all lower secondary schooling is in the public sector.

Overview of the Problem

The main objective of this exercise is to formulate a set of well-justified recommendations to the government on ways to rationalize public spending within lower secondary education. Your analysis should document the current pattern of costs, offer a diagnosis of the issues, and provide simulations of the impact of selected policy changes on the underlying parameters affecting costs.

In documenting the costs, consider first the average costs for the system as a whole, and assess how changes in the pupil–teacher ratio and the distribution of teachers by qualification affect those costs. How does the allocation of teachers—and the implied allocation of public spending—vary, on average, with school size? How much variation is there around the average pattern? Does the geographic location of the school affect the allocation? What policy conclusions emerge from your analysis?

Table 3.C.1.13: Annual Salaries of Teachers and Nonteaching Staff by Qualification[a]

Personnel	Wages and benefits (US$)
Qualified teachers	
qteach0	31,750
qteach1	34,500
qteach2	38,500
qteach3	42,900
Unqualified teachers	
uqteach0	
uqteach1	31,250
uqteach2	31,250
uqteach3	31,250
uqteach4	44,300
Nonteaching staff	31,250

a. Includes wages and benefits.

Beyond analyzing the actual pattern of costs and their financial implications, consider the scope for moving toward a more efficient allocation. For this purpose, costs as well as schooling outcomes should be taken into account. To what extent do well-resourced schools produce better outcome? What characteristics of schools appear to matter in determining outcomes? What policy recommendations can you support with your analysis?

Some Suggestions for Conducting the Analysis

There is, of course, no standard procedure for handling real data, so these instructions are intended merely as signposts to facilitate your analysis. Indeed, because field data are inevitably flawed or incomplete in one way or another, a key challenge for the analyst is to find ways to make the best use of what is available, always keeping in mind the key policy issues to be addressed.

Estimating and Analyzing the Costs

Prepare the data by first estimating for each of the 329 schools the annual public spending on staff (total and per student). You can accomplish this by multiplying the number of teachers in each qualification group by the corresponding salary. Sum up the total spending over all the schools and divide the result by the total number of students to obtain the (weighted) average cost of the system as a whole. Create new variables indicating the total number of teachers and nonteachers at each school.

Examine the cost data using graphs. Worksheet 2 labeled "GRAPHS" has been created for you to use to draw the graphs. In particular, consider the relationship between the number of students in a school and the following variables: the total number of teachers, the total number of nonteaching staff, total staff costs, and staff cost per student. Comment on the graphs.

Comment: _____

_____

_____

_____

_____

_____

Use regression analysis to evaluate the relationship between the numbers of teachers and students. Worksheet 3 labeled "REGRESSIONS" has been created for you to use to jot down the results. Expand the list of regressors to include regional dummies. Are there regional influences on the allocation of teachers across schools? What is your interpretation of the policy implications of your results? Repeat the procedure to evaluate the allocation of nonteachers. Similarly, use regression analysis to examine how the aggregate cost of personnel varies with the size of enrollments, and how unit costs vary with the size of enrollments.[2] Use your results to get a sense of what would be an optimal school size from the cost perspective. Comment on the current distribution of schools in light of this result.

Relating Costs and School Characteristics to Schooling Outcomes

3

Begin by calculating two possible outcome measures for each school: end-of-cycle examination passes as a percentage of the corresponding number of students, and repeaters as a percentage of enrollments. Outcome indicators such as these are of central interest to policymakers because good schools are characterized not so much by the quality of school inputs as by how smooth their students' schooling careers are, and how well the students perform on the national examinations.

Use regression analysis to relate the two outcome indicators to the characteristics of the schools. For this purpose, create new variables such as the pupil–teacher ratio, the pupil–nonteaching staff ratio, qualified teachers as a share of all teachers, and highly qualified teachers as a share of all teachers. Because all of these inputs are captured in the cost data, you also may relate outcomes to per-student spending on personnel, using graphs as well as regression analysis. In all of the above steps you may wish to assess the impact of school size on schooling outcomes, and the existence of regional differences in outcomes.

Forming Your Policy Recommendations

Considering your results from the analyses on costs and schooling outcomes, what can you say about options for rationalizing the allocation of spending in the system? What implications emerge from your analysis regarding strategies for implementing these options and for project design?

Endnotes

1. The unit costs of education, expressed as percentages of per capita income, for selected countries with comparable levels of per capita income are as follows:

Country	Primary education	Secondary education	Higher education
A	28	42	75
B	26	49	68
C	23	52	80
D	31	41	63
E	32	41	64
Average	28	45	70

2. In the second regression, unit costs are estimated as a function of the inverse of enrollments. The two regression specifications should yield approximately equivalent results.

Conducting Cost-Effectiveness Analysis in Education

A Two-Part Module

Alain Mingat and Jee-Peng Tan

Among educators and policy analysts alike, opinions vary on the best way to improve schooling outcomes. Because opinions, even those of experts, often are contradictory and inevitably subjective, they are an unsatisfactory basis for policy or project development. Needed instead are hard facts about the impact of alternative options and their costs. Not only do facts reduce the influence of personal perspectives in policy formulation but they also shift the focus away from inputs and processes alone, toward a situation in which outcomes also matter centrally. The purpose of this training module is to illustrate systematic evaluation of costs and impacts through cost-effectiveness analysis.

Cost-effectiveness analysis is superior to opinion-driven assessments on at least two counts, even though it has some limitations itself. The first advantage is that it compares policy options in terms of their *marginal* impact on outcomes relative to costs. The focus on the margin is relevant because all policy interventions involve incremental changes to an existing situation. For example, regarding policies on teacher qualification at a given cycle of education, the relevant question is not whether better-educated teachers are, on average, more effective than less-educated ones; we already know they are. Rather it is whether it would be worth the costs to expand recruitment of more highly educated teachers and to determine the optimal number of extra years of schooling that the new recruits should possess. Cost-effectiveness analysis can help shed light on both of these issues.

Another advantage of cost-effectiveness analysis is that it helps to sift out some of the ambiguity in policy formulation. To illustrate, consider the use of multigrade teaching in primary school. Some educators oppose such arrangements because they reduce the contact time between a pupil and his or her teacher, which effectively means that the child receives the services of a part-time instead of full-time teacher. They reason that because teachers are a key influence on learning, especially in the early grades, the implied reduction in pupil–teacher contact is almost certainly guaranteed to compromise learning.

Other educators argue, however, that multigrade teaching is likely to achieve precisely the opposite effect. One advantage, they feel, is that it explicitly encourages teachers to customize their teaching to the diverse learning styles and capabilities of pupils in their class. Even when pupils have been grouped by grade and ability, these educators argue that sufficient heterogeneity usually remains for smaller groupings within the same classroom to be helpful. A second advantage, they note, stems from the observation that pupils learn not only by listening to the teacher but also by working on their own and by interacting with peers. Because multigrade teaching inevitably involves allocating time to such activities, these educators argue that again the impact on learning is likely to be positive.

The arguments in favor of and against multigrade teaching are both persuasive, making it difficult for policymakers to decide on a policy. The only way to assess the arguments' validity is to bring into the discussion concrete facts about the impact on learning, recognizing at the same time that cost considerations also matter. Although such facts may ultimately constitute only part of the information that policymakers rely on, at least the facts offer a sound basis for initiating a productive policy debate regarding options for improving education outcomes.

Whether evaluating choices involving specific inputs or process (such as multigrade teaching, preschool education for selected populations, or remedial education for low achievers) or "staple" school inputs (such as teacher training or textbook availability), the analyst needs to identify the potential options for action and then to set priorities among them. Accomplishing these tasks requires three distinct steps in the analysis, as elaborated below.

The first step is to estimate the impact of alternative school inputs or processes on schooling outcomes. The procedure effectively involves relating variability in outcomes to variability in inputs. Because education systems differ in how inputs are used and processes are implemented, the analysis ideally should be context specific. Thus, although the results from studies in other settings are of interest, their relevance is at best limited to that of helpful background information.

The impact analysis generally will identify two types of inputs or processes: those with a positive influence on schooling outcomes and those whose impact is either nil or negative. For inputs in the latter category, the implications clearly are not to expand investments in them, and indeed to reduce investments to the extent possible, especially when the impact is negative. For inputs or processes with a positive influence the policy implications require further documentation. This is because a comparison on the basis of impact size alone ignores the fact that the impact of the inputs or processes being compared almost always entails different investment of resources.

The impact analysis therefore needs to be followed by cost analysis. The task is simple to accomplish using standard cost-analysis procedures. Finally, in the third step the separate analyses of impact and cost are consolidated through the calculation of cost-effectiveness ratios. Such ratios provide a common basis for making comparisons across investment options for improving schooling outcomes.

The module has two parts, with hands-on exercises in each part to illustrate how to perform the three steps in cost-effectiveness analysis. Part A focuses on basic techniques and part B addresses extensions of the techniques.

The CD-ROM contains two Excel files corresponding to the two parts of the module. Each Excel file contains worksheets corresponding to the exercises in the text write-up. For example, the Excel file "Cost_Effectiveness_Ex1" contains the exercises in part A, and the worksheet "problem 1" in that file refers to the first exercise.

The write-up is self-contained in the sense that it has all the information a reader needs to understand and accomplish the exercises. Because the analysis invokes regression estimation, it might be useful for readers unfamiliar with the technique to quickly scan appendix A on regression analysis before beginning on the problems, using the appendix as a reference as needed later on.

To complete the exercises, you need to work at a steady and relatively rapid pace. The first few operations in the Excel worksheets are kept simple to familiarize you with the hands-on approach; steps one and two in problem 1, for example, should require no more than 10 minutes to complete. Throughout the module, Excel procedures have been kept to a minimum to focus attention on the substance; thus most of the exercises have been partially completed and the participant's task is only to fill in the cells colored yellow. You are strongly encouraged to read the text relating to each exercise before attempting the computations.

Part A: Basic Techniques in Cost-Effectiveness Analysis

Suppose you have been asked to make recommendations for improving student learning in primary education. More precisely, your task is to assess whether it would be cost-effective to shift the allocation of resources across school inputs relative to the current allocation; if so, the task is to identify the specific directions for change. The discussion below shows how to conduct the analysis, examining impact analysis and cost analysis in turn, and then combining the two parts in cost-effectiveness analysis.[1]

Impact Analysis

Below we review some basic concepts and issues in impact analysis. If you are familiar with estimating education production functions, you may wish to proceed directly to problem 1; otherwise, simply read on.

Some Concepts and Issues

Given the policy focus of the analysis, the factors explicitly specified in the analysis would need to include features of the schooling context that potentially are open to policy manipulation. These features may include tangible school inputs (such as availability of textbooks) as well as classroom management practices (such as the use of periodic student evaluation). To illustrate the basic techniques we shall focus below on the following attributes of the schooling context: the classroom teacher's formal education and training, the availability of textbooks, and the class size.

To relate these factors to schooling outcomes typically requires regression estimation of what is known in the literature as an "education production function." On the left-hand side of the equation is the schooling outcome of interest, and on the right-hand side is a set of variables representing school inputs and other factors, including students' personal characteristics, that are expected to influence schooling outcomes.[2]

Before proceeding we need to be more specific about defining schooling outcomes. The problem is more complex than it appears at first sight. One reason is that policymakers often are interested in a broad range of outcomes, including achievement against curricula goals in the various subjects as well as pupils' behavior patterns. Even when the problem is simplified by focusing on a single measure of outcome, such as test scores in mathematics, policymakers are concerned not only about a policy's impact on the average pupil but also about its impact across pupils (for example, girls versus boys, high achievers versus low achievers, pupils in urban schools versus those in rural schools, pupils from rich families versus those from poor families, and so forth).

Thus, to be thorough in our analysis, we should define schooling outcomes broadly, focusing not only on average outcomes but also on their distribution. For the immediate purpose of the exercises in part A, however, we will use test scores across the core subjects (mathematics and language arts) as the measure of the schooling outcome of interest, and we will focus on the average scores. In part B we will extend the analysis to show how distributional aspects of schooling outcomes can be addressed.[3]

Another key issue in impact analysis is that the schooling outcomes observed at a given point in time represent the cumulative product of a process over time. The impact of a given set of schooling conditions on outcomes therefore needs to be gauged by how much it has improved the capabilities of the children exposed to it, relative to the initial level at which the children started. In other words, the correct basis for comparison is the value added by the various policy options.

Because our outcome measure here is test scores, it might seem reasonable to compute value added as the difference between initial and outgoing scores, and use the result as the dependent variable in the regression equation. The specification is invalid, however, because neither of the two tests measures student achievement on an absolute scale. For this reason, when estimating the (value-added) impact of alternative policies we typically specify a regression equation in which outgoing test scores (the dependent variable) are regressed against entering test scores among other regressors on the right-hand side. The coefficients on the variables representing school inputs can then be interpreted as the corresponding input's value added to learning outcomes, given a pupil's initial level of learning.

4

Problem 1: Estimating an Education Production Function

Your task here is to estimate an education production function using data pertaining to 301 classes of fourth graders. Insert the CD-ROM into the computer and open the file titled "Cost_Effectiveness_Ex1." Check the bottom of your screen to ensure that you are in the worksheet titled "problem 1." The text in red in the Excel sheet contains abbreviated instructions on how to proceed. Follow the text below to accomplish your analysis.

Table 4.A.1.1: Data on 301 Classes of Fourth Graders

Variable name	Definition	Mean	Standard deviation
OSCORE	Average outgoing test score	106.50	8.45
ISCORE	Average entering test score	100.20	13.89
TED	Class teacher's formal education (years)	10.00	1.23
EX38	Dummy variable = 1 if teacher has between three and eight years of teaching experience; 0 otherwise	0.47	0.50
EXM8	Dummy variable = 1 if teacher has more than eight years of teaching experience; 0 otherwise		
PSTT	Pre-service teacher training received by the teacher (years)		
ISTT	In-service teacher training received by the teacher in past five years (months)	1.40	1.38
CSIZE	Number of pupils in the class	42.50	7.78
TEXTBK	Textbook sets per pupil	0.52	0.33
LOWSES	Percent of pupils in the class from low socioeconomic backgrounds	30.40	14.97

Step 1: Defining the Variables   The worksheet contains data on the 10 variables defined in table 4.A.1.1. Read the definitions and then compute the mean and the standard deviation for the two variables for which the last two columns are blank. After completing this task go on to step 2.

Step 2: Understanding the Data   Your task here is simply to understand the nature of the data, particularly the two variables relating to teacher experience, EX38 and EXM8. They are defined according to the standard definition for dummy variables: they take on the value of one when the specified condition is satisfied, and zero otherwise. Because dummy variables are common in regression estimation, it is important to understand them well. To do so, try to answer the following questions:

(i)   What is the third category of teaching experience not covered by the definition of EX38 and EXM8?

Answer: _____

_____

_____

_____

(ii)   Given the means of EX38 and EXM8, what is the distribution of the full sample of teachers by years of teaching experience?

Answer: _____

_____

_____

_____

(iii) Why is the third category of teaching experience not explicitly included among the regression variables listed in table 4.A.1.1?

Answer: _____

_____

_____

_____

Step 3: Estimating the Regression   Scroll down the Excel sheet until you locate this step on the worksheet. Then follow the instruction printed in red to estimate the following education production function using the data for the 301 classes:

OSCORE = f (ISCORE, TED, EX38, EXM8, PSTT, ISTT, CSIZE, TEXTBK, LOWSES)

After the results appear, follow the rest of the instructions in red and then comment briefly on what they suggest about the impact of the various school inputs on student learning.

Comment: _____

_____

_____

_____

Step 4: Understanding the Regression Results Basing your responses on the regression results, answer the questions below regarding the magnitude of the impact of selected school inputs on outcomes:

(i) Suppose we have two classes of fourth graders who are identical in all respects expect that in one class the teacher is new on the job, and in the other class the teacher has been teaching for five years. By how much higher would OSCORE be in the class taught by the more experienced teacher?

4

Answer: _____

_____

(ii) Suppose now that the two classes are identical in all respects except that one class has 42.5 pupils, and the other class has 41.5 pupils. (i) What is the average difference in OSCORE between the two classes? (ii) What will be the difference if the smaller class becomes even smaller, with only 31.5 pupils?

Answers: _____

_____

(iii) What do you notice about your answers to (a) and (b[i]) above? What do they imply regarding interpretation of the regression coefficients in general? When the coefficient on variable X_1 is bigger than that on X_2 would it be valid to say that X_1 has more impact on OSCORE than does X_2?

Answers: _____

_____

_____

_____

_____

Step 5: Consolidating the Results   To facilitate your work on subsequent problems, the regression results are now organized in the format of table 4.A.1.2, to highlight the marginal unit of input with which each of the regression coefficients is associated. If you are familiar with regression analysis, scan the table quickly now and proceed to the next section on cost analysis; otherwise read the explanation below. We will recall the table for use in the final section on cost-effectiveness analysis.

Consider, for example, the teacher's formal education. Because the variable is measured in years, its coefficient estimate refers to the impact of an extra year of formal education for the class teacher, relative to the sample mean. All other variables in the table that are measured in continuous units have a similar interpretation. The marginal units on the two teacher-experience variables, EX38 and EXM8, are slightly different. Because they were specified as dummy variables, the marginal unit is a change relative to the omitted category of teacher experience (which in our case here is zero to three years). Thus the marginal unit of the EX38 variable is defined as changing from a teacher with only zero to three years of experience to one with three to eight years; and that of the EXM8 variable changes to a teacher with more than eight years of experience.

Table 4.A.1.2: Marginal Impact on Test Scores of Selected School Inputs

School input or characteristic	Marginal unit	Coefficient estimate	Statistical significance
Years of teacher's formal education	One extra year	0.19	n.s.
Years of teaching experience			
Zero to three years	Reference	—	—
Three to eight years	Relative to reference	2.81	***
Eight-plus years	Relative to reference	2.71	***
Years of pre-service teacher training	One extra year	0.22	n.s.
Months of in-service teacher training	One extra month	1.02	***
Number of pupils in the class	One fewer pupil	0.10	**
Textbook-to-pupil ratio	One extra set per pupil	6.00	***
Percent of pupils in class from low SES group	One percentage point drop in share of low SES pupils	0.039	*

— Not applicable.

*Statistically significant at the 10 percent level.

**Statistically significant at the 5 percent level.

***Statistically significant at the 1 percent level.

n.s. Not significant.

SES Socioeconomic status.

Cost Analysis

Because the regression variables in the impact analysis have been measured in different units, a direct comparison of the coefficients is not meaningful. To make valid comparisons we need to translate the physical units of the various inputs into their financial equivalents. The exercises below show how to accomplish the task, focussing on the inputs explicitly included in the impact analysis: teacher's formal education, pre-service teacher training, in-service teacher training, number of pupils per class, and availability of textbooks.[4]

Problem 2: Analyzing Teacher Salaries

In many countries teachers are paid according to a salary scale defined by such factors as teaching experience and formal qualification, with each point on the scale converting to financial amounts at preset rates. Because the pattern of teacher pay is a key influence on the cost of several of the inputs in the impact analysis, we will examine it as a first task in our cost analysis. The relevant data appear in table 4.A.2.3. Scan the table quickly and read on below for further instructions.

Step 1: Performing Some Simple Calculations   Tab over now to the worksheet titled "problem 2," which contains an electronic copy of table 4.A.2.3. As a reference for our cost analysis, we will use the salaries of teachers with 10–12 years of experience for all categories of qualification (even though the actual distribution by experience may differ across categories). Complete the cells colored yellow for teachers with 9 and 11 years of formal education, noting that each salary point currently converts to money terms at the rate of 216 rupees per year per point. We will use the data on salaries in some of the calculations below.

Step 2: Understanding the Data   Basing your responses on the data in the completed table, answer the following questions:

(i)   For teachers with 10 years of formal education, what is the average difference in pay between teachers with 2 years of pre-service teacher training and those with only 1 year?

Answer:

_____

_____

_____

_____

(ii)   Suppose teachers currently have, on average, 10 years of formal schooling and 1 year of pre-service teacher training. If the government were to raise teacher qualification by 1 extra year of pre-service

4

Table 4.A.2.3: Salary Scale of Teachers by Years of Formal Education, Pre-Service Teacher Training, and Teaching Experience

Teaching experience (years)	8 Years of formal education			9 Years of formal education			10 Years of formal education			11 Years of formal education			12 Years of formal education		
	Years of pre-service teacher training			Years of pre-service teacher training			Years of pre-service teacher training			Years of pre-service teacher training			Years of pre-service teacher training		
	0	1	2	0	1	2	0	1	2	0	1	2	0	1	2
0–2	100	118	136	118	136	154	136	154	172	154	172	192	172	192	220
2–4	106	124	142	124	142	160	142	160	178	160	178	198	178	198	226
4–6	112	130	148	130	148	166	148	166	184	166	184	206	184	206	234
6–8	118	136	154	136	154	172	154	172	190	172	190	212	190	212	242
8–10	124	142	160	142	160	178	160	178	196	178	196	220	196	220	248
10–12	130	148	166	148	166	184	166	184	202	184	202	226	202	226	254
12–15	133	154	170	154	170	187	170	187	208	187	208	232	208	232	260
15–20	138	157	174	157	174	192	174	192	214	192	214	236	214	236	264
20–25	140	160	178	160	178	195	178	195	218	195	218	242	218	242	268
25–30	142	164	183	164	183	198	183	198	222	198	222	248	222	248	272
30–35	145	172	188	172	188	202	188	202	226	202	226	252	226	252	278
35+	146	176	190	176	190	204	190	204	230	204	230	258	230	258	284
Reference salary points	130	148	166				166	184	202				202	226	254
Average annual salary (rupees)	28,080	31,968	35,856				35,856	39,744	43,632				43,632	48,816	54,864

Note: At the current conversion rate, each salary point is worth 216 rupees a year.

training, would your answer above represent the only cost associated with the new policy, given the present salary structure?

Answer: **Yes**   **No**

because

Problem 3: Computing Marginal Costs

These costs are defined as those associated with changing a school input by a given unit. Recall that for our purpose the relevant unit for each input is specified in table 4.A.1.2 above (in the final part of the section on impact analysis). The specific procedure for estimating marginal costs depends on the nature of the input, as the steps below show; in all cases we will be evaluating the costs at the sample means of the relevant variables. Follow the instructions in each step to complete the calculations.

Step 1: Computing the Cost of Raising Pre-Service Teacher Qualification   In our example there are two possible ways to raise pre-service teacher qualification: through formal education or through pre-service teacher training. The marginal cost associated with either of these options can be computed using the same procedure.

To continue with the results you obtained in problem 2, we will focus on pre-service teacher training. Your results there indicate that raising teacher qualification by one year of pre-service training relative to the sample mean entails 3,888 rupees a year in incremental salary for the teacher. The increase is only part of the marginal cost, however, because the extra training also requires extra investment in the training itself.

For our purpose we have the following data relating to the cost per participant in a year-long pre-service teacher training program: 18,120 rupees in direct costs (covering the cost of trainers, materials, and so on), and 21,600 rupees in opportunity cost for the trainee.[5] The latter is assumed to be the same as the starting salary of teachers with eight years of formal education and no pre-service training. The total cost therefore amounts to 39,720 rupees per trainee.

Because we expect the training to remain useful for several years, the amount represents the investment cost of the training. It must therefore be annualized before it can be added to the increment in salary to obtain the full marginal cost of increasing pre-service teacher training by one year.

The standard formula for annualizing investment costs is:

$$AC = \frac{IC \cdot k \cdot (1 + k)^n}{(1 + k)^n - 1}$$

where AC is the annualized cost and IC is the investment cost (that is, 39,720 rupees); k is the interest rate (or equivalently, the opportunity cost of capital, usually assumed to be 10 percent a year); and n is the useful lifetime of the investment in years (assumed here to range between 15 and 20 years).

Apply this formula to annualize the investment costs of the year-long teacher training course. For your convenience the data are organized in the top part of table 4.A.3.4. Tab over now to the worksheet titled "problem 3" where you will find a copy of the table. Complete the calculations for $n = 15$ in the yellow cells. Then add the result to the incremental salary associated with raising teacher qualification by one year of pre-service training. The sum is the full marginal cost implied by the policy.

The marginal cost of increasing teacher qualification by one year of formal education is computed in the same way. Complete the calculations and enter your answers in the yellow cells in the column for $n = 15$ years.

Step 2: Computing the Cost of Increasing In-Service Training and Textbook Availability Neither of these inputs entails an increase in teacher salaries, but they both have useful lifetimes exceeding one year. As

Table 4.A.3.4: Computing the Annual Marginal Cost of Increasing Teacher Qualification (rupees per teacher)

Cost components	Investment cost			Annual/ annualized cost	
	Direct cost	Opportunity cost	Total	$n = 20$	$n = 15$
One year of pre-service teacher training					
Pay raise associated with the qualification	—	—	—	3,888	3,888
Cost of the training	18,120	21,600	39,720	4,665	
Total marginal cost	—	—	—	8,553	
One year of formal education					
Pay raise associated with the qualification	—	—	—	3,888	
Cost of the education	6,500	21,600	28,100	3,301	3,694
Total marginal cost	—	—	—	7,189	

— Not applicable.

Note: With reference to the formula for annualizing investment cost, the total cost of the year of training or education corresponds to IC, and the useful lifetime of the year of training or schooling corresponds to n. We assume an interest rate of 10 percent a year, so that the value of k in the equation is 0.10.

4

before, the costs of these inputs represent investment outlays that need to be annualized to render them comparable to other costs in our analysis.

The relevant data appear in table 4.A.3.5. Locate them by scrolling down your worksheet. Note that the opportunity costs of a month-long in-service course for teachers are estimated at one-twelfth of the salary at the sample mean teacher qualification (that is, 10 years of formal education and 1 year of pre-service training). This works out to be 3,312 rupees per trainee based on the salary scale in table 4.A.3.5. We make two alternative assumptions for the durability of in-service teacher training and textbooks, ranging, respectively, from 5 to 10 years and from 3 to 5 years. In the interest of saving time, the annualized costs of both inputs corresponding to these assumptions have been completed for you. Simply review the results in the table and then proceed to the next step.

Step 3: Computing the Marginal Cost of Changing Class Size
Although class size is not a tangible school input, it does reflect the amount of pedagogical resources effectively available to each pupil in a class. This is because inputs such as a teacher's time, pedagogical materials, and the classroom building itself are shared across pupils in the class. An increase in the number of pupils in the class implies spreading the shared resources over more pupils, and therefore corresponds to a decline in the resources available per pupil. Class size and resource availability per pupil are therefore inversely related.

Assuming that we have one teacher per class, we can express the resource availability per pupil using the following equation:

$$\text{Resources per pupil} = \frac{\text{Teacher salary}}{\text{Class size}} + \text{Materials per pupil}$$

Table 4.A.3.5: Annualized Cost of Increasing In-Service Teacher Training and Textbooks Availability

Cost component	Cost per unit (rupees)			Assumed useful lifetime, n	Annualized costs (rupees)
	Direct costs	Opportunity costs	Total costs		
One month of in-service training per trainee	1,500	3,312	4,812	10	783
				5	1,269
Per set of textbooks	110	—	110	5	29
				3	44

— Not applicable.

Note: With reference to the formula for annualizing investment cost, the total cost of the year of training or education corresponds to *IC*; and the useful lifetime of the year of training or schooling corresponds to *n*. We assume an interest rate of 10 percent a year, so that the value of *k* in the equation is 0.10.

Furthermore, assuming that teacher costs amount to about 95 percent of total unit costs, we can simplify the equation to:

$$\text{Resources per pupil} = \frac{\text{Teacher salary}}{\text{Class size}} \times \frac{1}{0.95}$$

We can use this equation to estimate resources per pupil for any class size and level of teacher salary. For our purpose we will assume class size to be at the sample mean of 42.5 pupils per class, and vary teacher salaries from the lowest to the highest point across categories of teacher qualification, the former corresponding to the salary of teachers with 8 years of formal education and no pre-service teacher training, and the latter corresponding to that of teachers with 12 years of formal education and 2 years of pre-service training.

To compute the marginal cost of reducing the class size by one pupil below the sample mean, we simply calculate the unit costs corresponding to 42.5 and 41.5 pupils for the assumed level of teacher salary, and take the difference between the resulting estimates. Table 4.A.3.6 has been arranged to facilitate your calculation, and the upper-bound column has been completed as an example. Locate the table now by scrolling down your current worksheet and complete the cells colored yellow.

Step 4: Consolidating the Cost Analysis   As a final step in this analysis we consolidate the foregoing marginal cost estimates in table 4.A.3.7 below. In preparation for the cost-effectiveness analysis we also compute the marginal cost per pupil of manipulating the various school inputs. Scroll down the worksheet to locate the table and follow the instructions printed in red to complete the table. Take a moment to review all of the entries and then proceed to the next section on cost-effectiveness analysis.

Cost-Effectiveness Analysis

In this section we bring together the impact and cost analyses to evaluate the cost-effectiveness of the various inputs. To facilitate the task, we

Table 4.A.3.6: Marginal Cost of Reducing Class Size

Cost component	Alternative assumptions or estimates	
	Lower bound	Upper bound
Teacher's annual salary (rupees)	28,080	54,864
Unit cost (rupees per pupil)		
With class size of 42.5 pupils		1,359
With class size of (42.5–1) pupils		1,392
Marginal cost of expanding class size by one pupil (rupees)		33

Note: For our sample the mean class size is 42.5 pupils.

Table 4.A.3.7: Marginal Cost of Changing the Various School Inputs (rupees)

School input	Marginal unit	Cost of marginal unit[a]		Marginal cost per pupil[b]	
		Lower bound	Upper bound	Lower bound	Upper bound
Teacher's formal education (years)	One extra year per teacher	7,189	7,582	120	303
Pre-service teacher training (years)	One extra year per teacher				
In-service teacher training (months)	One extra month per teacher	783	1,269	13	51
Number of pupils in the class	One fewer pupil in the class	17	33	17	33
Percent of pupils in class with a textbook set	One extra set per pupil	29	44	29	44

a. The upper and lower bounds correspond to alternative assumptions about the useful lifetime of the investment. For class size they correspond to the extreme ends on the teacher salary scale.

b. For the first three inputs, the upper and lower bounds correspond, respectively, to classes of 25 and 60—these being the extremes in the spectrum of class size in the sample.

4

repeat in table 4.A.4.8 the estimates of marginal impact and marginal costs from the preceding sections. For completeness in the analysis, we also repeat impact estimates for two other factors: teaching experience and share of pupils from disadvantaged socioeconomic backgrounds.

Tab over now to the worksheet titled "problem 4" where you will find a copy of the table. Follow the instructions printed in red in the Excel sheet and then go on to the problem below to evaluate the policy implications of your results.

Problem 4: Evaluating the Policy Implications

Basing your responses on the data in table 4.A.4.8, try to answer the following questions:

(i)   For which input or inputs are there clear-cut policy implications?

Answer:

_____

_____

_____

_____

_____

Table 4.A.4.8: Comparing Cost-Effectiveness across School Inputs

Input/factor	Marginal impact on test scores (points)		Marginal cost per pupil (rupees)		Impact per unit cost (points per rupees)	
	Coefficient estimate	t-Statistics	Lower bound	Upper bound	Lower bound	Upper bound
Teacher's formal education	0.192	n.s.	120	303	0.6	1.6
Pre-service teacher training	0.221	n.s.	143	364	0.6	1.6
In-service teacher training	1.015	***	13	51	20.0	77.8
Number of pupils in class	0.101	**	17	33	3.1	6.0
Textbook availability	6.000	***	29	44	135.6	206.8

Teacher's teaching experience

Zero to three years (reference)	—	—			—	—
Three to eight years	2.807	***				
Eight-plus years	2.713	***				
Percent of low SES pupils in class	0.039	*			—	—

— Not applicable.

*Statistically significant at the 10 percent level.

**Statistically significant at the 5 percent level.

***Statistically significant at the 1 percent level.

n.s. Not significant.

SES Socioeconomic status.

(ii) Regarding teacher qualification and training, what overall policy conclusions would you draw from the results?

Answer:

_____

_____

_____

_____

_____

(iii) Note the coefficient estimates on the teacher experience variables in the table. What do they suggest about the effectiveness of pre-service teacher training as it is currently designed? In what ways would it probably be cost-effective to modify the design of such training?

Answers:

_____

_____

_____

_____

(iv) What does the cost-effectiveness ratio for in-service teacher training suggest regarding policies involving the use of this input to improve student learning?

Answer:

_____

_____

_____

_____

(v) Regarding class size, what overall policy conclusions do your results suggest?

Answer:

_____

_____

_____

_____

(vi) Note the coefficient estimate on the "share of low socioeconomic status (SES) pupils" variable. Its magnitude implies that an increase in the share of low SES pupils from 20 percent to 60 percent would cause test scores to drop by 1.56 points [= $0.039 \times (60 - 20)$]. Because the coefficient on the class size variable is estimated to be -0.101, a decline in class size can compensate for the adverse effects of having a high concentration of low SES pupils in the class. By how much should class size be reduced to offset the drop of 1.56 points in test scores? What does this calculation imply about targeting reduction in class size as a policy lever?

Answers:

_____

_____

_____

_____

Part B: Extensions of the Basic Techniques

We now extend the basic tools to address policy design issues in two situations commonly encountered in education. These relate to the existence of diminishing marginal returns in the impact of school inputs, and the likelihood of differences in the impact of policies across population groups. The analytical procedure involves the same generic steps as before: impact analysis, cost analysis, and consolidation of the two parts to compare cost-effectiveness across inputs. Implementing the analysis requires some extensions to the basic tools in part A, however, particularly in conducting the impact analysis. They are the focus of the exercises below.

The Policy Context

4

The need to go beyond the basic tools can be illustrated by a specific example. Suppose that in country A about 25 percent of the children currently attend preschool programs lasting one, two, or three years. The ministry of education is considering expansion of preschool education for several reasons. One reason stems from the general observation that the earlier children start formal schooling, the better they seem to perform in primary school. Equally important is the observation that learning difficulties in the initial grades currently cause many children in the minority ethnic group to drop out. A major source of difficulty for many of the dropouts is that the language of instruction in school is not their home language. Under these circumstances the ministry of education believes that expanding preschool education will help reduce pupils' language difficulties in first grade, and therefore help reduce learning disparities across ethnic groups and generally raise overall student achievement.

Is the ministry's plan to expand preschool education a good one? If so, should it focus on programs lasting one year, two years, or three years? And should the programs be targeted at children from the minority ethnic group only or should the programs be provided to all children? Addressing these issues in the design of the policy requires careful documentation of the following questions:

- What is the impact of preschool education on student learning in grade one?
- How does its impact differ across ethnic groups?
- To what extent does the impact of preschool differ according to the duration of the program?
- Which design of preschool programs would be cost-effective relative to other interventions to improve schooling outcomes?

The methods of cost-effectiveness analysis in part A can address only the first of these four questions. To answer the other questions we need to modify the impact analysis. The extensions discussed below generally are applicable for situations in which the impact of an input is likely to vary according to the intensity with which it is used, and in which its impact may differ across population groups.

Data for the Analysis

Suppose the available data relate to a sample of 4,043 first graders from 126 classes. The sample contains a good cross-section of pupils from both ethnic groups, and within each group there is sufficient variation across pupils in terms of preschool experience and the characteristics of their schooling environment in grade one. For each pupil, information also is available on his or her score on an achievement test administered at the end of grade one, and on his or her personal and family background. The data for the analysis appear in table 4.B.1.9, along with the variable definition, mean, and standard deviation.

Take a moment now to review the table. Note that preschool experience has been defined with two alternative variables: years of preschool (YRSPRES) is a continuous variable, and preschool (PRESCH) is a dummy variable. Note also that teacher qualification has been defined as three mutually exclusive dummy variables. The one corresponding to the lowest level of qualification, category C (TEACH-C), is the reference category.

Impact Analysis

Recall that the general procedure is to estimate a regression equation with test scores on the left-hand side (the dependent variable) and a set of regressors on the right-hand side representing a pupil's personal and family background and the characteristics of his or her learning environment.[6] If we merely want to determine whether preschool education affects first graders' academic performance, we need only estimate a regression equation with either of the two preschool variables defined in table 4.B.1.9 as one of the regressors. The coefficient on the preschool variable would indicate the impact of preschool averaged across programs spanning one to three years, and across children from both language groups. Although the result may be of general interest, it has limited application in policy design. Needed for this purpose are more specific results regarding the number of years of preschool it would be cost-effective to provide, as well as the target population for which the intervention would be especially effective. The problems below illustrate the procedure for obtaining these results.

Problem 1: Redefining the Preschool Variable

As preparation for the regression analysis we need to make two modifications to the preschool variable. The first is to allow for nonlinearity in the

Table 4.B.1.9: Data on a Sample of 4,043 First Graders

Variable	Definition	Sample mean	Standard deviation[a]
School outcome			
YETS	Pupil's year-end test score	100	15
Pupil background			
GIRL	Dummy variable = 1 if pupil is a girl; 0 if a boy	0.45	—
MOED	Mother's years of schooling	3.40	2.3
FAED	Father's years of schooling	2.60	1.8
LANGA	Dummy variable = 1 if pupil's home language is the language of instruction in school; 0 otherwise	0.40	—
Preschool experience			
YRSPRES	Years of preschool education	1.20	
PRESCH	Dummy variable = 1 if pupil has ever attended preschool; 0 otherwise	0.70	
Teacher characteristics			
TEACH-A	Dummy variable = 1 if class teacher has category A qualification; 0 otherwise	0.25	—
TEACH-B	Dummy variable = 1 if class teacher has category B qualification; 0 otherwise	0.45	—
TEACH-C	Dummy variable = 1 if class teacher has category C qualification; 0 otherwise. This is the omitted variable.	0.30	—
TEACH-FE	Dummy variable = 1 if class teacher is a woman; 0 if a man	0.62	—
TEACH-EX	Teacher's years of teaching experience	6.30	4.4
Conditions of the learning environment			
CSIZE	Number of pupils in the class	38.0	25–60
PEDMAT	Spending on pedagogical materials per pupil	5.2	3.5

— Not applicable.

a. For simplicity, only the standard deviations for continuous variables are shown in the column. For class size the data refer to the range; the information will be used in one of the exercises.

relationship between preschool attendance and learning outcomes in grade one, and the second is to allow for possible interaction between the preschool variable and ethnicity (that is, to allow for the impact of preschool to vary according to the ethnicity of the child who receives it). Follow the explanation given below for accomplishing the modification, and answer the questions posed in steps 1 and 2.

Step 1: Allowing for Nonlinearity There are two possible approaches. One is to specify a regression equation that includes *YRSPRES* and *YRSPRES²*. Under this specification the marginal impact of preschool on learning outcomes is given by the expression $(a + 2b \times YRSPRES)$, where a is the coefficient estimate on *YRSPRES* and b is the coefficient estimate on *YRSPRES²*. A negative value for b implies that there are diminishing returns to years of preschool.

Although the quadratic specification may be convenient to implement, it probably would be more straightforward to use a set of dummy variables corresponding, respectively, to programs lasting one, two, or three years. Moreover, these are the options effectively available to the policymaker. We define the dummy variables as listed in table 4.B.1.10.

To appreciate the meaning of these definitions, complete the last two columns of the table, which show the data for two observations in the sample. Retrieve now the file titled "Cost_Effectiveness_Ex2" from your CD-ROM and make sure you are in the worksheet labeled "problem 1." Complete the yellow cells and then try to answer the following questions:

(i) Which of the four dummy variables would you choose as the omitted variable?

Answer:

_____

_____

_____

_____

_____

_____

Table 4.B.1.10: Defining Dummy Variables for Preschool Exposure

Variable name	Definition	Sample means	Examples Observation 1: YRSPRES=0	Observation 2: YRSPRES=2
PRESCH0	Equals 1 if YRSPRES = 0; otherwise equal to 0	0.30		0
PRESCH1	Equals 1 if YRSPRES = 1; otherwise equal to 0	0.30		0
PRESCH2	Equals 1 if YRSPRES = 2; otherwise equal to 0	0.20		1
PRESCH3	Equals 1 if YRSPRES = 3; otherwise equal to 0	0.20		0

YRSPRES Years of preschool.

(ii) Given your choice, how would you interpret the regression coefficient on PRESCH3?

Answer: _____

_____

_____

(iii) With the preschool variable entering the regression model as a vector of three dummy variables, would the estimated impact of preschool on learning in grade one be the same for children from both ethnic groups?

Answer: **Yes**   **No** _____

because _____

_____

_____

4

Step 2: Incorporating Interaction Effects So far, all of the right-hand-side variables in our regression equation appear as additive variables. The specification carries the implicit assumption of infinite substitutability among the various school inputs in the equation. In reality, complete substitution is impossible. Indeed, some school inputs may be complements rather than substitutes. To take an extreme example, consider computers in the classroom and computer training for the classroom teacher. It is clear that computers in classrooms with teachers who do not know how to operate them will have no impact on student learning. The same outcome also can be expected in computerless classrooms where the teacher has had computer training. Because of complete complementarity between the two inputs, a multiplicative rather than additive specification would be a better model in that it would capture a relationship in which the absence of either input would nullify the impact of the other input on learning.

In reality, complete complementarity is just as rare as complete substitutability. Most school inputs are substitutable to some extent and all of them complement each other to produce learning outcomes. Because the additive model is easier to handle in impact analysis, the standard procedure is to specify a regression equation in which most of the variables enter additively and in which complementarity is incorporated on an as-needed basis. In the language of regression analysis, we would be allowing for interaction effects in what is globally an additive model.

In our problem we face precisely this type of interaction effect with regard to the influence of preschool programs on children from the two ethnic groups. Recall that in the standard additive model these variables enter separately; the coefficient estimates on the preschool variables (corresponding to programs of various duration) measure their impact *averaged* across pupils from the two language groups; and the coefficient on the language variable measures its impact *averaged* across pupils, irrespective of their exposure to preschool programs.

To allow for interaction between the preschool variable and a child's home language we can modify the additive regression specification in various ways. For our purpose we choose a simple method in which each of the dummy variables for preschool defined in step 1—PRESCH1, PRESCH2, and PRESCH3—are further split into two, according to the home language of the child. The full list of new dummy variables and their definitions appears in table 4.B.1.11. Take a moment to skim the table and then proceed to the next paragraph.

Scroll down the worksheet to locate the table. Enter in the cells colored yellow the values of the new dummy variables for observation num-

4

Table 4.B.1.11: Defining Interaction Variables for Preschool and Language Group

| | | | Examples | |
Variable name	Definition	Sample mean	Observation 1: YRSPRES=2 LANGA=0	Observation 2: YRSPRES=3 LANGA=1
PRESCH0	Equals 1 if YRSPRES = 0; otherwise equals 0	0.30		0
PRESCH1A	Equals 1 if YRSPRES = 1 and LANGA = 1; otherwise equals 0	0.20		0
PRESCH1B	Equals 1 if YRSPRES = 1 and LANGA = 0; otherwise equals 0	0.10		0
PRESCH2A	Equals 1 if YRSPRES = 2 and LANGA = 1; otherwise equals 0	0.12		0
PRESCH2B	Equals 1 if YRSPRES = 2 and LANGA = 0; otherwise equals 0	0.08		0
PRESCH3A	Equals 1 if YRSPRES = 3 and LANGA = 1; otherwise equals 0	0.13		1
PRESCH3B	Equals 1 if YRSPRES = 3 and LANGA = 0; otherwise equals 0	0.07		0

YRSPRES Years of preschool education.
LANGA Dummy variable = 1 if pupil's home language is LANGA, the language of instruction in school; 0 otherwise.

ber 1 whose value for YRSPRES and LANGA are indicated in the table. Then try to answer the following questions:

(i) What would you choose as the omitted dummy variable in your regression specification?

Answer: _____

_____

(ii) Given your choice, how would you interpret the regression coefficient on PRESCH2A?

Answer: _____

_____

_____

(iii) For children from language group A who are already in a one-year-long preschool program, how would you compute the impact of adding another year to their preschool exposure?

Answer: _____

_____

_____

Problem 2: Estimating the Regression Equation

Our regression equation has the following general functional form:

$$YETS = f(GIRL, MOED, FAED, LANGA, TEACH\text{-}A, TEACH\text{-}B,$$

$$TEACH\text{-}FE, TEACH\text{-}EX, CSIZE, PEDMAT, PS)$$

where *PS* refers to the preschool variable variously defined as (a) YRSPRES (years of preschool); (b) PRESCH (dichotomous dummy variable to indicate preschool attendance); (c) a vector of three dummy variables corresponding to programs lasting one, two, or three years; or (d) a vector of six dummy variables corresponding to interaction of the two language groups with the three types of preschool programs.

The regression results appear in table 4.B.2.12 for three alternative definitions of the preschool variable; definitions listed as (a) and (b) in the previous paragraph are comparable, so we show only the results for the latter. Take a moment now to scan the table and then proceed to the steps below.

Step 1: Understanding the Overall Results Write down the key features in the regression results regarding the influence of pupil background, teacher characteristics, the schooling environment, and preschool educa-

Table 4.B.2.12: Regression Estimates of the Correlates of First Graders' Year-End Test Scores

Variable	Model 1 Coefficient	t-Statistic	Model 2 Coefficient	t-Statistic	Model 3 Coefficient	t-Statistic
Pupil background						
GIRL	−1.12	0.66	−0.99	0.54	−1.21	0.71
MOED	0.53	2.54	0.59	2.19	0.81	2.31
FAED	0.24	0.58	0.33	0.43	0.31	0.54
LANGA	4.52	2.11	4.21	1.97	4.32	2.24
Teacher characteristics						
TEACH-A	4.21	1.99	4.07	2.10	4.62	1.91
TEACH-B	3.02	1.68	3.34	1.73	3.68	1.82
TEACH-FE	1.41	1.22	1.13	1.11	1.32	1.44
TEACH-EX	0.28	2.14	0.31	2.22	0.32	2.21
Learning environment						
CSIZE	−0.06	2.33	−0.04	2.43	−0.08	2.14
PEDMAT	2.21	2.88	2.07	2.98	2.44	2.64
Preschool experience						
PRESCH	10.89	4.43	n.a.	n.a.	n.a.	n.a.
PRESCH1	n.a.	n.a.	9.11	4.61	n.a.	n.a.
PRESCH2	n.a.	n.a.	11.21	4.26	n.a.	n.a.
PRESCH3	n.a.	n.a.	12.13	3.98	n.a.	n.a.
PRESCH1A	n.a.	n.a.	n.a.	n.a.	2.71	1.63
PRESCH1B	n.a.	n.a.	n.a.	n.a.	16.22	6.71
PRESCH2A	n.a.	n.a.	n.a.	n.a.	3.10	1.92
PRESCH2B	n.a.	n.a.	n.a.	n.a.	15.43	5.34
PRESCH3A	n.a.	n.a.	n.a.	n.a.	4.14	1.82
PRESCH3B	n.a.	n.a.	n.a.	n.a.	17.32	6.23
Intercept	3.45		2.98		3.16	
R^2	0.25		0.36		0.37	
Number of observations	4,043		4,043		4,043	

See table 4.B.1.9 for variable definitions.

tion on learning outcomes in grade one. Note the differences in impact across the preschool programs of different duration, as well as the differences in the impact across children in the two language groups.

Comment:

Step 2: Consolidating the Impact Estimates   To anticipate the cost-effectiveness analysis in a later problem, we now consolidate the results from the regression estimates in table 4.B.2.13. It shows the impact of the following inputs on test scores: (a) a change in teacher qualification; (b) improvement in the learning environment in the form of smaller classes and increased spending on pedagogical materials; (c) preschool programs averaged across all durations and across children from both language groups; (d) the impact of the first, second, and third year of preschool programs averaged across children from both language groups; and (e) the impact of the first, second, and third year of preschool programs for children from each of the two language groups. Scroll down the worksheet to locate the table. Complete the cells colored yellow and review the whole table for a moment before going on to the next problem.

Cost Analysis

The cost analysis follows the same procedures as in part A. The relevant data for our example appear in table 4.B.3.14. To save time, the data have

Table 4.B.2.13: Consolidating the Regression Results

Input	Impact estimate	Statistical significance
Teacher qualification		
C (reference level)	—	
B (relative to C)	3.68	*
A (relative to B)	0.94	n.s.
Learning environment		
Number of pupils in class	0.08	**
Per-pupil spending on pedagogical materials	2.44	**
Preschool programs		
Average impact	10.89	***
First year	9.11	***
Second year	2.10	*
Third year	0.92	n.s.
First year for language group A		*
Second year for language group A		n.s.
Third year for language group A		n.s.
First year for language group B	16.22	***
Second year for language group B	−0.79	n.s.
Third year for language group B	1.89	n.s.

— Not applicable.

*Statistically significant at the 10 percent level.

**Statistically significant at the 5 percent level.

***Statistically significant at the 1 percent level.

n.s. Not significant.

Table 4.B.3.14: Data for Computing the Marginal Cost of Inputs per Pupil

Item	Unit	Unit cost (Fcfa)
Teachers		
Category C (least qualified)	Per teacher per year	450,000
Category B (moderately qualified)	Per teacher per year	750,000
Category A (most qualified)	Per teacher per year	1,200,000
Class size		
Average	One fewer than sample average of 38 pupils per class	—
Upper bound	One fewer than upper bound of 60 pupils per class	—
Lower bound	One fewer than lower bound of 25 pupils per class	—
Preschool programs[a]	Per pupil per year	12,000

— Not applicable.

Fcfa Franc de la Communauté Française d'Afrique.

a. The cost of preschool programs is the same in the first, second, and third years.

already been adjusted to reflect annualized costs where appropriate. Thus, the difference in teacher costs between qualification categories A, B, and C include both the salary differential and the annualized investment costs associated with the implied difference in qualification. Similarly, the expenditure on pedagogical materials corresponds to the annualized cost of textbooks and other material inputs.

Problem 3: Assembling the Marginal Cost Data

As before, the cost-effectiveness comparison is based on costs per pupil. We therefore need to assemble the relevant cost data in the format of table 4.B.3.15. Your task is to complete the cells colored yellow in the table. Note that for teacher qualification the marginal cost per pupil depends on the class size. We compute the average marginal cost by using the average class size in the sample (38 pupils), and the upper and lower marginal costs per pupil by using the corresponding bounds on the range of the class-size variable (that is, 25 and 60 pupils, respectively). To compute the average per-pupil marginal cost of changing class size, we assume teacher salaries corresponding to category B qualification and an initial class size corresponding to the sample mean (38 pupils). The upper and lower bounds are computed with teacher salaries set at qualification C and B, respectively, and initial class size set at the corresponding bounds on the range of the

Table 4.B.3.15: Marginal Cost per Pupil of Various School Inputs (Fcfa)

| Input | Marginal unit | Cost of the marginal unit | Marginal cost per pupil[a] | | |
			Average	Lower bound	Upper bound
Teacher qualification[a]					
Category C (reference)	—	—	—	—	—
B	Change from qualification C to B	300,000	7,895	5,000	12,000
A	Change from qualification B to A	450,000			
Learning environment					
Number of pupils in class:[b]	One fewer pupil per class	—		212	1,250
Pedagogical materials	One Fcfa per pupil	1.0	1	1	1
Preschool programs					
Sample average in duration	1.2 years per pupil	14,400	14,400	—	—
First year	1 year per pupil	12,000	12,000	—	—
Second year	1 year per pupil	12,000	12,000	—	—
Third year	1 year per pupil	12,000	12,000	—	—

Fcfa Franc de la Communauté Française d'Afrique.

— Not applicable.

a. See text in Excel worksheet for explanation on computing the upper and lower bounds in the estimates of marginal cost per pupil.

b. See text in Excel worksheet for explanation.

class size. The reason for computing these bounds is to illustrate the scope for targeting improvements in teacher qualification and class size.

Cost-Effectiveness Analysis

We now are ready to consolidate the impact and cost analyses to compare the cost-effectiveness of investments in preschool programs relative to other interventions for improving learning outcomes. The relevant estimates on marginal impact and costs from the preceding two sections appear in table 4.B.4.16. In the problem below, you are asked to complete the table and assess the policy implications of the results.

Problem 4: Assessing the Policy Implications

Tab over now to the worksheet labeled "problem 4" and compute the ratio of impact to cost corresponding to an improvement in teacher qualification from category C to category B. Notice that you need to divide the impact estimate by the lower-bound cost estimate to obtain

Table 4.B.4.16: Comparing Cost-Effectiveness across Inputs

Input	Marginal impact (points)		Marginal cost (000 Fcfa)			Ratio of impact to cost		
	Coefficient estimate	Statistical significance	Average	Lower bound	Upper bound	Average	Lower bound	Upper bound
Teacher qualification								
C (reference)	—		—	—	—	—	—	—
B	3.68	**	7,895	5,000	12,000	—	—	—
A	0.94	n.s.	11,842	7,500	18,000	0.08	0.05	0.13
Learning environment								
Class size	0.08	**	533	127	2,000	0.15	0.04	0.63
Per-pupil spending on pedagogical materials	2.44	**	1,000	—	—	2.44	—	—
Preschool programs								
On average	10.89	***	14,400	—	—	0.76	—	—
Averaged across language groups								
First year	9.11	***	12,000	—	—	0.76	—	—
Second year	2.10	n.s.	12,000	—	—	0.18	—	—
Third year	0.92	n.s.	12,000	—	—	0.08	—	—
For language group A								
First year	2.71	***	12,000	—	—	0.23	—	—
Second year	0.41	n.s.	12,000	—	—	0.03	—	—
Third year	1.04	n.s.	12,000	—	—	0.09	—	—
For language group B								
First year	16.22	***	12,000	—	—	1.35	—	—
Second year	-0.79	n.s.	12,000	—	—	-0.07	—	—
Third year	1.89	n.s.	12,000	—	—	0.16	—	—

— Not applicable.

*Statistically significant at the 10 percent level.

**Statistically significant at the 5 percent level.

***Statistically significant at the 1 percent level.

Fcfa Franc de la Communauté Française d'Afrique.

n.s. Not significant.

the upper-bound ratio, and vice versa to obtain the lower-bound ratio. The same calculations for the other inputs have been completed for you. Examine the results for their policy implications, focusing on the following questions:

(i)   For which input or inputs is the justification for increased investment strongest? What can the government do to enhance the use of such inputs in the system?

Answers: _____

_____

_____

_____

_____

(ii) Regarding teachers, what do the results imply for policies on teacher recruitment, deployment, and in-service training?

Answer: _____

_____

_____

_____

_____

(iii) What implications, if any, do the results have for policies regarding class size?

Answer: _____

_____

_____

_____

_____

(iv) Review the impact-to-cost ratios for preschool programs in table 4.B.4.16 and note the following: the first item listed refers to preschool programs averaged across all durations and both language groups; the second block refers to preschool programs of one, two, and three years averaged across both language groups; and the third and fourth blocks refer to programs of one, two, and three years for each of the two language groups. What do the results imply for investment priorities in preschool education?

Answer: _____

_____

_____

_____

_____

Conclusion

Although conceptually simple, cost-effectiveness analysis requires the use of tools that may not be readily accessible to policy analysts in the education sector. These involve regression estimation of the impact of school inputs or policies on school outcomes as well as careful cost analysis. The purpose of this module has been to illustrate the application of generic tools for both steps in the analysis, using concrete quantitative examples as a pedagogical device. Armed with these tools the user of this module should now have a better understanding of the requirements for cost-effectiveness analysis, and be in position to apply the tools for assessing priorities in various policy contexts.

As the exercises have shown, cost-effectiveness analysis is demanding, requiring much effort in both data collection (some specifics are provided in the annex to this module) and analysis. Is it worth the effort? The answer is a clear "yes" in a sector generally characterized by vast inefficiencies in resource allocation and where policy debate is all too often dominated by strongly held opinions. In this context the main contribution of cost-effectiveness analysis is to facilitate systematic comparison of the costs and benefits of alternative policy options. Although political feasibility and the manageability of implementation may be decisive influences in the choice of policies, the results of cost-effectiveness analysis provide a key input into the policymaking process, especially in the early phases. At the very least they help set an agenda for productive policy debate by making available to policymakers context-specific facts about the impact and costs of alternative choices. Used as a diagnostic device, cost-effectiveness analysis also can identify current aspects of the education system that produce too few benefits for the resources they absorb and therefore warrant attention in sector management.

4

As a conclusion to the course, you might wish to jot down your thoughts concerning cost-effectiveness analysis as an approach for policy analysis in education, noting both its potential and its limitations.

Comment: _____

_____

_____

_____

_____

_____

_____

4

Annex: Data for Cost-Effectiveness Analysis

Because cost-effectiveness analysis is inherently comparative in nature, it requires data with sufficient variability in each of the relevant variables. For example, to comment meaningfully on changing class size to improve schooling, we need data from settings in which the class size does indeed vary. If in the data actually collected the variable ranges between, say, 15 and 30 pupils per class, the analysis would yield valid implications regarding class size only within this range. To say something about policies to reduce class size to 10 or to raise it to 40, for example, would require new data spanning these extremes in class size.[7]

Ensuring sufficient variability in the relevant variables is therefore an important preparatory task in cost-effectiveness analysis. Although the details of data collection will differ according to the problem being analyzed and the policy context, there generally are three approaches for data collection: random sampling, stratified sampling, and experiments. The first method is the least demanding to implement, but may not generate the desired data because of the population characteristics; the third is the most demanding but is unavoidable for evaluating the cost-effectiveness of new policy instruments.

Random Sampling

Suppose the issue is to compare the impact of male teachers on student learning with that of female teachers. If the distribution of teachers in the system is relatively even across gender, random sampling will likely include sufficient male and female teachers in the resulting sample.

Stratified Sampling

Continuing with the foregoing example, suppose that most of the female teachers work in urban schools. A random sample most likely would yield too few female teachers from rural schools. As a result, the data would be inadequate for separating the impact of teacher's gender from that of geographic locality. To forestall this possibility requires the use of stratified sampling in which male and female teachers from urban and rural areas are sampled separately. As another example, suppose that we are interested in assessing the impact on student learning of varying class size in the range of 15 to 40 pupils per class. If few classes in the population contain fewer than 20 pupils or more than 30 pupils, it would be wise to stratify the population by class size first, and then to take random samples within each range.

Experiments

In some situations we may be interested in assessing the cost-effectiveness of entirely new policy instruments. By definition, the desired data for evaluating the instruments' impact are nonexistent and must therefore be generated by actually implementing the new instruments through pilot activities. Although it is beyond the scope of this module to address experimental evaluation in detail, an obvious point is that the sample should contain observations from both the treatment and control schools.

Two additional points are noteworthy when generating evaluation data through experiments. The first concerns the possible influence of the "Hawthorne effect"—the natural tendency of people to alter their behavior when they know they are being monitored or observed. Ignoring the possible presence of the effect—both during data collection and in the course of data analysis—would make it impossible to isolate the impact of the pilot activities alone, thereby compromising the validity of the results for policy design.

The second point is to recognize that often there is scope for variation in the way a contemplated policy instrument is implemented. For example, the label "in-service teacher training" can encompass various activities ranging from general courses that prepare teachers for formal examinations to obtain their teaching diplomas, to special courses related to the implementation of a new curriculum, to practical courses in grading techniques and classroom management. Given the scope for

4

differences in implementation, the actual content and nature of an intervention clearly matters much more than the conceptual label with which it is associated.

Endnotes

1. As in any analysis, data collection is an integral part of the work. Because our focus here is on analytical concepts and techniques we refer the reader to appendix A for an overview of the main approaches to data collection for cost-effectiveness analysis.

2. To review the main concepts, as well as the key statistical indicators for interpreting the regression results, consult the regression analysis in the annex to this chapter.

3. The reader also may wish to consult the hands-on module, "Analyzing Equity in Education" by Alain Mingat and Jee-Peng Tan, with Stella Tamayo, for further details on how to perform the analysis.

4. The cost calculations can be accomplished in one of two ways: (a) using cost functions, which also are estimated through regression analysis (for example, by regressing teacher years of education against pay); or (b) through application of the classical procedure of piecing together the composite parts of costs. A more detailed discussion of the various methods can be found in two other hands-on modules: "Analyzing Costs in Education" by Jean-Pierre Jarousse, Alain Mingat, Stella Tamayo, and Jee-Peng Tan and "Performing Economic Analysis of Educational Technology" by Alain Mingat and Jee-Peng Tan, with Stella Tamayo.

5. Opportunity costs refer to the cost of the time people spend in training or in school.

6. Normally, we also would include the entering test score as one of the regressors. The variable is excluded here for lack of data. In real-life situations, such data for first graders are usually scarce, in part because of the difficulty in collecting the data from young children who have just started school.

7. The same requirement for data variability applies when evaluating policy changes regarding more specialized school inputs. For example, to assess the impact of a new method in teaching reading we would need to compare it with the traditional method. The data sample should therefore include pupils taught by both methods.

Managing Teacher Deployment and Classroom Processes

A Two-Part Module

Alain Mingat and Jee-Peng Tan, with Shobhana Sosale

Education is a complex social undertaking. Although there is no easy way to analyze the many dimensions of policy involved, we can begin with a simple characterization of education as a process involving the allocation and use of available resources to achieve certain educational, social, or economic objectives. The policy choices fall into two broad categories: (a) allocations across levels (and types) of education—which generally affect the macro structure of the education system; and (b) allocations within each level of education—which affect the operational arrangements in schools and classrooms. In this chapter we focus on the second class of policy choices, taking as a given the macro pattern of resource allocation across levels of education. Within that class of problems, we can analyze the management of overall spending at a given level of education, or focus on specific components of spending. Because teachers typically represent the single most important component of education costs, particularly at the lower levels of schooling, managing the resources embodied in them warrants especially close attention.[1] Teachers and their management are therefore the focus of this chapter.

In most education systems, a common observation is that some schools are better endowed than others—for example, in terms of the number and qualifications of the teaching staff and the availability of books and other materials. The better-endowed schools tend to produce better results, as measured by such indicators as student achievement and schooling careers, but the pattern is not necessarily a tight one. Some teachers are simply more skillful than others, enabling them to achieve better outcomes despite having fewer resources than other teachers. This result underlines the fact that, although tangible resources may affect schooling outcomes through their impact on the quality of the classroom environment, the interaction between the teacher and his or her pupils also plays an important role. For the policymaker, the management of teachers therefore requires attention to two types of problems: efficiency in the deployment of teachers across schools (or classrooms), and efficiency of teachers' management of the pedagogical process within the classroom. Part A of this chapter addresses the first problem, and part B deals with the second. The focus in both parts is to illustrate methods for evaluating options to improve management of the system.

As in the other hands-on modules, this training module includes exercises on the CD-ROM: two Excel files corresponding to the two parts of the module. Each of the Excel files contains worksheets for the exercises indicated in this write-up; for example, the file "teacher_mgt_Ex1" contains all the exercises for part A, and the worksheet "problem 1" in that file refers to the first exercise. The emphasis is on the concepts and interpretation of the analytical results, rather than on the mechanics of the computations. Accordingly, participants are encouraged to complete the exercises as a follow-up self-paced activity.

Part A: Analyzing Teacher Deployment Issues

In a well-managed education system, we expect teachers to be deployed across schools in numbers that are more or less proportionate to the size of enrollments; and within each school, we expect teaching assignments to be allocated among teachers so that the school operates at a reasonable level of efficiency. These ideas suggest some benchmarks for evaluating the deployment of teachers across and within schools. The problems below elaborate on ways to operationalize the assessment.

Documenting the Problem

Problem 1: Understanding Teacher Deployment across Primary Schools

The data for this problem pertain to a sample of 51 primary schools.[2] Your task here is twofold: to examine the relationship between the number of teachers at each school and the corresponding size of enrollment, and to evaluate the implications regarding teacher deployment in the system. Follow the steps below to accomplish the analysis.

Step 1   Open the file titled "teacher_mgt_Ex1" on the CD-ROM, checking the bottom of the screen to see that you are in the worksheet titled "problem 1." For each of the 51 schools in the sample, we have data in table 5.A.1.1 on the number of pupils and teachers.

Review the plot of number of pupils against number of teachers in figure 5.A.1.1, the regression results (in the lilac block), and the data sorted by pupils (in the light blue block) and teachers (in the aqua blue block). What do the results reveal about the relationship between size of enrollment and number of teachers employed at the school? Write your comments in the yellow box on the Excel sheet, or here:

Comment on the relationship between size of enrollment and number of teachers:

_____

_____

_____

_____

Step 2   Using the regression estimate as a basis, it is now possible to identify the over- and underendowed schools (in terms of teacher deployment against size of enrollment). Scroll down to step 2 on the same Excel sheet, locate table 5.A.1.2, and complete the following tasks, which also appear in red on the Excel sheet:

(i)   Use the regression result in equation 5.A.1.1a to compute the number of teachers that would be consistent with the overall relationship between numbers of students and teachers. To avoid repetitive Excel manipulation, you need only perform the calculation for the cells colored yellow in table 5.A.1.2.

(ii)   Calculate the average pupil–teacher ratio in the system.

(iii) Compute the number of teachers that would need to be reassigned to rationalize deployment based on enrollments, assuming the overall pupil–teacher ratio remains unchanged.

(iv) Suppose the government decides to lower the overall pupil–teacher ratio to 30. The predicted number of teachers at each school would then be given by $(32.5/30) \bullet ([0.37 + 0.29] \bullet \text{pupils})$. Apply this formula to the first school in table 5.A.1.2 in the Excel file and compute the predicted surplus or shortfall of teachers.

(v)   With the lower pupil–teacher ratio, how many teachers would now be needed systemwide? How many more teachers would need to be reassigned from the overendowed schools?

Step 3   Although any redeployment exercise would clearly benefit from wide consultation to build support and acceptance, some simple analysis of available data can help improve understanding of the situation. In particular, we can use some commonly available data to examine the correlates of the current pattern of teacher deployment. For example, to the extent that better-qualified teachers tend to request and obtain assignments in better-endowed schools, and to the extent that better-endowed schools attract students from more advantaged backgrounds, we also can expect these factors to relate in a systematic fashion to the allocation of teachers across schools. Suppose that the data for our 51 schools also include information on the number of teachers by qualification and the percent of children from high socioeconomic backgrounds.[3] For simplicity we distinguish between two categories of teacher qualification, A and B; the average salary of teachers are US$1,200 and US$1,500 a year, respectively, in the two categories.

Given these data, what indicators do you think can be used as a proxy for teacher quality?

(a) _____

(b) _____

5

For the purpose here, we will use the average cost per teacher as a proxy for teacher quality. Scroll down the Excel sheet to locate table 5.A.1.3 where the data for the 51 schools appear. Review the data and the regression results based on them. Then comment on what they imply about the current pattern of teacher allocation in the system, and possible difficulties in and opportunities for rationalizing the pattern. You may write your answer below or directly on the Excel sheet in the cell colored yellow. To facilitate the evaluation you may wish to examine the data in the working table (shown on the right-hand side of the Excel sheet) where the 51 schools are ranked according to teacher surplus and deficit and to the socioeconomic composition of the student population.

Comment: _____

_____

_____

_____

Problem 2: Understanding Teacher Deployment across Secondary Schools

Your task here is to contrast the pattern of teacher deployment at the primary and secondary school levels, identify and understand the differences in results between the two levels of education, and distill potential policy issues in teacher deployment in secondary education. Follow the steps below to accomplish the assignment.

Step 1 Tab over to the worksheet labeled "problem 2" in the same Excel file (teacher_mgt.Ex1) where you will find the data pertaining to enrollments and number of staff in table 5.A.2.4 and the regression results for 57 secondary schools. Take a moment to review the regression results, and then compare the regression results for primary and secondary education. Write your comments below or directly in the yellow cell in the Excel sheet. Take a moment to review the plot of number of students and number of staff in figure 5.A.2.2a.

Comments:

_____

_____

_____

_____

Step 2 Here we re-estimate the regression for the sample of 57 secondary schools with the total salary cost of teachers instead of the number of teachers as the dependent variable. The purpose of this step will become clear below. For simplicity, we convert the data on number of teachers into monetary terms at the average rate of US$1,200 per teacher. Scroll down now to this step in the worksheet where you may view the regression results.

If we divide both sides of the regression equation by the number of students, we obtain the following relationship between salary cost per student and the size of enrollment at the school:[4] salary cost per student = (10,531.1/students) + 32.4.

The relationship between the cost per student and the size of enrollment follows a hyperbolic shape, as shown in figure 5.A.2.2b in the Excel sheet. Comment on what this graph implies for the management of the size distribution of schools in the system. For your evaluation, you may wish to consider such options as (a) do nothing (with a comment on the justification), (b) amalgamate small schools (with a comment on how equity concerns can be addressed), and (c) reduce the fixed costs for operating a secondary school (with a comment on how this might be achieved).

Comment:

_____

_____

_____

Assessing Potential Gains from Greater Consistency in Staffing Decisions

Inconsistency in teacher deployment juxtaposed against disparities in the size distribution of schools is common in most education systems. The pattern raises two management concerns: (a) how to identify and apply standards for teacher deployment, in order to minimize ad hoc decisions motivated by patronage and political considerations; and (b) how to manage the costs of service delivery to students living in areas with low population densities and typically small schools. The problems below illustrate analytical techniques for addressing these issues.

Problem 3: Setting Criteria for Improved Consistency in Teacher Deployment

In this problem you are asked to evaluate the impact on efficiency of applying consistent staffing norms that reflect prior decisions on the pedagogical arrangements for delivery of the curriculum.

Continuing with the 57 schools from the previous exercise (which we assume to be lower secondary schools for our purpose here), we note that the following arrangements currently prevail at this cycle of schooling:

- Lower secondary schooling lasts four years.
- Students receive instruction in seven subjects during a 28-hour week.
- Teachers' normal workload is 20 hours a week.
- Beyond the normal workload, teachers receive overtime pay for a maximum of four hours a week.
- The maximum class size is set at 40 students.
- Schools operating with one section of students per grade are entitled to one administrative position (that is, school head), whereas those with more sections per grade are entitled to two administrative positions.

For our immediate purpose, we take these arrangements as given and examine the efficiency gains that can result simply from increased consistency in the application of staffing norms. The underlying parameters are amenable to change and therefore represent additional policy levers for improved management of teacher deployment in the system.

Step 1 Tab over now to the next Excel sheet titled "problem 3" where you will find data in table 5.A.3.6 on the time allocation across subjects taught in the four grades of lower secondary school. Take a few minutes to scan the data, then follow the instructions to complete table 5.A.3.7. (To save time, only two cells in the table are left for you to complete.)

Step 2 Here your task is to compute the number of full-time-equivalent teachers required to deliver the desired number of teaching hours in the various subjects. We assume that teachers specialize by subject, that they teach a normal load of 20 hours weekly, and receive overtime compensation for up to four hours of extra work a week. For example, in one-section schools, 21 hours of teaching in math are required to deliver the curriculum, entitling the school to 1.05 full-time-equivalent teachers (that is, one teacher who would teach the normal load plus one hour of overtime a week). To make sure you understand the calculation, try to compute the number of full-time-equivalent math teachers needed in schools with three sections of students and enter your answer in the yellow cell in table 5.A.3.8 in the Excel sheet.

Scroll down to table 5.A.3.9 where the calculations from the preceding operations, aggregated across all subjects, are repeated in the first two rows. Use these results to compute the average hours of teaching per teacher per week in schools with only one section, and compare the utilization rate of teachers in such schools with the normal load of 20 hours per teacher per week. Comment on your results so far regarding the efficiency of resource use in small schools, relative to large schools.

Comment: _____

_____

_____

_____

_____

5

Step 3   We now are in a position to evaluate the gains in system efficiency that would follow from consistent application of staffing norms across all the 57 schools in the system. To proceed we first establish the school sizes that correspond to the various levels of staffing entitlements; then we apply these entitlements to each of the 57 schools according to their size; and finally we compare the resulting aggregate staff requirements with the actual allocation to obtain a measure of the potential efficiency gains from increased consistency in staffing. Follow the instructions in the Excel sheet relating to table 5.A.3.10 to complete the exercise, and summarize any concluding remarks here.

Concluding remarks: _____

_____

_____

_____

Assessing Policy Options for Managing the High Costs of Small Schools

We have seen from the foregoing calculations that small schools, especially those with enrollments below 100 pupils, remain significantly more costly than larger schools, even when the allocation of teachers across schools is perfectly consistent with staffing norms. The reason is twofold: in small schools there are fewer sections of students, which inevitably leads to less than full utilization of the teachers; and in smaller schools the fixed costs (which are determined by the number of sections of students) are spread over fewer students. In the next two problems, we will assess policies to manage the costliness of small schools (a) by rationalizing teacher utilization through multisubject rather than single-subject teaching and (b) by relocating students from the small schools to the larger ones, with adequate arrangements to compensate for the increase in private costs for transport and lodging faced by the affected students. Using the results from problems 4 and 5, problem 6 will focus on the formulation of an overall strategy for managing the costs of small schools.

Problem 4: Moving to Multisubject Instead of Single-Subject Teaching

Suppose that instead of being trained for specialized teaching, teachers are trained to teach more than one subject. For our purpose, teachers of physics also teach biology, and teachers of the national language also teach the arts. Your assignment is to assess the cost savings that can be expected under the new arrangements. Follow the steps below to complete the exercise.

Step 1   Tab over to the next worksheet, titled "problem 4" in your Excel file. Review tables 5.A.4.11 through 5.A.4.14 in which the calculations from the previous problem are repeated with the new assumptions about the use of multisubject teaching for physics and biology and for the national language and the arts. Comment briefly on the results regarding the rate of teacher utilization.

Comment: _____

_____

_____

_____

Step 2   Scroll down to table 5.A.4.15, which shows the staff utilization rates under multi- and single-subject teaching. Follow the instructions to answer the questions below, which also are printed in red on the Excel sheet:

(i)   By how much will the salary cost per student fall if multisubject teaching is used in place of single-subject teaching?

Answer: _____

_____

_____

_____

(ii) How does the overall salary cost of the sample of 57 schools compare under single- and multisubject teaching?

Answer: _____

_____

_____

_____

(iii) Among the 20 smallest schools, how do the costs per student compare under the two arrangements for teaching?

Answer: _____

_____

_____

_____

In addition to multisubject teaching, the other option for managing the costs of small schools is to distribute their students to the bigger schools where costs per student are predictably smaller, as our calculations thus far have shown. The following problem illustrates one method for assessing this option.

Problem 5: Relocating Students from the Small Schools to the Larger Ones

We assume that the 57 sample schools are staffed according to the norms for specialized teaching, so the number of staff at each school is the same as those computed in problem 3 above. Your tasks below are to identify schools for which the relocation policy might be justified on economic grounds and to evaluate the cost savings that such a policy would generate. Follow the steps below to accomplish your assignment.

Step 1 Tab over to the worksheet titled "problem 5" where you will find a working table to facilitate calculation of the salary cost per student at each of the 57 schools, assuming that teachers are remunerated at the average annual rate of US$1,200 each. Review the graph based on the results from the working table, which shows the relationship between size of enrollment and cost per student. Review the graph, using it to answer the following question (either here or on the Excel sheet): For what size schools would a policy of student relocation potentially be justified on economic grounds?

Answer: _____

_____

_____

Step 2 Scroll down to this step in the Excel sheet. Here the task is to evaluate the potential gross savings in unit costs from relocating students in the small schools to larger ones. Follow the instructions printed in red in the worksheet to answer the following questions:

(i) To measure the potential cost savings we need a benchmark against which to compare the costs of the small schools. What in your opinion would be a reasonable cost benchmark?

Answer: _____

_____

_____

_____

(ii) What is the average cost per student in schools with 100 or more students?

Answer: _____

_____

_____

(iii) On the basis of the above results, compute the gross savings per student that can materialize from a policy of relocating students. You need only do the calculations for the smallest school in the sample;

the rest of the cells have been completed for you to avoid repetitive operations in Excel.

Answer:

_____

_____

_____

_____

(iv) Against the gross savings the government must also consider the potential costs of the policy. What in your opinion are some of the costs?

Answer:

_____

_____

_____

_____

Step 3 Your task in this step is to compute the net savings from relocating students, taking into account the cost of compensating the affected students. This compensation can take the form of a direct cash subsidy or the provision of boarding services. Suppose that in this example a stipend of US$90 per student would be sufficient for students to find their own accommodations, and that the cost function of boarding services is as described in equation (1):

(1) $$tbcost = 4{,}000 + 70 \bullet nboarders$$

or equivalently,

$$ubcost = 4{,}000/nboarders + 70$$

where *tbcost* is the total cost of a boarding facility, *nboarders* is the number of boarders it serves, and *ubcost* is the cost per boarder. Scroll down now to step 3 in the Excel sheet to answer the following questions:

(i) What does equation (1) imply about the marginal cost of boarding services?

Answer:

_____

_____

_____

(ii) What is the minimum number of students for which it would be economically justified to organize boarding services instead of providing students with a cash subsidy of US$90 each to find their own accommodations?

Answer: _____

_____

_____

_____

(iii) What are the upper and lower bounds on the cost per student of a policy involving the relocation of students away from their school districts?

Answer: _____

_____

_____

_____

(iv) For which schools would there be net savings from relocating students to larger schools?

Answer: _____

_____

_____

_____

In the last two problems above we have considered two separate options for managing the high cost of small schools: using multisubject teachers instead of specialists, and relocating students from small schools to larger ones. We are now in a position to compare the two options and to formulate an overall strategy for managing the high costs of small schools.

Problem 6: Forming a Policy Strategy

Your tasks are to review the relevant results from earlier exercises and to reflect on their policy implications.

Step 1 Tab over to the Excel sheet titled "problem 6" where you will find the relevant results from the previous two problems consolidated for convenient viewing. Take a moment now to examine the data and comment on the economic justification for the two options for managing the high costs of small schools.

Comment:

_____

_____

_____

_____

_____

Step 2   Scroll down to this step and follow the instructions printed in red to answer the following questions pertaining to the underlying assumptions in our assessment:

(i)   In assessing options A (relocation of students) and B (use of multi-subject teaching) we have so far ignored the time perspective. Why would taking account of this factor be important in our analysis?

Answer:

_____

_____

_____

_____

(ii)   Are there hidden costs associated with multisubject teaching that we have ignored?

Answer:

_____

_____

_____

_____

(iii) What other assumptions are implicit in the data presented so far concerning the impact of options A (relocation of students) and B (use of multisubject teaching) above?

Answer:

_____

_____

_____

_____

(iv) Briefly summarize your conclusions regarding a strategy to manage the costs of small schools.

Answer:

_____

_____

_____

_____

_____

Part B: Improving Teacher Management of Classroom Processes

The teacher deployment and utilization policies considered in part A are an example of system-level decisions that affect the management of the system. Like other such decisions the focus is on how the system is organized (for example, regulations about class size, grouping and streaming of students, curriculum options, and so on) and on the quantity and quality of inputs supplied to support teaching and learning (for example, investments in teacher training and development, textbooks, physical facilities, and so on). Although it is obvious that these dimensions of educational management warrant attention, they need to be complemented by an equally close scrutiny of what takes place within classrooms and schools. This is because it is at these levels in the education system, especially within the classroom, that the process of transforming the resources devoted to education into schooling outcomes actually occurs.

Teachers and (to a lesser extent) school administrators are the key agents concerned. Their effectiveness in managing classroom activities and processes determines how much students learn, and their assessment of a child's progress during the school year typically is the key factor in year-end decisions about the child's grade assignment for the following year. Yet what goes on within the classroom and the school is largely opaque to outsiders, especially to casual observers. In recent years, educators have devised classroom observation techniques and other methods for looking more systematically into the "black box." This approach is particularly effective for identifying specific examples of good and poor practices in classroom and school management. Its focus on detail and on concrete examples of behavior in individual classrooms or schools brings numerous advantages, but as a gauge on the whole system's performance, these features impose obvious limitations.

Thus, although direct classroom observation has its place in policy work, it needs to be preceded by a broad-brush diagnosis of systemic patterns of deficiencies in the management of the schooling process. Such a diagnosis can be used to identify both the lagging and leading schools in the system, with the former helping to sharpen the targeting of follow-up efforts to improve performance, and the latter providing context-specific models for possible emulation. The purpose of the exercises below is to elaborate on methods for implementing the broad-brush diagnosis. To provide a context for the quantitative analysis we begin by focusing briefly on the nature of classroom processes.

Clarifying Our Understanding of Classroom Processes

Problem 1: Role of the Teacher, the Key Manager of Classroom Processes

Your tasks here are simply to reflect on the nature and scope of the teacher's role in the classroom and to offer possible explanations why schooling outcomes may differ across classes of students who are similar in access to pedagogical and physical resources and in socioeconomic composition. To guide your thinking, try to answer the following questions briefly, either in the space below or in the worksheet titled "problem 1" in the file titled "teacher_mgt_Ex2" on the accompanying CD-ROM.

(i) Itemize some of the activities that teachers perform as managers of classroom processes. What do they do daily? What do they do at selected junctures over the course of a school year?

Answer:

_____

_____

_____

_____

_____

(ii) What leeway do teachers have in discharging their day-to-day teaching responsibilities?

Answer:

_____

_____

_____

_____

5

(iii) What scope is there for teachers to influence a child's schooling career in terms of grade-to-grade progression?

Answer: _____

_____

_____

_____

(iv) In your opinion, what is the desirability and feasibility of moving toward greater uniformity in teachers' management of the various processes in the classroom?

Answer: _____

_____

_____

_____

5

Diagnosing Possible Problems in Classroom Management

Teachers are likely to vary widely in how they teach and in how they manage students' progression through the current school year and into the next. The concern of policymakers is not so much that there is diversity in classroom practices, but that the diversity may produce systemic patterns of inequities and inefficiencies. Such problems are hinted at when students with comparable levels of academic achievement follow substantially different schooling careers, depending on the school they happen to be attending; and when wide disparities exist in student achievement across schools. Below we explore ways to diagnose these problems, using two indicators for which the data can be assembled or collected relatively easily in the context of developing countries: the pattern of students' grade-to-grade progression, and the pattern in student learning outcomes. Our purpose here is simply to provide the policymaker with a broad-brush diagnosis of the functioning of the entire system in terms of teachers' management of classroom processes.

Problem 2: Diagnosing Management Problems as Revealed by Disparities in Students' Grade-to-Grade Progressions

Here we focus on the only decision over which teachers and the school administration have complete control: the decision at the end of each school year (except the terminal year in a cycle, where selection to the next cycle is often regulated by a national examination) whether to hold back a student in the same grade for another year or to promote the child to the next grade. How consistent are such decisions across schools? To what extent are students with comparable levels of learning held back in some schools but promoted in others?

Step 1 Tab over now to the worksheet titled "problem 2" in the Excel file "teacher_mgt_Ex2" where you will find data for 47 classes of fifth-grade pupils, showing the average rate of repetition across classes and the average test scores of students on two separate tests: *tchr_score* refers to scores on year-end evaluation tests set by the various class teachers for their own classes; *std_score* refers to scores on a single standardized test administered at the end of the school year for the sample as a whole.[5] Take a moment now to scan the data, answer the following question briefly, and then proceed to the next step. How difficult, or how easy, would it be to compile a similar data file for the countries you work in or are familiar with? Where might you find the needed data?

Answer:

_____

_____

_____

_____

5

Step 2 Your task here is to examine the relationship between the year-end average test score across classes and the share of pupils who are asked to repeat the grade at the end of the year. Scroll down to the relevant part of the Excel sheet, follow the instructions printed in red, and answer the following questions as best you can:

(i) What are the main similarities between the two graphs (which relate test scores to the repetition rate) and their corresponding regression estimates? *Hint:* Consider the overall shape of the graph, the dispersion of the scatter plot, and the range across classes with similar average scores on the two tests, in the share of pupils being asked to repeat.

Answer:

_____

_____

_____

_____

(ii) In your opinion, why do classes with similar average scores differ so much in the proportion of students who are asked to repeat the grade?

Answer: _____

_____

_____

_____

(iii) What is the key difference between the two graphs and their corresponding regression estimates?

Answer: _____

_____

_____

_____

(iv) In your opinion, why is the relationship in the first graph much tighter than that in the second graph?

Answer: _____

_____

_____

_____

Step 3   Your task here is to examine the relationship between the scores on the test set by each class teacher and those based on the standardized test. As before, locate this section in the Excel sheet and answer the following questions: Why do the scores on the two tests relate so weakly to each other? What does the weak link suggest about the management of classroom processes in the system?

Answers: _____

_____

_____

_____

Step 4   Here the assignment is to draw together the diagnosis as a whole and to suggest possible next steps in policy development. Respond to the following questions:

(i)   By way of summary, how would you characterize the nature of the management deficiencies in the system?

Answer: _____

_____

_____

_____

(ii)   What next steps would you recommend to help develop a strategy for addressing the management problems identified?

Answer: _____

_____

_____

_____

_____

Problem 3: Diagnosing Management Problems as Revealed by Disparities in Student Learning

We turn now to the diagnosis of possible management deficiencies as revealed by disparities in learning outcomes across pupils.[6] The disparities reflect the impact of two broad sets of factors—those having to do with pupils' personal, family, and community characteristics; and those having to do with their schooling environments. The learning achieved by pupils at any given point reflects the cumulative impact of these factors over time; in other words, a child's achievement at the end of, say, fourth grade is the result of a progressive accumulation of skills acquired at home and at school, from birth through fourth grade. In view of the cumulative nature of the learning process, it would not be valid simply to relate student learning at a given point in time to conditions that prevailed during the corresponding school year. Because these conditions can only be expected to influence pupils' *progress* in learning during that school year, the relationship needs to be expressed in value-added terms, as follows:

(2) $$e\_score = f(s\_score, pfc, ped)$$

where *e_score* and *s_score* refer, respectively, to pupils' test scores at the end and at the start of the school year; *pfc* refers to the pupils' personal, family, and community characteristics; and *ped* refers to the pedagogical environment in which the pupils were taught during that school year. Below we will apply this conceptual model, appropriately modified, to diagnose possible gaps in the management of student learning in the classroom. The R^2 statistic, a product of regression estimation that measures the explanatory power of the regression model, is especially relevant to our purpose here.

Step 1 Your task is to understand specifications of the model in equation (2) in order to tease out a diagnostic indicator for assessing the management of learning processes. Examine the following specifications and try to interpret them, using the questions below to guide your thinking. Enter your comments in the spaces after each question or on the Excel sheet labeled "problem 3."

Specification A:	$e\_score = f(s\_score, pfc)$	$R^2 = A$
Specification B:	$e\_score = f(s\_score, pfc, class\_dummy)$	$R^2 = B$

where *class_dummy* is a vector of $N-1$ variables corresponding to the N classes of pupils in the sample, with each of the variables defined as having a value of 1 if a pupil belongs to the class represented by it, and 0 otherwise.

Specification C:	$e\_score = f(s\_score, pfc, class\_log)$	$R^2 = C$

where *class_log* refers to a vector of variables that captures the logistical or tangible aspects of the pedagogical environment, including such aspects as the physical condition of the facilities; the teacher's gender, education and training, and experience in teaching; the number of pupils in the class; and the availability of textbooks and pedagogical materials for teachers and pupils.

(i) Would you expect the R^2 statistic for specification A to exceed those of the other two regressions? Briefly explain your answer.

Answer: _____

_____

_____

_____

_____

(ii) How would you interpret the coefficient on the dummy variables?

Answer:

(iii) Would the R^2 statistic for specification B exceed that for specification C? Briefly explain your answer.

Answer:

(iv) In specification C, what important set of factors could have been incorporated in the model? Would you place great importance on collecting data on these factors to include in the regression analysis?

Answer:

5

Step 2   Here your task is to examine how the R^2 statistic from the three specifications can be used to identify the existence and nature of management deficiencies at the school or classroom level. To accomplish the task, try to answer the following questions (which appear also on the Excel sheet):

(i)   Recall that the R^2 statistic is a measure of the proportion of variability in the dependent variable—year-end test scores in this case—that is explained by the regressors on the right-hand side of the equation. Given this understanding, how would you interpret the following quantities (which are defined in step 1 above): $[C-A]$, $[B-A]$, and $[B-C]$?

Answer:

(ii) What would large values of [C – A] and [B – C] signify regarding the management of education at the classroom level?

Answer: _____

_____

_____

(iii) In a system with good management at the classroom or school level, would you expect students to perform equally well on year-end tests? Why or why not?

Answer: _____

_____

_____

_____

(iv) Consider the R^2 statistics below that correspond to regression estimates using data from three countries—X, Y, and Z. The lilac block in the Excel file shows the differences in R^2 values corresponding to [B – A], [C – A], and [B – C]. Place your cursor on these cells to reveal their definitions. Using your results as a basis, how would you rate the management of the three countries' education systems at the class or school level?

Answer: _____

_____

_____

_____

Responding to the Identified Management Problems

The foregoing two problems elaborated on methods for diagnosing possible gaps in the management of classroom processes. By providing information on the location, magnitude, and nature of these deficiencies, the diagnostic analysis is an indispensable first step in finding solutions for them. Clearly, however, it needs to be followed by additional work to inform the design of the solutions. Although it is beyond the scope of the present module to elaborate in detail on the follow-on analysis, a few ideas can be explored regarding the types of analysis that potentially are helpful.

Problem 4: Moving from Diagnosis toward a Plan of Action

An important ingredient of a plan of action is choosing appropriate interventions and targeting them accurately. Follow the steps below to see how some progress can be made in this regard. We emphasize that the work involved in the steps below is only a component of a broader set of follow-on analysis that is needed to inform the development of a strategy for improved management.

Step 1 Your task here is to identify possible directions for follow-on work to support policy development. To guide your thinking, answer the following question as best you can, either in the spaces below or on the Excel worksheet labeled "problem 4":

(i) Suppose your diagnosis suggests that schools use substantially different criteria for making decisions about grade promotion, so that pupils who have similar marks but who are in different schools face widely different probabilities of being promoted or held back in the same grade. Comment on how this outcome might affect the efficiency of learning from grade to grade. What information and analysis can help policymakers define guidelines that teachers and school administrators can use to make decisions about grade promotion?

Answer:

_____

_____

_____

_____

_____

(ii) Suppose that your diagnosis suggests that the system also suffers from poor management of classroom processes. One possible approach is to set norms and standards. How promising is this approach? What additional information would policymakers need to define the norms?

Answer:

_____

_____

_____

_____

_____

_____

Step 2 A useful direction for the follow-on analysis is to examine more closely the relationship between per-pupil investment of resources and student achievement, taking classes of pupils in the sample schools as the relevant unit of aggregation. With the same data used to estimate the value-added education production specified in equation (2) above, we can estimate for each sample class the average spending per pupil by costing out the inputs and averaging the aggregate cost over the number of students in the class. It would not be useful, however, to relate the resulting unit cost directly to the average year-end test score of the class because the raw test score reflects the combined influence of three factors: initial test scores, pupil characteristics, and the effectiveness of classroom management processes. For our purpose, we are interested mainly in the last factor, so we need a year-end test score that has been standardized across all sample classes for differences in initial test scores and pupil characteristics. In other words, we need a conditional test score.

To estimate the conditional test score we proceed as follows. First we estimate the regression equation of the form specified in equation (2). Then we use the resulting equation to simulate the desired conditional scores by substituting into the equation the sample averages for initial scores and pupil characteristics while retaining the school-specific values of the variables pertaining to the logistical dimensions of the schooling environment (that is, *class_log*). Assuming that this analysis has been completed, the relationship between the conditional test score and spending per pupil is as shown in figure 5.B.4.1. Your task here is to distill

Figure 5.B.4.1: Relationship between Unit Spending and Test Scores

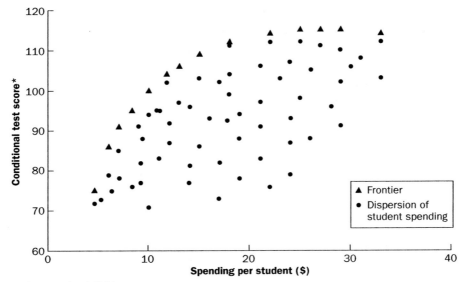

* See text for definition.

implications from the results to support the development of a strategy for improved management at the class or school level.

Take a moment now to review the graph in figure 5.B.4.1. If you wish, you may view the graph in color on the Excel sheet. Each diamond represents a class of pupils in the sample. The triangles connect points on the "frontier" representing the most efficient classes in the system. Proceed to answer the question posed below.

Indicate on the graph above the following four clusters of classes in the sample:

- Cluster 1: classes that are reasonably efficient and could benefit from increased funding
- Cluster 2: classes that are clearly inefficient and whose internal operations warrant close scrutiny
- Cluster 3: classes that are efficient and are overresourced
- Cluster 4: classes that can be considered good models for the rest of the system

What implications does your analysis so far have for developing a strategy to improve management of the system?

Answer: _____

_____

_____

_____

_____

Step 3　Beyond identifying individual schools for various interventions, the relationship depicted above also allows us to evaluate broader policy choices for the system as a whole. To perform this evaluation we add three more details to the graph, as shown in figure 5.B.4.2: the open circles connect points on a straight-line regression relating the variables on the two axes; the vertical and horizontal squares connect lines through the sample mean, which is represented by a large circle. Take a moment to review the graph and then proceed to the items below.

(i)　Suppose the government would like to raise student learning for the system as a whole. What would this require if classroom processes and the efficiency of their management remain essentially unchanged? Indicate on your graph the direction in which the position of the point representing the system average would shift.

(ii)　Indicate on your graph how the government can improve student learning or expand coverage without necessarily increasing the average level of spending per pupil.

Figure 5.B.4.2: Relationship between Unit Spending and Test Scores (with Three Details Also Shown)

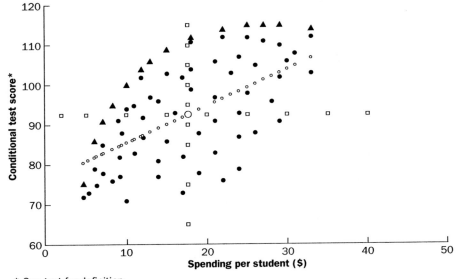

* See text for definition.

5

Conclusion

In this chapter we have considered various dimensions of management in education. For our purpose, we began with a simple perspective on education, viewing it as a process involving the allocation and use of available resources to achieve certain educational, social, or economic objectives. A well-managed system would be characterized by at least two qualities: the resources are allocated in a consistent manner across schools and classes, and educational outcomes are achieved as efficiently and equitably as possible. How can one gauge whether an education system is being managed well? How can a broad-brush assessment of management performance be made using readily available data? How can the results of such an assessment help policymakers form a strategy for action or a plan for more focused follow-up analysis? In this module we have explored methods for conducting the broad-brush assessment and examined how the results can be used to inform policy design.

The methods elaborated above rely on data pertaining to teachers. The focus on teachers is appropriate because they account for the bulk of costs associated with delivering education services—at all levels of education but especially at the basic levels. Moreover, teachers are the main agents of management in the classroom, and their effectiveness as a moderator of all that goes on in the classroom—on a day-to-day basis as well as over the course of the school year—matters enormously for the performance of the system as a whole.

The chapter considered first the deployment of teachers as a management issue. The focus was on documenting the possible gaps in management on this front and on evaluating the existence of scale economies and their implications for teacher deployment in small schools, particularly at postprimary levels of instruction. The chapter then moved to the next lower level of aggregation by looking at management issues within the classroom. Again the aim was to develop broad indicators to diagnose the system as a whole rather than to delve into the details of specific teacher practices and behavior. Taken as a whole, the various methods offered above can provide a sufficiently good basis for gauging management performance and can direct policymakers' attention toward more strategic choices in addressing possible management deficiencies in the education system.

Endnotes

1. The cost of teachers can make up as much as 95 percent of total spending at the lower levels of education in poor countries; even in rich countries, where spending on other schooling inputs is generally larger, teacher costs seldom fall below 80 percent of total spending.

2. In most countries the government collects similar data on the number of teachers and students at the school level, often for the purpose of producing the annual publication on education statistics. Although the publication shows only aggregated data, it may be possible with little extra effort to obtain data at the school level to conduct the type of analysis described here.

3. School-level data on such characteristics often are collected to prepare education statistical yearbooks. Because they usually are not published, access to the data often requires a specific request from potential users. Other correlates, such as regional location of the school or ethnicity of the school population, also might be included as appropriate to the context of the analysis.

4. The estimated regression equation in the Excel worksheet is totals = 10,531.1 + 32.4 • students.

5. The unit of observation in this example is the class. If data on individual pupils are available, the analysis also can be conducted with individuals as the unit of observation. Although the techniques required for the latter will be more demanding, the basic ideas remain the same.

6. Where data on individuals are available, the analysis also can be accomplished using individual pupils rather than classes of pupils as the unit of observation.

5

Assessing Policy Options for Teacher Training and Pay

A Two-Part Module

Alain Mingat and Shobhana Sosale

The road to education for all (EFA) presents an enormous challenge in many countries. Many governments need to hire and train (and retain) massive numbers of new teachers over the next decade to reach the EFA goals. Their success in this endeavor will largely determine whether EFA efforts are successful and sustainable.

The relationship between teacher pay and teacher quality has been analyzed often in the literature on education research, with inconclusive results. Many factors, including the nature of the labor market as well as various political factors, come into play, making direct connections—for instance, a doubling of teacher salaries with a subsequent doubling of outputs—difficult to discern. Yet there are linkages and a delicate balance to be found—where teacher salaries are too low, countries are often unable to attract or retain qualified teachers; where salaries are too high, costs become unmanageable, and countries are unable to afford the numbers of teachers needed.

Teacher salaries currently represent 80 percent of total spending on education, and teachers constitute a crucial input in the quality of education. To ensure that qualified individuals are attracted to the teaching profession and that they deliver the expected services, teachers should be adequately paid. Teachers also should be trained correctly so that they can master the many professional skills and competencies required by their work.

Policies pertaining to teacher training and teacher pay need to be assessed. Analyzing teacher-training policies separately from teacher-pay policies is worthwhile, even though the two sets of policies are somewhat interrelated. The purpose of this learning module is to illustrate the principles, concepts, and methodology and techniques needed to accomplish the analyses.

The chapter consists of two parts, with hands-on exercises. Part A focuses on identifying a teacher-training policy. The hands-on exercises will involve the use of techniques to estimate the impact of teacher education and training on student outcomes, estimate the costs associated with changes in inputs, and arrive at a cost-effectiveness analysis. The exercises will progress from simple to complex calculations. Part B focuses on the economics of teacher pay. Here the emphasis is on introducing you to techniques for using international and national comparative perspectives for salary-related issues and for projecting the resources that would have to be available for education in the future. The module can be completed in one day by those who already have a basic understanding of regression analysis and who are competent in using Excel; those without such background will need pretraining in order to benefit fully from the module.[1]

The module includes this write-up and the CD-ROM with Excel data files for the exercises. The Excel files are distinctly labeled to correspond to each of the two parts, and individual exercises within each part can be found in worksheets identified with a name corresponding to the exercise. For example, the file "tchr_trg_pay_1.xls" refers to exercises in part A of the module, and the worksheet "problem 1" in that file refers to the first exercise.

The write-up is self-contained in the sense that it includes all the information that a reader needs to understand and accomplish the exercises. The first few problems are deliberately kept simple in order to acclimatize the user to the hands-on pedagogical method. Excel procedures are invoked in the exercises, but are kept to a minimum so as to focus attention on the substance. Because the exercises are arranged in sequence, it is best to proceed systematically from problem to problem. Learners are thus strongly encouraged to read the text relating to each exercise before attempting the computations.

Part A: Identifying a Teacher-Training Policy

Basic Principles to Justify Policies on Teacher Training

Problem 1

Insert the CD-ROM into the computer and retrieve the file "tchr_trg_pay_1.xls." Check the bottom of the screen to make sure that you are in the worksheet marked "problem 1." Follow the steps below to complete the exercises. The exercises in the problems are specifically designed to lead you to understand the principles and concepts, analyze data, and finally combine the principles with the analytical results to come up with an optimal teacher-training policy.

Step 1   There are some basic principles to consider in order to justify policies on teacher training. Prior to defining the principles, however, some critical questions need to be investigated in the context of teacher training and education. What are some of the questions? Use the yellow block in the Excel worksheet or the space here to answer the question.

Answer:

_____

_____

_____

_____

_____

_____

Five principles govern the structure of this learning module:

- **Principle 1:** *Factual analysis is by necessity a comparative analysis.* This implies gathering facts with respect to student learning and levels across different types of teacher training.
- **Principle 2:** *Facts about impact on student learning need to be contrasted with costs.* Choosing education and training for teachers is related to both pedagogical issues and economic aspects that also need to be taken into account.

Step 2   What might be two complementary dimensions of cost that require attention? Provide your answer here or in the yellow block under "problem 1, step 2."

Answer:

_____

_____

_____

_____

_____

_____

- **Principle 3:** *A marginal perspective is appropriate for many teacher issues, where certain policies may have diminishing returns beyond a given value.* Refer to diagrams A and B in figure 6.A.1.1.

6

Figure 6.A.1.1: Understanding the Marginal Perspective

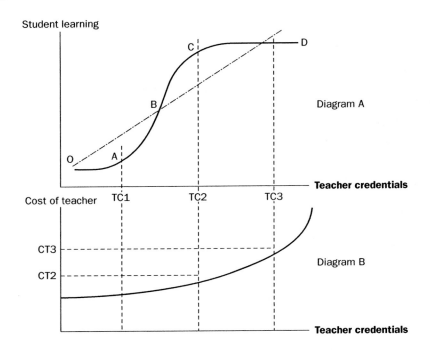

Step 3   Comment on the relationship between student learning and teacher credentials. Use the yellow block under "problem 1, step 3" in your Excel worksheet or the space below.

Answer:

_____

_____

_____

_____

_____

- **Principle 4:** *Opportunity costs will need to be taken into consideration; investments need to be made where benefits are greatest.* This principle is arrived at by blending principles 1, 2, and 3 to identify a cost-effective strategy for teacher education and training (the opportunity cost argument). If the benefits to student learning increase as a result of greater allocations for teacher training, this expenditure is justi-fied—particularly if expenditures to increase the number of tutorials or learning materials or to reduce class size have less of an impact on student learning.

  If we focus on increasing teacher credentials, we are confronted with the patterns of the marginal diminishing impact of teacher credentials on student learning; and of the marginal increase in the cost of doing so. It follows that this strategy becomes progressively less attractive. It will remain attractive as long as the marginal cost-efficiency ratio associated with increasing teacher credentials exceeds that of expanding the provision of any other school inputs.

- **Principle 5:** *Teacher education may vary widely in content and purpose, making cost-effectiveness comparisons difficult.* A label such as "pre-service" or "in-service teacher training" may be used to describe activities whose design or content may be quite different. For example, under the label of in-service training we may find activities ranging from academic courses intended to help primary school teachers get a higher pay scale or to teach in secondary schools, to very practical activities designed to help teachers manage their classes and respond to the difficulties they encounter in their day-to-day work. Similarly, pre-service teacher training may correspond to a general education type of studies completed with some general courses in child psychology and in the history of pedagogical movements. It also may be targeted at practical aspects such as concrete pedagogical techniques, evaluation of students, and so forth. It is clear that one month, one year, or one dollar spent in either pre-service or in-service teacher training may be associated with quite different outcomes (marginal impact on student learning), whether the training is of one type of content or another.

For this reason, when assessing the impact of teacher training (and deriving cost-efficiency indicators), we need to be conscious that the results of the assessment are indexed on the particular content of the activities undertaken under the generic label of teacher training. It follows that if teacher training corresponds to different "approaches" and ways of training in a certain country, it may be useful to conduct the assessment in parallel for the alternative modes implemented. If only one mode exists, and if the assessment results in a low level of cost efficiency, it does not imply that the approach is inadequate; rather, the low level might be caused by the way the approach is being implemented.

Overview of the Steps in the Analysis

Generally speaking, following the five principles outlined above—that is, relating what is done at the margin of existing conditions with the marginal costs on the one hand, and with the marginal impact on student outcomes on the other (cost-effectiveness techniques[2])—should be fundamental to analyzing the potential options for action and then to setting priorities among them. The cost-effectiveness context involves three steps in the analysis, as elaborated below.

The first step is relating education and training characteristics of teachers with the amount of learning that students have acquired over a period of time (for example, a school year). The second step is determining the costs of the different components of education and training. And the third step is determining ratios of benefits to costs and identifying a strategy.

It should be stressed that it is not advisable to aim at analyzing the targeted teacher characteristics in isolation from the other main elements that together define the context in which education is imparted to students. Two reasons prevail. First, to assess the impact on student learning of a given input (for example, the amount and type of professional training the teacher has received prior to taking the position), it is preferable to control for the influence of other elements that together play a role on outcomes—for example, textbooks and learning materials. Second, when designing a strategy for teacher training, we need to compare the impact on outcomes of putting more resources in training with the impact of using the same resources in another input in the context of schooling (the opportunity cost argument). Therefore, to form a really justifiable strategy on teacher training, we need information on schooling inputs.

Estimating the Impact of Teacher Education and Training on Student Outcomes

We begin by reviewing some basic concepts and issues in impact analysis. If you are familiar with estimating education production functions you may wish to proceed directly to problem 2; otherwise, simply read on.

To assess the impact of a school factor affecting student outcome, there should be some variability in that factor. We can evaluate its impact by measuring the extent to which outcomes are significantly better (or worse) when more (or less) of the factor is provided or used. In most education systems, particularly in developing countries, we find a fair variation in schooling conditions across different schools and classes. This applies to a great extent to teacher education. For example, teachers may have between 8 and 14 years of general education, between 1 and 2 years of pre-service teacher training, or no education. Class size may range from 15 to 80 pupils. Such variability in learning conditions may not be good for the system as a whole. The preference is obviously for a system in which the learning conditions are fairly homogeneous across different schools and across different geographical locations. It is helpful, however, to underscore that the variability makes for favorable conditions to analyze the relationship between variable inputs and outcomes.

Let us assume that a country in which primary school teachers are recruited with 12 years of general education and 2 years of pre-service teacher training is considering extending the requirements for teacher recruitment to 14 years of general education and keeping pre-service teacher training at 2 years. The focus of our analysis is in documenting whether such a plan is justified.

6

To conduct the analysis, we need a sample of classes with fair variation in the duration of both education and training of teachers.[3] We also need to collect data on student learning at the beginning and at the end of the school year. We assume that 125 classes of grade four have been sampled, and that 30 students have been selected randomly to participate in the study. For each pupil, we have data on gender and parents' occupations, as well as on his or her entering and outgoing test scores. With regard to school and class, we have data on location (rural or urban), number of pupils registered, proportion of pupils with a textbook, and an index of availability of teaching materials. With respect to teachers, we know the gender, the number of years of general education, number of years of pre-service teacher training, and the number of years of teaching experience.

After the data have been collected, we can conduct the empirical analysis. To relate the factors to schooling outcomes typically requires regression estimation of what is known in the literature as "an education production function." On the left-hand side of the equation is student learning (outgoing score). In the regression specification it is important to recognize that the schooling outcomes observed at a given point in time represent the cumulative product of a process over time. The impact of a given set of schooling conditions on student learning therefore needs to be gauged by how much it has improved the capabilities of the children exposed to it, relative to the level at which the children started. In other words, the correct basis for comparison is the value added by the various policy options. On the right-hand side is a set of variables representing schooling conditions that are amenable to policy manipulation, as well as policy-sensitive factors that also are expected to affect student learning, including students' personal characteristics, family background, and regional location.[4]

The general framework involves regressing the outgoing score on (a) the incoming score of students (value-added perspective); (b) the individual pupil variables (for gender, a dummy variable[5] of one if a girl or zero if a boy; for location, a dummy of one for rural and zero for urban; a set of three dummy variables for father's occupation: farmer, informal craftsman, or salesman; low-qualification wage earner; and qualified wage earner); (c) the class or school variables (number of pupils registered, percent of pupils with textbooks, and index of availability of teaching material—all three variables being continuous[6]); and (d) the teacher variables (gender; a dummy variable: years of general education in dummy variables for 9 years or less, 10 years, 11 years, 12 years, 13 years and more; two dummy variables for pre-service training: one year and two years, with zero used as the reference, and the number of years of teaching experience a continuous variable).

6

Problem 2

Click on the worksheet marked "problem 2." Follow the steps below to complete the exercises. Results of the regression are provided in table 6.A.2.1 below. Take a moment to scan the table.

Table 6.A.2.1: Regression Results of Outgoing Scores against a Set of Explanatory Variables

Regression variable	Sample values	Coefficient	t-Statistics
Pupil variables			
Entering score	$N(100,15)$	+0.67	8.5
Girl/boy	0.43	−2.30	2.1
Father: farmer/qualified wage earner	0.45	−1.24	0.7
Father: informal sector/qualified wage earner	0.30	−1.71	1.2
Father: unqualified wage earner/qualified wage earner	0.20	−2.15	1.9
Class/school variables			
Location: rural/urban	0.69	−3.56	2.6
Number of pupils in class	(46.15) [15–82]	−0.07	2.2
Percent of pupils with textbooks	39 [5–100]	+0.11	3.1
Index of teaching materials	(3.6, 1.8) [1–6]	+1.15	1.9
Teacher variables			
Female/male	0.30	−1.31	0.8
10 years of general education/9 years or less	0.15	+3.24	1.7
11 years of general education/9 years or less	0.20	+6.51	2.7
12 years of general education/9 years or less	0.35	+5.98	2.2
13–14 years of general education/9 years or less	0.15	+7.34	2.0
1 year of pre-service teacher training/no pre-service teacher training	0.25	+5.25	3.0
2 years of pre-service teacher training/no pre-service teacher training	0.35	+4.21	2.4
Number of years of teaching experience	(11, 7.2) [1–26]	+0.15	1.4
Constant	n.a.	+25.36	n.a.
Share of variance accounted by the model (%)	n.a.	43.2	

n.a. Not applicable.

Note: Outgoing score $N(100,15)$. Figures in parentheses are the mean and the standard deviation. Figures in brackets give the range of the variable in the sample. Figures alone correspond to the proportion of the considered category for dummy variables: the proportion of the omitted category is the complement to one of the sums of the different categories of the same output.

(i)   On the basis of the information provided in table 6.A.2.1, comment on the performance of girls versus boys.

Answer:

_____

_____

_____

_____

_____

(ii) Using data in table 6.A.2.1 as the basis, comment on the performance of pupils by location (rural versus urban).

Answer:

_____

_____

_____

_____

_____

(iii) If you use the information provided in table 6.A.2.1 as a basis, what effect do school input variables (other than teacher variables) have on student learning?

Answer:

_____

_____

_____

_____

_____

6

(iv) Focusing on the target variables in table 6.A.2.1, describe your observations about teacher variables (in particular, general education and pre-service training) on student learning.

Answer:

_____

_____

_____

_____

_____

Cost Estimation—Estimating the Costs Associated with Changes in Inputs

From the regression results in problem 2 we get a sense of the effective impact on student learning of the different factors analyzed. This constitutes an important step (generally the most difficult) toward identifying some educational policies. Because the regression variables in the impact analysis have been measured in different units, a direct comparison of the coefficients is not meaningful. For policy purposes we need to compare instead the impact per unit of resources expended, unless we have a variable bearing a cost but showing no impact on outcomes. To do so, we first need to translate the physical units in which the regression variables have been measured into their financial equivalents (see table 6.A.3.2 below). For example, we need to know the costs of such items as an extra year of teacher education, an extra month of in-service teacher training, and an extra year of pre-service teacher training. To identify the cost of changing the provision of each of the inputs considered (for example, the cost of reducing class size by one pupil, of providing students with textbooks, of expanding the level of general education of teachers from 12 to 14 years, and so forth), let us now examine how we can do this. We start the analysis by focusing on the costs associated with teacher education and training.

The exercises below show how to accomplish the cost estimation, focusing on the inputs explicitly included in the impact analysis: teachers' formal education, pre-service teacher training, and in-service teacher training.[7]

Problem 3

In many countries teachers are paid according to a salary scale generally based on the initial level of education and training, and on seniority. According to these criteria, the scale defines the number of points for any individual. The points relate to a value, which when converted can be expressed in prevailing wage scales (for example, the current value of a point in country X is 26.5 shillings a month, or 318 shillings a year). The wage scales may vary over time, but the point scale may be relatively stable. Because the pattern of teacher pay is a key influence on the cost of several of the inputs in the impact analysis, we will examine it as a first task in our cost analysis. Table 6.A.3.2 provides relevant data in the country under consideration. The calculation of average annual salary based on level of education and years of experience has already been completed for your convenience. Scan the table quickly and read on below for further instructions. (The purpose here is not to arrive at a conclusion as to whether ministries of education should reduce the

6

Table 6.A.3.2: Data on Teacher Salary, Experience, and Training Level in Country X

Years of teaching experience	9 years of general education Years of pre-service TT			10 years of general education Years of pre-service TT			11 years of general education Years of pre-service TT			12 years of general education Years of pre-service TT			14 years of general education Years of pre-service TT		
	0	1	2	0	1	2	0	1	2	0	1	2	0	1	2
0–2	100	118	136	118	136	154	136	154	172	154	172	192	172	192	220
2–4	106	123	142	123	142	160	142	160	178	160	178	198	178	198	226
4–6	112	124	148	124	148	166	148	166	184	166	184	206	184	206	234
6–8	118	130	154	130	154	172	154	172	190	172	190	212	190	212	242
8–10	124	136	160	136	160	178	160	178	196	178	196	220	196	220	248
10–12	130	142	166	142	166	184	166	184	202	184	202	226	202	226	254
12–15	133	148	170	148	170	188	170	188	208	188	208	232	208	232	260
15–20	140	154	176	154	176	192	176	192	214	192	214	236	214	236	264
20–25	142	158	182	158	182	196	182	196	218	196	218	242	218	242	268
25–30	146	164	188	164	188	202	188	202	222	202	222	248	222	248	272
Reference salary point	130	142	166	142	166	184	166	184	202	184	202	226	202	226	254
Average salary/year (shillings)	41,340	45,792	52,788	45,792	52,788	58,512	52,788	58,512	64,236	58,512	64,236	71,868	64,236	71,868	80,772

TT Teacher training.

Note: At the current conversion rate, each salary point is worth 318 shillings a year.

6

number of graduated seniority and qualification-based scales. Where there is a long history of such approaches, this is unlikely to happen. Almost all countries are confronted with the issue of raising teacher qualification levels. It seems unlikely that countries will do this purely on a cost basis.)

Our first task is to understand the data. In the Excel file tab over to the worksheet titled "problem 3," which contains an electronic copy of table 6.A.3.2. Scroll down the worksheet to view the table. What are your observations based on the information provided in table 6.A.3.2?

Answer: _____

_____

_____

_____

_____

Now let us assume that the issue confronted by policymakers in country X is whether to increase the level of general education of teachers from 10 to 11 years. If you were the policy analyst in the ministry of education in country X, what would you identify as the most important information that would be useful in the policymaking process?

Answer: _____

_____

_____

_____

Problem 4

Here you learn to calculate the marginal costs of increasing teachers' level of general education. Marginal costs refer to the costs associated with changing a school input by a given unit, taking the current level of the input as the base from which the change is made. Consider teachers' formal schooling, for example. Because we have measured the variable in years, the marginal cost of the input would be the cost of raising teacher's formal schooling by 1 year from the current average of 10 years. For the variables included in our analysis the relevant marginal costs refer to the cost of the units of teacher inputs specified in table 6.A.3.2 above, which has been reproduced in the Excel worksheet in problem 4 for your convenience.

The procedure for estimating marginal costs varies across inputs, depending on the nature of the inputs. Some inputs entail both recurrent and investment costs, and others entail only one of the two types of costs. Where investment costs are involved they would need to be annualized in order to render them comparable to recurrent costs. The steps below identify both types of costs and show how they can be analyzed. For all inputs considered here, we will evaluate upper- and lower-bound marginal costs, both to reflect a reasonable range in the underlying assumptions and to test the sensitivity of the cost estimates to their assumptions.

Step 1　Let us begin by determining the marginal costs of raising teachers' level of general education from 9 to 10 years. Table 6.A.4.3 provides information on the marginal cost figures, the average, and the range, drawing on information provided in table 6.A.4.2. Using table 6.A.4.2 it is possible to determine the additional annual salary cost in country X. Go to the worksheet marked "problem 1.4" and complete in table 6.A.4.3 the blank yellow cells for teachers with no teachers' training and with one year of training. For your convenience a copy of table 6.A.4.2 has been reproduced in the Excel worksheet.

Step 2　Now turn to the case of pre-service teacher training. Its impact on cost has two components: (a) teachers who have received more pre-service training are entitled to a higher salary scale, and (b) there is a cost implication related to the spread of the initial investment for pre-service training that needs to be amortized over the period during which the investment is used. These two components should be added. A standard way to proceed with the latter component consists of calculating the total investment cost incurred during the period of training and of annualizing that cost and adding it to the marginal salary cost.

Because we expect the training to remain useful for several years, the amount in fact represents the investment cost of the training. It must therefore be annualized before it can be added to the increment in salary

6

Table 6.A.4.3: Marginal Cost of Increasing Level of General Education of Teachers in Country X

General education	No teacher training	1 Year of teacher training	2 Years of teacher training	Average (range)
From 9 to 10 years			5,724	5,724 (4,452–6,996)
From 10 to 11 years		5,724	5,724	6,148 (5,724–6,996)
From 11 to 12 years	5,724	5,724	7,632	6,360 (5,724–7,632)
From 12 to 14 years	5,724	7,632	8,804	8,413 (5,724–8,804)

(the marginal cost or the value-added cost) to obtain the full cost of increasing pre-service teacher training by one year (from 9 to 10 years). The general formula to determine the annualized cost of a given initial capital spending or investment cost is as follows:

$$AC = \frac{ICS \bullet K \bullet (1 + k)^n}{(1 + k)^n - 1}$$

where AC is the annualized cost, ICS is the initial capital spending, k is the opportunity cost of capital (interest rate), and n is the useful lifetime of the year of training or schooling.

For our purpose we have the following data relating to the cost per participant in a year-long pre-service teacher-training program: direct cost per trainee-year is 22,000 shillings, and the opportunity cost is 31,800 shillings.[8] The latter is assumed to be the same as or equal to the starting salary of a teacher with eight years of general education. The total investment cost of one year of teacher training is therefore 53,800 shillings per trainee. This amount should be annualized. In order to do this we assume that teacher training may be amortized over 10 years and the yearly opportunity cost of capital (interest rate) is 5 percent.

For convenience the data are organized in table 6.A.4.4. Now apply the formula above to annualize the investment costs of the year-long teacher-training course. Complete the calculation for one year of investment in teacher training.

Step 3   We now can move to estimate the marginal costs associated with other school inputs, which might not entail an increase in teacher salaries but which have useful lifetimes exceeding one year. As above, the costs of the inputs represent investment outlays that need to be annualized to render them comparable to other costs in our analysis. Let us assume with regard to the availability of textbooks that the price of a pupil's set of textbooks is 500 shillings, the textbooks need to be replaced every four years, and the yearly opportunity cost of capital (interest rate) is 5 percent. Let us also assume that the index of teaching material has been estimated with one point of the index worth, on average, 600 shillings, that the material so acquired lasts for five years, and that the yearly opportunity cost of capital (interest rate) is 5 percent. In the interest of saving time, the annualized costs of both inputs corresponding to these assumptions have been completed for you in table 6.A.4.5. Simply review the results in the table and then proceed to the next step.

Step 4   Now we'll consider the cost of changing class size. Although class size is not a tangible school input, it does reflect the amount of pedagogical resources effectively available to each pupil in a class. This is because inputs such as the teacher's time, pedagogical materials, and the

6

Table 6.A.4.4: Computing the Total Cost of Increasing Teacher Qualification (shillings)

	9 Years of general education	10 Years of general education	11 Years of general education	12 Years of general education	14 Years of general education	Average [range]
From 0 to 1 year of TT						
Salary cost[a]			5,724	5,724	7,632	6,106 (4,452–7,632)
Annualized capital cost[a]						
Total cost[b]						12,546 (10,901–14,081)
From 1 to 2 years of TT						
Salary cost[a]		5,724	5,724	7,632	8,904	6,996 (5,724–8,904)
Annualized capital cost[a]						
Total cost[b]						13,445 (12,173–15,353)

TT Teacher training.

a. Information obtained from table 6.A.4.3.

b. Total cost = salary cost + annualized capital cost.

classroom building or infrastructure itself are shared across pupils in the class. An increase in the number of pupils in the class implies spreading the shared resources over more pupils, and therefore corresponds to a decline in the resources available per pupil. Class size and resource availability per pupil therefore are inversely related.

Table 6.A.4.5: Marginal Cost of Increasing Textbooks and Teaching Material

	Cost per unit (shillings)				
Item	Direct costs	Opportunity costs	Total costs	Assumed useful lifetime, n	Annualized costs (shillings)
Per set of textbooks	500	n.a.	500	4	141
Index of teaching materials	600	n.a.	600	5	139

n.a. Not applicable.

Note: Opportunity cost of capital (interest rate) is assumed to be 5 percent.

6

Assuming that we have one teacher per class, we can express the resource availability per pupil using the following equation:

$$\text{Resources per pupil} = \frac{\text{Teacher salary}}{\text{Class size}} + \text{Materials per pupil}$$

Furthermore, assuming that teacher costs amount to about 90 percent of total unit costs, we can simplify the equation to:

$$\text{Resources per pupil} = \left(\frac{\text{Teacher salary}}{\text{Class size}} \right) \Big/ 0.90$$

We can use this equation to estimate per-pupil expenditure for any class size and level of teacher salary. In order to obtain the marginal cost associated with variation in class size, we will assume class size to be at the initial or sample mean of 46. We do this because marginal cost depends on the characteristics and salary level of the teacher. We use the same approach as above—that is, we assess the impact of class size for "extreme" cases as far as the salary of teachers is concerned, getting therefore the upper and lower bounds of the range of the marginal cost associated with the factor.

To compute the marginal cost of reducing the class size by one pupil below the sample or initial mean, we simply calculate the unit costs corresponding to 46 and 45 pupils for the assumed level of teacher salary, and take the difference between the resulting estimates. Table 6.A.4.6 has been arranged to facilitate your calculation and the upper bound has been completed as an example. Locate the table now by scrolling down your current worksheet, and complete the yellow cells.

Step 5   As a final step in this analysis we consolidate the foregoing marginal cost estimates in table 6.A.4.7 below. In preparation for the

Table 6.A.4.6: Calculating the Marginal Cost of Changing Class Size

	Alternative assumptions or estimates	
Item	*Lower bound*	*Upper bound*
Teacher's annual salary (shillings)	41,340	80,772
Unit cost (shillings per pupil)		
With class of 46 pupils		1,755.9
With class of 45 pupils		1,794.9
Marginal cost of reducing class size by one pupil (shillings)		39.0

Note: For our sample, the mean class size is 46 pupils.

Table 6.A.4.7: Marginal Costs of Changing the Various School Inputs

School input	Marginal unit	Cost of marginal unit		Marginal cost per pupil	
		Lower bound[a]	Upper bound[a]	Lower bound	Upper bound
School-class variables					
Number of pupils in class	One fewer pupil		39		39
Percentage of pupils with textbooks	One extra set	141	141	141	141
Index of teaching materials	One extra point	139	139	139	139
Teacher variables[b]					
General education	9 to 10 years			64	350
	10 to 11 years	5,724	6,996	82	350
	11 to 12 years	5,724	7,632	82	382
	12 to 14 years	5,724	8,804	82	440
Pre-service teacher training	0 to 1 year			156	704
	1 to 2 years			174	768

a. The lower and upper bounds correspond to alternative assumptions about the useful lifetime of the investment. For class size they correspond to the extreme ends on the teacher salary scale.

b. For these variables we have a lower and an upper bound for the cost of the marginal unit. But we also take into account variations in class size from 20 to 70, to get the lower and upper bound of the marginal cost per pupil.

cost-effectiveness analysis we also compute the marginal cost per pupil of manipulating the various school inputs. Scroll down the worksheet to locate the table and complete the yellow cells. Take a moment to review all of the entries and then proceed to the next section on cost-effectiveness analysis.

Step 6   Three principles underlie the procedures for our cost analysis above. The first principle is to ensure that the cost estimates relate directly to the units in which the inputs have been specified in the impact analysis. The second principle is to ensure consistency in the time dimension of the cost estimates through the application of annualization techniques as appropriate. And the third principle is to standardize all the cost estimates to a per-student basis. Consider how you might apply these principles to your current work, jotting down your ideas below. As an option, you might wish to review your comments in the earlier section on impact analysis where you were asked to jot down your observations about the information on impact analysis provided in table 6.A.2.1.

Comments: _____

_____

_____

_____

_____

Cost-Effectiveness Analysis

Before bringing together the impact and cost results from the preceding sections, it may be of interest to stress that there exists in general a substantial variation in the way the inputs can be mixed within each level of per-pupil expenditure. Under average schooling conditions in country X (which we have been using for our example), the recurrent unit cost is estimated at 1,365 shillings [$(59,757 / 46) + (141 \times 0.39) + (139 \times 3.6 / 46)$]. If 600,000 children out of 800,000 in the population are currently enrolled, this indicates that the coverage of the system is about 75 percent (600,000 / 800,000) and that overall recurrent spending for primary schools is estimated to be 819 million shillings.

Therefore, two dimensions of educational policy decision need to be analyzed. The first implies the distribution of total spending over the population and the tradeoff between the number of children that can be put through school and the spending that can be earmarked for each of them. We obviously would like to have both the maximum number of children in primary schooling and to allocate to each of them a level of spending that is conducive to the best quality of education. Unfortunately, given budgetary constraints, the two objectives are not compatible. The decisionmaker will have to determine whether, for example, she or he prefers to have universal coverage with a level of spending per pupil of 1,024 shillings (819 million shillings / 800,000 children), or only 50 percent coverage for an education for which per-pupil spending is 2,048 shillings (or any other compatible combination). The actual tradeoff (75 percent of coverage with per-pupil spending of 1,365 shillings) may in this regard be considered to be reasonable or be subject to change).

The second decision dimension has implications for the distribution of per-pupil spending across various school inputs. In this regard it should be stressed that considerable variations in the mix of inputs would be possible within a given level of per-pupil spending. For example, better qualified teachers may be hired, but this will be at the cost of either increasing class size or of reducing the provision of nonsalary inputs. Less costly teachers can be used, allowing, therefore, for more materials, a

6

smaller number of pupils in the class, or both. As an illustration, table 6.A.4.8 shows some of the variations that can be accommodated within the average per-pupil expenditure of 1,365 shillings in country X.

Let a be the percentage of students with textbooks, b be the number of points of the index of pedagogical material, S be the salary or the average salary of teachers, and N be the number of students accommodated, given the budget constraint or given the unit cost of 1,365 shillings. Therefore,

$$\text{Unit cost } 1,365 \text{ shillings} = (S/N) + (139 \times b) + (141 \times a)$$

$$S/N = 1,365 - (139 \times b) - (141 \times a)$$

$$N = S/[1,365 - (139 \times b) - (141 \times a)]$$

Table 6.A.4.8 shows that with the same recurrent unit cost of 1,365 shillings, the organization of schooling conditions can be quite different—for example with class size varying from 32 to 73. From a pedagogical point of view, opinions will differ about which of the alternative mixes of inputs is preferable. A factual approach would be to simulate the production function equation estimated in the section on "Estimating the Impact of Teacher Education and Training on Student Outcomes" above. The numbers obtained are given in the last row of table 6.A.4.8. We can see that different combinations of school inputs, if they lead to the same unit cost, are not equivalent in terms of student learning (average student test score being used as the proxy), and that some of them are associated with higher student learning than are others.

6

Table 6.A.4.8: Variations in Per-Pupil Spending in Country X

Variation	Case 1	Case 2	Case 3	Case 4	Case 5	Case 6	Case 7
Years of general education	9	10	11	12	14	14	14
Years of teacher training	0	0	1	1	2	1	2
Number of pupils in the class	32.1	36.1	48.5	57.9	59.1	64.7	72.9
Percentage of pupils with textbooks	50	60	100	100	0	100	100
Index of teaching material	2	3	6	6	0	6	6
Average student test score	92.6	97.8	113.3	110.6	94.4	113.0	111.4

Having understood the possibility of variations in student outcomes arising from changes in the mix of inputs keeping the level of spending constant, in the exercises below we bring together the impact and cost results from the preceding sections on impact and cost analysis. In other words, we have to relate the marginal impact of the different variables to the corresponding marginal costs, and then calculate the cost-effectiveness ratios. To facilitate evaluation of the cost-effectiveness of the various inputs, table 6.A.4.9 below shows the relevant estimates of marginal impact and costs from those sections.

Problem 5

In table 6.A.4.9 the last two columns have been computed by dividing the coefficient estimate in the second column by the lower- and upper-bound cost estimates in the fourth and fifth columns. Considering the lower-bound estimates, for example, we note that the impact of an

Table 6.A.4.9: Comparing Cost-Effectiveness across School Inputs

School input or factor	Marginal impact on test scores (points)		Marginal cost per pupil (shillings)		Impact per unit of cost (points per 1,000 shillings)	
	Coefficient estimate	t-Statistics	Lower bound	Upper bound	Lower bound of cost	Upper bound of cost
School-class factors						
Number of pupils in class	−0.07	**	20	39	3.5	1.8
Textbooks	+0.11	**	141	141	78.0	78.0
Teaching materials	+1.15	**	149	139	8.3	8.3
Teacher's factors						
9 to 10 years of general education	+3.24	**	64	350	50.6	9.3
10 to 11 years of general education	+3.27	**	82	350	39.8	9.3
11 to 14 years of general education	+0.89	n.s.	164	822	5.4	1.1
0 to 1 year of pre-service TT	+5.25	***	156	704	33.7	7.5
1 to 2 years of pre-service TT	−1.04	n.s.	174	468	0	0

n.s. Not statistically significant from zero.
*Statistically significant at the 10 percent level.
**Statistically significant at the 5 percent level.
***Statistically significant at the 1 percent level.
TT Teacher training.

increase in teacher's formal education from 11 to 14 years is only 5.4 points per 1,000 shillings, compared with 78 for textbooks. This means that increasing textbook availability would be much more cost-effective than increasing teacher's formal schooling from 11 to 14 years as an option for improving student learning outcome.

Use the data in table 6.A.5.9 to answer the following questions:

(i)   For which input(s) are there clear-cut policy implications?

Answer: _____

_____

_____

(ii) Regarding teacher education, what overall policy conclusions would you draw from the results?

Answer: _____

_____

_____

_____

(iii) Note the coefficient estimates on teacher's factors in the table. What do they suggest about the effectiveness of pre-service teacher training as it is currently designed? In what ways would it probably be cost-effective to modify the design of such training?

6

Answer: _____

_____

_____

_____

(iv) What does the cost-effectiveness ratio for teaching materials suggest regarding policies involving the use of this input to improve student learning?

Answer: _____

_____

_____

_____

(v) Regarding class size, what overall policy conclusions do the results in table 6.A.5.9 suggest?

Answer: _____

_____

_____

_____

(vi) What would be the optimal input mix given the results in table 6.A.5.9?

Answer: _____

_____

_____

_____

Implications and Summary of Cost-Effectiveness Analysis

Acknowledging the possible presence of nonlinearity and interaction effects is critical to cost-effectiveness analysis.[9] Ignoring it can seriously compromise the validity of the analysis, as well as reduce its application in policy design.

Teachers, like other professionals, deserve appropriate pay for the work they perform. Teacher pay policies involve taking into consideration a number of variables, such as the formal credentials of teachers, their teaching experience, and the schooling context—class size, availability of teaching materials, cognitive and social characteristics of students, and so forth. We now will turn to the economics of teacher pay and proceed to analyze teacher pay issues.

Part B: The Economics of Teacher Pay

In part B of this learning module we analyze the economics of teacher pay. Teacher salaries are a major cost in education. Policies affecting teacher pay are therefore key concerns in the sector. Some of the important questions are these: Are teachers adequately paid, relative to other workers? Is their pay high enough to motivate effective teaching? To what extent is teacher pay consistent with the educational policy in terms of coverage of the system and its budgetary constraints? Although these and other questions concerning teacher employment and pay are best addressed through microeconomic analysis of the labor market for teachers, comparative analysis can offer some insights based on relatively simple data requirements, particularly as an entry into in-depth analysis.

The analytical focus in this section of the module is positive and comparative in approach (that is, how does actual teacher pay compare with that in other professions?), rather than normative and absolute (that is, what do teachers deserve, given the important social task they perform?). The focus will be on two complementary perspectives: (a) international—trying to compare actual teacher pay in one country with that in comparable countries; and (b) national—trying to compare the remuneration of teachers with that of other professions in the same country, and to compare the remuneration of teachers over time. We will analyze these two perspectives in turn before synthesizing the results for a policy assessment.

Your task in this section is to evaluate the directions for policy development regarding teacher pay in primary education in selected countries in our sample. Follow the steps below to accomplish your task.

Understanding the Policy Context: Concepts and Arguments

Problem 1

In this section of the module we will concentrate on the classical angle of teacher pay based on teachers' credentials and the type of work they perform, rather than on the newer and more controversial issue of merit pay, although the angles are complementary. We know from a number of empirical studies that teachers with similar characteristics (same formal credentials, same duration of teaching experience) teaching in a similar schooling context (similar logistic conditions, such as class size, availability of teaching materials, with students of similar cognitive and social characteristics) may differ widely in their abilities to impart knowledge to their students, thereby demonstrating wide disparities in teaching effectiveness.[10] If we are more interested in student outcomes (learning), there may be some validity in not tying teacher-pay policy to teachers' credentials and the type of work they perform.

Step 1   Insert the CD-ROM into the computer and open the file titled "tchr_trg_pay_II.xls." Check the bottom of your screen to ensure that you are in the worksheet titled "problem 1." Now proceed with the exercises. What would be the reasonable pay for a teacher with a certain educational background, pre-service teacher training, and teaching experience? Often working in resource-constrained environments, policymakers are confronted with two contradictory objectives. What are they?

Answer: _____

_____

_____

_____

Empirical Analysis: The International Comparative Perspective

Step 2 Let us assume that we want to assess the level of remuneration of primary school teachers in country X (in terms of current gross national product [GNP] per capita—US$1,800), where teachers get an annual average salary of, say, 30,000 in the currency units of the country. How would you go about deciding whether levels of remuneration for primary school teachers in country X are high or low by international standards? We cannot directly compare the 30,000 units in country X with 900,000 units earned by counterparts in another country because the two figures do not refer to a common currency unit. One can think of a relatively straightforward technique—using the exchange rate between the two currencies, or converting the exchange rate of each of the two countries into a single common currency such as the U.S. dollar (particularly if we want to extend the comparisons to a number of countries). An alternative is to measure the average level of teacher remuneration in units of a country per capita GNP. We get a measure that we can compare across countries, and this would be consistent with the country context.

For comparative analysis the data on teacher pay first must be standardized into the same unit of measure. The simplest procedure is to convert teacher pay denominated in the national currency into its equivalent in a common currency, such as the U.S. dollar, using the current exchange rate. The resulting data have limited use in comparative analysis, however, because wide differences in economic context make it difficult to interpret cross-country comparisons of teacher salaries in absolute terms. For example, in Bangladesh, where the per capita GNP is US$220, a salary of US$1,000 would make teachers a relatively expensive input, but the same salary in Brazil, where the per capita GNP is US$2,770, would make teachers a relatively inexpensive input. To improve the basis for comparative analysis, a common approach is to express teacher salaries (and other financial indicators in education) as ratios of the per capita GNP (this unit is consistent with the fact that the

6

resources of the country for its system of education depend primarily on its level of per capita GNP).

Now, scroll down to step 2 in worksheet "problem 1." In the working table you will find data on teacher salaries and per capita GNP (pc_gnp) for a sample of 31 countries. To save time the data on teacher salaries in dollar units (t_salaryd) already have been converted to per capita GNP units (t_salary). Table 6.B.1.10 below shows selected data for C3 and C19, two countries in the sample. Comment briefly on the data, noting any implications regarding the difficulty of expanding enrollments in the two countries, and possible reasons for the differentials in teacher salaries.

Comment: _____

_____

_____

_____

Step 3 Your task here is to explore the relationship between teacher salaries and per capita GNP, and thereby to identify a world pattern. The latter variable is more meaningful in comparative analysis. The method is to use a logarithmic scale so that an increase in per capita GNP from, say, US\$500 to US\$1,000 implies the same magnitude as an increase from US\$1,000 to US\$2,000, or indeed as any twofold increase.

In your worksheet, convert per capita GNP into logarithmic units. Then plot a scatter graph with lnpc_gnp (per capita GNP) on the *x*-axis, and primary school teacher salaries in per capita units (variable labeled "Tsal") on the *y*-axis. Comment on the general pattern in the relationship between the two variables, elaborating on the factors you think might account for the observed pattern.

6

Comment: _____

_____

_____

_____

Table 6.B.1.10: Primary School Teacher Salaries in Two Countries

Country	Per capita GNP (US$)	Teacher salaries as ratio of per capita GNP
C3	200	4.7
C19	1,160	1.8

Step 4 Your task here is to perform a more precise evaluation of the relationship between teacher salaries and per capita GNP based on regression analysis. Because the relationship has the appearance of a hyperbolic curve rather than a downward-sloping straight line, it is more appropriate to specify the following functional form for the regression equation than to use a straight line:

$$Tsal = a + b \, / \, lnpc\_gnp$$

or equivalently

$$Tsal = a + b \times ilnpc\_gnp$$

where *tsal* is primary school teacher salary in per capita GNP units, *lnpc_gnp* is the natural logarithm of per capita GNP, and *ilnpc_gnp* is the inverse of *lnpc_gnp* (that is, 1 divided by *lnpc_gnp*).

Scroll down your worksheet to the working table for this step in the problem, where you will find the relevant data for the regression analysis. Create a new column in the table showing the values of *ilnpc_gnp*. Then invoke Excel's regression command to estimate the desired equation. Enter your coefficient estimates in the blank spaces below or those highlighted in yellow in your worksheet and comment on the results.

$$Tsal = \underline{\hspace{2cm}} + \underline{\hspace{2cm}} \times ilnpc\_gnp \qquad R^2 = \underline{\hspace{1.5cm}}$$

Comment: _____

_____

_____

Step 5 Using the regression equation you have just estimated, simulate $ptsal_1$, the value of *tsal* predicted by the above equation on the basis of each country's per capita GNP. Enter the results in the yellow column yellow in the working table for step 5.

The overall pattern is described in table 6.B.1.11. Review the data and comment on the results.

Comment: _____

_____

_____

_____

6

Table 6.B.1.11: International Primary School Teacher Salaries in Comparative Perspective

Per capita GNP (US$)	200	400	600	800	1,000	1,500	2,000	2,500
Estimated yearly teacher salary								
Per capita GNP unit	4.55	3.82	3.39	3.09	2.85	2.43	2.12	1.88
US$	910	1,528	2,034	2,472	2,855	3,645	4,224	4,700

Beyond the comparability argument, it can be shown that evaluating teacher salary in per capita GNP units is consistent with assessing the effort to improve education in a country, using spending on education as a proportion of its GNP. Assume, for example, that in country X the average primary education teacher salary is 30,000 units of the country (UC) (in current international per capita GNP units—US$1,800), and the national per capita GNP is 9,000 UC. It follows that teacher salary corresponds to 3.33 (30,000 / 9,000) per capita GNP units of the country. The issue now is to determine whether this figure is high or low by international standards. For country X, which stands at an international per capita GNP of US$1,800, the point estimate for primary teacher pay is 2.23 units of per capita GNP. As the current average teacher remuneration is observed to represent 3.33 times the per capita GNP of the country, we can conclude that by international standards primary school teachers in country X appear to be overpaid by about 49 percent [(3.33 – 2.23) / 2.23]. This approach is interesting, but it obviously constitutes only one yardstick by which we can assess the current level of teacher salaries in a given country. The analysis can be considered to be complete only after doing a comparative analysis of teacher salaries in the context of country X itself.

What are your observations about paying teachers at 3.33 times the per capita GNP instead of paying teachers at 2.23 times the per capita GNP in terms of coverage of primary education, assuming that the current gross enrollment ratio in country X is 42 percent?

Answer and comments for educational policy:

_____

_____

_____

_____

6

Empirical Analysis: The National Comparative Perspective

We now move on to assess primary teacher salaries in the national context. The relevant comparators are individuals who have reasonably similar education and experience as teachers, but who are not in the teaching profession. The focus is often on teacher pay in the civil service. A comparator of particular interest in this context would be teachers employed in private schools.

To conduct the analysis, we need data on education, training, occupation, job experience, and pay of a reasonably large sample of individuals. The standard way to proceed might be using an existing household or labor force survey in which the required pieces of information are generally available. In relatively high-income countries, or in countries where the modern sector makes up a reasonably high proportion of the labor market, an analysis in the manner of Mincer can be undertaken. The general specification of a corresponding earnings function can be estimated as follows:

$$LnEarnings = a_0 + a_1 \bullet Yeduc + a_2 \bullet Yexp + a_3 \bullet Yexp^2 + a_4$$
$$\bullet\ Privteach + a_5 \bullet Pubteach + a_6 \bullet Pub$$

6

where *LnEarnings* is the logarithm of individual yearly earnings, *Yeduc* is the number of years of education, *Yexp* is the years of work experience, *Privteach* is a dummy variable for private school teachers, *Pubteach* is a dummy variable for public school teachers, and *Pub* is a dummy variable for nonteachers or civil servants (the omitted category for other cases— private sector). Estimates can be made separately for males and females.

Problem 2

Now we focus on interpreting the empirical results of the earnings function.

Step 1 Tab over to problem 2 in the Excel worksheet. The empirical estimates obtained in country X are provided in the equation. Consider the results and interpret them in the context of country X. Jot down your answers below or in the space marked in yellow in your worksheet.

$$LnEarnings = 8.54 + 0.11 \bullet Yeduc + 0.05 \bullet Yexp - 0.0008$$
$$(t = 3.2) \qquad (t = 2.1) \qquad (t = 1.9)$$

$$\bullet\ Yexp^2 - 0.02 \bullet Privteach + 0.26 \bullet Pubteach + 0.32 \bullet Pub$$
$$(t = 0.8) \qquad (t = 2.4) \qquad (t = 2.2)$$

$R^2 = 0.38$ (2,400 observations)

Interpretation of empirical estimates in the context of country X:

_____

_____

_____

_____

Empirical estimates of similar type can also be usefully conducted in countries in which the labor market is "segmented" and characterized by a high degree of "dualism." In such circumstances, it is often quantities rather than prices that help regulate the labor market. We usually find individuals who possess relatively high educational credentials but who are not employed in the modern wage sector of the economy. They are generally in some form of informal sector jobs or in family-owned businesses. At the same time, wages in the modern sector (often dominated by the civil service) tend to be fairly rigidly in line with demand-and-supply conditions.

In this type of an economy, it is useful to estimate an earnings function in the modern sector and identify where teachers' earnings are located, given their individual credentials, in the distribution of earnings. But this does not tell the full story. To get a better understanding of the reality, first it is interesting to evaluate the number of individuals who have the basic credentials to become primary or secondary teachers and then to arrive at some estimate of their current earnings. From that we may have a sense of the magnitude of the excess supply and of the level of minimum wages they could consider if they were offered the opportunity to become a teacher. And it may be useful to run a Mincerian earnings function on the whole adult population whose earnings (in the modern or informal sector) can be reasonably estimated at the individual level. This would help to provide more directly an estimate of the extent to which teachers may be under- or overpaid, given the broad demand-and-supply conditions on the labor market in the country. Results of a simulation are provided below. Peruse the results and proceed to answer the question in step 2.

$$LnEarnings = 8.31 + 0.09 \bullet Yeduc + 0.04 \bullet Yexp - 0.02$$
$$(t = 3.2) \qquad (t = 2.1) \qquad (t = 0.8)$$

$$\bullet \ Privteach + 0.26 \bullet Pubteach + 0.32 \bullet Pub - 0.55 \bullet Inform$$
$$(t = 2.4) \qquad (t = 2.2) \qquad (t = 4.3)$$

$R^2 = 0.48$ (6,400 observations)

Step 2 Note that beyond this analytical perspective some other information might be useful. What could that be?

Answer: _____

_____

_____

Problem 3

To blend the international and national perspectives, it is convenient to locate teacher salary in country X in figure 6.B.3.2.

How would you interpret the location of country X in the figure in terms of macroeconomic versus sectoral policies to be undertaken?

Answer: _____

_____

_____

_____

Projecting the Resources Likely to Be Made Available for the Sector in a Future Time

Trying to get a sense of what a country's system of education could be like some years in the future (for example, in the context of designing a 10-year plan, or simulating a "vision 2020"), we will have to examine two

Figure 6.B.3.2: Locating Teacher Salary of Country X in National and International Perspectives

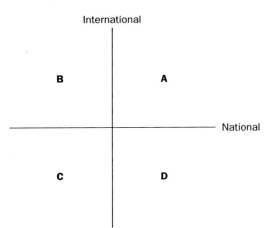

aspects: (a) What are the policies that could be justified to foster efficiency and equity? and (b) What are the likely public resources that could be mobilized for education during the period? This exercise often takes the form of assessing the amount of additional resources that could be made available, with a reference point being current allocations. Before doing the analysis, we have to make some assumptions about the rate of growth of the economy, the share of government budget in GNP, the share of education within the government budget, and the rates of growth of the overall population and the school-age population.

Problem 4

Step 1 Tab over to the next worksheet in the file "tchr_trg_pay_II.xls." Peruse the data in table 6.B.4.12 and try to answer the questions following the table in the CD-ROM.

If no change in education policy was undertaken between 2000 and 2015, what would be the budget for education to help keep enrollment rates constant in the system?

Answer: _____ **billion in 2000 currency units.**

The resources freed for new policies (expanding coverage, per-pupil spending, or both at different levels and types of education) thus can be estimated to be what amount?

Answer: _____ **billion in 2000 currency units.**

From this point onward, let us consider some educational policies based on the assumption that the overall resource implications do not

Table 6.B.4.12: Basic Data for Projecting Resources for the Sector

	2000	2015
Rate of growth of the economy between 2000 and 2015 (%)		6.5
Rate of growth of the population between 2000 and 2015 (%)		2.2
Rate of growth of the school-age population between 2000 and 2015 (%)		2.4
GNP (billions; year 2000 currency units)	1,000	2,572
Population (millions)	12	16.6
GNP per capita (year 2000 currency units)	83,000	154,900
GNP per capita (year 2000 US$)	430	803
Share of budget in GNP (%)	15	18
Share of Education in government budget (%)	20	22
Government budget (billions; year 2000 currency units)	150	463
Education budget (billions; year 2000 currency units)	30	102

6

exceed the figure that you have calculated directly above. The assumption may not be the relevant way to proceed, but we should not forget that if economic growth brings new resources to the sector, it also will bring a change in domestic costs, particularly in teacher salaries that currently make up the bulk of spending in education budgets. Documenting the magnitude of that change is a good practice, but is not common in conducting the analysis.

Step 2 First, let us consider the salary component of spending on education. Assume that salaries account for 75 percent of the total current education budget. How will these salaries evolve with the growth of the economy? A starting point may be to examine the actual level of teacher salaries (from both the national and international perspectives as demonstrated in problems 1, 2, and 3 above), and to get a sense of whether actual salaries are above or below some desirable yardstick. Before considering any other policies, it is probably relevant to set the salary point. To this end, you may find it useful to locate the country under consideration in figure 6.B.4.3. Doing so helps you understand the extent to which average teacher salary in the country is above or below the international standard of remuneration, given the country's current per capita GNP.

Using the data provided in table 6.B.4.12, under current conditions, let us assume that the country's per capita GNP is E1 (US$430) and the level of primary teacher salary is TS* (representing, say, 4.2 per capita GNP units), whereas the reference point estimate (by world standard) is TS1 (3.75). In 15 years from year 2000, per capita GNP of the country is estimated at E2 (US$803) for which the reference world standard would be TS2 (3.10 per capita GNP units). The exercise is to determine the level of teacher salaries in 2015.

Figure 6.B.4.3: Locating Teacher Salary of Country X in an International Perspective

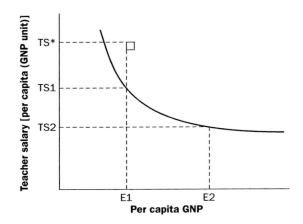

Scroll down the worksheet in problem 4 and answer the following question, jotting down your response here or in the space marked in yellow in the worksheet. Given current labor supply and demand conditions in the country, how would you determine the level of teacher salaries in 2015?

Answer:

_____

_____

_____

_____

Step 3   Now let us consider the nonsalary portion, which in our example is 25 percent of total spending on education. We will assume the following:

- International prices are stable, although domestic prices for goods and services produced locally tend to increase with economic growth.
- Domestic inflation equals the growth rate of the economy. Domestically and internationally purchased goods each account for 50 percent of spending on nonsalary items. That is, 12.5 percent of nonsalary spending is on domestic goods and services and 12.5 percent is on international goods and services.
- Goods and services grow at the same rate as the coverage of the system.

Scroll down the worksheet and answer the following questions, jotting down your answers here or in the space marked in yellow in the worksheet.

(i)   With no variation in enrollment rates and other things being equal, what would be the nonsalary expenditure in the year 2015?

Answer:

_____

_____

(ii)   Without changing the actual enrollment rates (but coping with demographic growth) and with other things being equal, what is the total spending on education?

Answer:

_____

_____

6

(iii) What are your observations about spending on education?

Answer: _____

_____

_____

_____

Conclusion

The chapter has helped you assess the tradeoffs between quantity and quality, determined by identifying the best choices in terms of teacher credentials and pay so as to maximize the outcome of the system in both quantitative and qualitative terms within the budgetary constraints a country faces.

Endnotes

1. To review the basic concepts in regression analysis readers may wish to consult appendix A at the end of this book.

2. The reader also may wish to consult the hands-on module titled "Conducting Cost-Effectiveness Analysis in Education" by Alain Mingat and Jee-Peng Tan for further details on how to perform the analysis.

3. Data collection is an integral part of any analysis. Because our focus here is on analytical concepts and techniques, for an overview of the main approaches to data collection for cost-effectiveness analysis we refer the reader to the annex to the module "Conducting Cost-Effectiveness Analysis in Education," chapter 4 of this volume.

4. A general note on regression analysis appears in appendix A of this volume. Please consult it to review the main concepts involved, as well as the key statistical indicators for interpreting regression results.

5. A dummy variable takes on the form of zero or one. For example, to differentiate for gender you could assign zero for boys and one for girls. The coefficient of the variable indicates the differential impact on the outcomes, all things being equal, of girls versus boys.

6. A continuous variable can take any value in a given range (for example, from 0 to 100 for the percent of pupils with textbooks).

7. The cost calculations can be accomplished in one of two ways: (a) using cost functions, which are estimated through regression analysis (for example, by regressing teachers' years of education against pay); or (b) through the application of the classical procedure of piecing together the composite parts of costs. A more detailed discussion of the various methods can be found in two other hands-on modules: "Analyzing Costs in Education" by Jean-Pierre Jarousse, Alain

Mingat, Stella Tamayo, and Jee-Peng Tan, and "Performing Economic Analysis of Educational Technology" by Alain Mingat and Jee-Peng Tan, with Stella Tamayo.

8. Opportunity costs refer to the time cost of people who are in training or in school.

9. Refer to part 2 (Extensions to the Basic Techniques) of the hands-on module "Conducting Cost-Effectiveness Analysis in Education" (chapter 4 of this volume) to understand the procedures involved in conducting analysis to address nonlinearity and interaction effects.

10. See the module "Managing Teacher Deployment and Classroom Processes" (chapter 5 of this volume) by Alain Mingat and Jee-Peng Tan, with Shobhana Sosale.

6

Analyzing Equity in Education

A Two-Part Module

Alain Mingat and Jee-Peng Tan, with Stella Tamayo

Equity in education attracts interest in public policy for several reasons. In most countries the government subsidizes education, so access to education determines who benefits from the subsidies. Because spending on education represents a substantial share of government budgets in both industrial and developing countries, the education system effectively is a major conduit for the distribution of public subsidies. Furthermore, education affects people's life chances as adults in terms of their earning capability as well as social mobility. Equity in educational opportunity therefore influences the future distribution of income, wealth, and status in society. Beyond its economic significance, education is viewed widely as a good in itself, and indeed a basic human right with regard to the lower levels of education. For this reason, too, equity in education often is a focus of public policy debate.

This chapter offers some methods for analyzing equity in education. As context, we note four broad approaches suggested by the vast literature on the subject:[1]

1. Comparison of differences in access to a specific level or type of education across population groups, using such indicators as relative rates of entry, transition, and completion. The analysis assumes that education is a good in itself without elaborating on the specific nature or value of the benefits.

2. Comparison of the benefits from education received by various population groups. The benefits materialize in two forms: (a) as public subsidies for education received as a student, and (b) as increased earnings (or income) and upward social mobility after the student exits from the education system.

3. Comparison of who pays for and who benefits from education. The analytical focus is clearly on the distributional implications of financing arrangements in education. The analysis may involve cross-sectional comparison of the taxes paid by various population groups to finance public spending on education relative to how much each group receives in education subsidies. It also may involve longitudinal comparison of individuals' lifetime contributions in taxes relative to the education subsidies they received as students.

4. Comparison of differences in achievement or learning across students. Here the analysis concerns the education process itself, rather than access to education or financial arrangements per se. It focuses on the influence of the pedagogical environment on the distribution of student learning. The pedagogical environment is defined by such factors as the physical conditions in the classroom, the number of children in the same class, and the teacher's personal attributes and pedagogical method. Because no schooling environment produces the same progress in learning across all students, initial disparities in achievement may widen or narrow over time depending on the specific pedagogical environment to which the students have been exposed.

All four approaches are relevant to the analysis of equity in education, but this chapter does not address them all. It excludes comparison of access to education across population groups (number 1 above) because the analysis is relatively straightforward and needs little elaboration. It also excludes analysis of the distribution of benefits from education in the form of increased earnings or social mobility (number 2 above), and analysis of who pays for and who benefits from public subsidies for education (number 3 above). Both of those topics are more feasible in the context of long-term research.

The chapter has two parts. Part A analyzes the incidence of public spending on education, highlighting the influence of the structure of enrollments as well as that of public subsidies; it falls under approach number 2 above. Part B turns from the financial aspects of equity to consider disparities in learning associated with policy choices affecting the pedagogical environment; it belongs in number 4 above. Each part is self-contained and can be attempted separately.

This module contains the write-up and Excel files on the accompanying CD-ROM corresponding to the exercises in the two parts: "Equity_Subsidy1," "Equity_Subsidy2," "Equity_Subsidy3," and "Equity_Subsidy4" for part A; and "Equity_Learn1" and "Equity_Learn2" for part B. The computations in part A can all be accomplished using a handheld calculator for those who prefer to do so; computations in part B are best done in Excel or other data analysis software.

7

Part A: The Distribution of Public Subsidies for Education

The distribution of public subsidies for education depends on two complementary factors:

1. The structure of the education system itself in terms of enrollments and subsidies across levels of education. The steeper the enrollment pyramid, the more equitable will be the distribution of a given amount of subsidies for education; similarly, the smaller the differences in subsidies per student across levels of education, the more equitable will be the distribution.

2. The social characteristics (for example, gender, parental education and income, locality of residence, and so on) of the students enrolled at each level of education. The more skewed the composition of enrollments, the more inequitable will be the distribution of public spending on education.

Distinguishing between these factors helps to clarify the sources of observed patterns in the distribution of public spending on education. Social selectivity in the access to education clearly matters in shaping the distribution, but the education system's structural characteristics exert an even more basic influence: it is through them that social disparities in the distribution of spending are mediated and produced.

The analysis can be conducted in two ways according to the scope of the aggregate subsidies that are being distributed. The first includes the subsidies accumulated by a population cohort as it passes through the entire range of schooling ages; the second includes total public spending across all levels of education in a given year. The beneficiaries in the second approach are members of different cohorts who happen to be enrolled in the year for which the calculations are made.

Both approaches rely on data that can be compiled from existing sources, and both offer useful insights for public policy in education. They can be used to document differences in the distribution of public spending over time or across countries; they can also be used to simulate the impact of potential policy options in education. The four problems below illustrate how the various analyses can be accomplished.

Structural Aspects of Education and the Distribution of Subsidies

Two aspects of the structure of education systems combine to influence the distribution of subsidies in a population cohort. The first is the relative amount of subsidies per student by level of education, which determines the cumulative size of subsidies according to a student's terminal level of schooling. The second is the structure of enrollment ratios, which determines the distribution of educational attainment. The problem below shows how these basic ideas can be used to analyze equity in the distribution of public spending on education.

Problem 1

The relevant data for a hypothetical education system appear in table 7.A.1.1. Retrieve the Excel file labeled " Equity_Subsidy1," check that you are in worksheet 1, and continue below for further instructions.

Two features in the data warrant some elaboration. First, with regard to the structure of subsidies, our interest is in the *average* pattern across levels of education. The annual subsidy per student therefore refers to the average across all types of schools in the system, weighted by the corresponding share of enrollments. Second, with regard to the structure of enrollments, we focus again on the *average* enrollment rate across all grades at each level of education. Note that the enrollment rate refers to the percentage enrolled among the relevant population, this population being defined as those in the same age group as nonrepeaters among the students. As a rough approximation, the gross enrollment ratio may be used, but the results can be compromised in situations where over-age students represent a large share of enrollments.[2]

Step 1   Using the data in table 7.A.1.1, compute the distribution of educational attainment in a cohort of 100 people and enter your results in table 7.A.1.2 (column 1). For example, given that the enrollment ratio is 45 in primary education, we know that 45 of the 100 children will enter primary school, leaving 55 (= 100 – 45) with no schooling. In lower secondary education, the enrollment ratio is 20. Thus, of the 45 people who enter primary school, 20 will enter lower secondary school, which implies that 25 (= 45 – 20) will exit the education system with primary schooling as their terminal level of education. Continue with this line of reasoning to complete the calculations and enter your results in table 7.A.1.2 (column 3).

Step 2   Again using the data in table 7.A.1.1, compute the subsidies accumulated by each person exiting the education system at each level

Table 7.A.1.1: Enrollment Rates and Public Subsidies per Student in a Hypothetical Country

Level of education	Length of cycle (years)	Enrollment rate (%)	Public subsidy per student per year (US$)
Primary	6	45	200
Lower secondary	4	20	400
Upper secondary	3	8	700
Higher	4	3	2,400

**Table 7.A.1.2: Distribution of Educational Attainment
and Public Subsidies for Education in a Population Cohort of 100**

Terminal level of education	Distribution of cohort by educational attainment	Subsidies per person accumulated up to time of exit from school (US$)	Aggregate subsidies accumulated by the cohort over its entire schooling career	
			Absolute (US$)	Share (%)
No schooling				
Primary				
Lower secondary				
Upper secondary				
Higher				
All levels		—		100.0

— Not applicable.

and enter your results in table 7.A.1.2 (column 2) in the same worksheet. For example, the subsidies accumulated by each person attaining lower secondary education on leaving the system would amount to US$2,800 (= 6 × 200 in primary cycle + 4 × 400 in lower secondary cycle).

Step 3   Multiply columns 2 and 3 in table 7.A.1.2 to obtain the subsidies received in aggregate by each group in the cohort according to the group's terminal level of schooling. Enter your results in column 4 of the table, and use them to compute the percentage share of the total subsidies received by the entire cohort of 100 (column 5).

Step 4   Complete table 7.A.1.3 as preparation for plotting a Lorenz curve that shows the distribution of public subsidies received by the cohort according to educational attainment. In column 2, for example, the cumulative share of the cohort that attains lower secondary education would be the sum of cohort shares up to this level of education. Similarly, the cumulative share of aggregate subsidies (column 3) would be the sum of the shares up to this level of education. Plot your result in the

7

**Table 7.A.1.3: Cumulative Distributions of Cohort Population
and the Corresponding Education Subsidies Accumulated
by the Cohort**

Educational attainment	Cohort population	Accumulated subsidies
No schooling		
Primary		
Lower secondary		
Upper secondary		
Higher		

box labeled figure 7.A.1.1 in the CD-ROM, with column 2 on the *x*-axis and column 3 on the *y*-axis. Comment briefly on the graph.

Comment: _____

_____

_____

_____

Step 5 Compute a Gini coefficient to summarize the distribution of subsidies in the population cohort by educational attainment, following the instructions in this and the next paragraph.[3] The definition of the coefficient can be understood in terms of the graph you have just completed, as the ratio of *A* to *B*, where *A* is the area between the left-to-right diagonal and the curve representing the distribution of subsidies, and *B* is the area of the triangle below the left-to-right diagonal. The closer the distribution lies relative to the diagonal, the smaller the Gini coefficient and the more equitable the distribution of subsidies.

To implement the calculation here, we can take advantage of the fact that the curve representing the distribution in this problem is made up of a series of straight lines. Follow these steps to obtain the magnitude of *A*:

1. Divide the area bounded by the curve and the horizontal axis into one triangle and three trapezoids.
2. Calculate the magnitude of the triangle and trapezoids according to the following formulas:

$$\text{Area of triangle} = 0.5 \times \text{base} \times \text{height}$$

$$\text{Area of trapezoid} = 0.5 \times (\text{sum of parallel sides}) \times \text{height}$$

3. Sum up the area of the triangle and trapezoids, and subtract it from the magnitude of *B*, defined as the triangle below the left-to-right diagonal in the figure. The result gives the value of *A* referred to above.
4. Calculate the Gini coefficient by taking the ratio of *A* to *B* and report your result below:

$$\text{Gini coefficient} = \underline{\hspace{2cm}}$$

Distribution of Education Subsidies across Population Groups

As noted above, education subsidies may refer to public spending during a given calendar period (typically a year) or to spending on a population cohort accumulated over the cohort's entire schooling lifetime. The fol-

7

lowing two problems illustrate the calculations for analyzing equity in education under these two definitions.

Problem 2

This problem concerns the distribution of aggregate public spending on education in a given year. Before presenting the data, note that the amount of subsidies, X_j, received by population group j is given by:

$$X_j = \sum_{i=1}^{3} E_{ij} \cdot \frac{S_i}{E_i} = \sum_{i=1}^{3} E_{ij} \cdot u_i$$

where E_{ij} = number of children from group j enrolled in education level i; S_i = aggregate government spending on level i, net of cost recovery; E_i = total number of students enrolled in level i; and u_i = subsidy per student (net of cost recovery) at level i.

The j group's share of total education subsidies, x_j, is given by:

$$x_j = \sum_{i=1}^{3} \frac{E_{ij}}{E_i} \cdot \frac{S_i}{S}$$

where S = the total public education subsidy.

The relevant data for this problem can be found in worksheet 1 of the Excel file "Equity_Subsidy2." Retrieve the data now and continue reading for further instructions. Table 7.A.2.4, the first table in the worksheet, shows the share of enrollments in primary, secondary, and higher education across four population groups by household income in a hypothetical country. A common source for such data are household surveys (for example, the World Bank–supported Living Standards Measurement Studies). In the table, Q1 is the bottom 25 percent of households by income, whereas Q4 is the top 25 percent. In primary education, for example, 19 percent of the students come from the poorest 25 percent of all households.

Table 7.A.2.5, the second table in the worksheet, shows the data on total enrollments and average public subsidies per student by level of

Table 7.A.2.4: Distribution of Enrollments by Level of Education and Income Group in a Hypothetical Country (percent)

Income group	Primary	Secondary	Higher
Q1	19	15	10
Q2	23	20	19
Q3	26	30	31
Q4	32	35	40
All groups	100	100	100

Table 7.A.2.5: Enrollments and Public Subsidies by Level of Education

	Primary	Secondary	Higher
Number of students	1,750,000	720,000	144,000
Average public subsidies per student (US$)	100	250	650

education in the hypothetical country. Data similar to these normally can be extracted or compiled from statistical yearbooks issued by the ministry of education or other government agencies.

Step 1 Compute the aggregate subsidies received by each income group, performing the calculation separately for primary, secondary, and higher education, and then for all three levels taken together. Enter your results in table 7.A.2.6 here or in the same Excel worksheet.

Step 2 Compute the distribution of the aggregate subsidies again for each level of education and then for all three levels taken together. Enter your results in table 7.A.2.7.

Step 3 Use your results to plot in the Excel worksheet box labeled figure 7.A.2.2 a Lorenz curve illustrating the distribution of public subsidies for education in this country, with the x-axis showing the cumulative share of households (starting with those ranked lowest in household income), and the y-axis showing the corresponding cumulative share of subsidies. Recall that each quartile contains 25 percent of the households. Plot the graph for each level of education, as well as for all three levels taken together. Comment briefly on your results and discuss how you might apply the method to analyze equity in public spending on education in a country with which you are familiar.

Comment:

_____

_____

_____

_____

Table 7.A.2.6: Aggregate Public Subsidies for Education Received by Each Income Quartile

Income group	Primary	Secondary	Higher	All levels
Q1				
Q2				
Q3				
Q4				
All groups				

Table 7.A.2.7: Distribution of Public Subsidies for Education by Income Group (percent)

Income group	Cumulative share of households	Primary		Secondary		Higher		All levels	
		%	Cumulative %	%	Cumulative %	%	Cumulative %	%	Cumulative %
Q1									
Q2									
Q3									
Q4									
All groups	n.a.	100.0	n.a.	100.0	n.a.	100.0	n.a.	100.0	n.a.

n.a. Not applicable.

147

Problem 3

We turn now to consider the distribution of education subsidies in a population cohort by income group. Begin by retrieving worksheet 1 from the Excel file "Equity_Subsidy3," and continue reading for further instructions. The basic data for the calculation are in table 7.A.3.8. The distribution of enrollments by income group and the amount of subsidies by level of education are the same as in problem 2 above. The table also shows the distribution of all school-age children by income group, the length of each cycle of education, as well as the corresponding overall enrollment rates.

Step 1   Go now to worksheet 2. As in problem 1, the calculations are based on a cohort of 100. Begin by completing the structure of student flow in the cohort by income group, using table 7.A.3.9 to organize your calculations. The boxes are lettered to indicate a convenient sequence for performing the calculations. The top row of boxes can be completed using the data from table 7.A.3.8; the results in turn provide information for completing the bottom row.

Step 2   Go now to worksheet 3. To obtain the desired incidence of public subsidies in the cohort, complete table 7.A.3.10 by following these instructions:

- Columns 2–5:   Copy the relevant results from table 7.A.3.9 (if you are doing this exercise in Excel, the cells have been linked to the previous table, so you can skip this step).

Table 7.A.3.8: Distribution of Enrollments and School-Age Population by Income Group and Selected Features of Primary, Secondary, and Higher Education

Indicator	Primary	Secondary	Higher	All school-age children
Percentage of students by income group:				
Q1	19	15	10	28
Q2	23	20	19	26
Q3	26	30	31	23
Q4	32	35	40	23
All groups	100	100	100	100
Average public subsidy per student per year (US$)	100	250	650	n.a.
Length of cycle (years)	5	6	4	n.a.
Overall enrollment rate (%)	70	30	10	n.a.

n.a. Not applicable.

7

Table 7.A.3.9: Student Flow by Income Group in a Population Cohort of 100

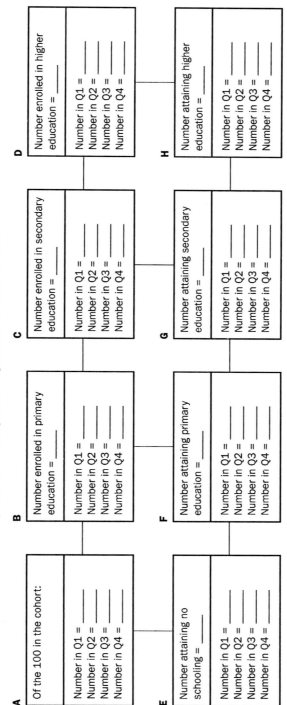

A

Of the 100 in the cohort:

Number in Q1 = _____
Number in Q2 = _____
Number in Q3 = _____
Number in Q4 = _____

B

Number enrolled in primary education = _____

Number in Q1 = _____
Number in Q2 = _____
Number in Q3 = _____
Number in Q4 = _____

C

Number enrolled in secondary education = _____

Number in Q1 = _____
Number in Q2 = _____
Number in Q3 = _____
Number in Q4 = _____

D

Number enrolled in higher education = _____

Number in Q1 = _____
Number in Q2 = _____
Number in Q3 = _____
Number in Q4 = _____

E

Number attaining no schooling = _____

Number in Q1 = _____
Number in Q2 = _____
Number in Q3 = _____
Number in Q4 = _____

F

Number attaining primary education = _____

Number in Q1 = _____
Number in Q2 = _____
Number in Q3 = _____
Number in Q4 = _____

G

Number attaining secondary education = _____

Number in Q1 = _____
Number in Q2 = _____
Number in Q3 = _____
Number in Q4 = _____

H

Number attaining higher education = _____

Number in Q1 = _____
Number in Q2 = _____
Number in Q3 = _____
Number in Q4 = _____

7

7

Table 7.A.3.10: Distribution of Resources in a Population Cohort by Income Group

Income group	Distribution of educational attainment in the cohort				Cumulative subsidies per person by educational attainment (US$)[a]				Aggregate cumulative subsidies by educational attainment and income group (US$)				Aggregate cumulative subsidies by income group	
	NS	P	S	H	NS	P	S	H	NS	P	S	H	Amount (US$)	%
All groups														100.0
Q1														
Q2														
Q3														
Q4														

NS No schooling.

P Primary education.

S Secondary education.

H Higher education.

a. The size of the subsidies is assumed to be the same for all income groups.

- Columns 6–9:   Compute the subsidies accumulated by each person exiting the education system at each level of education, and enter your results here. (Note that this step is accomplished in the same way as in problem 1, step 2 and step 3.)
- Columns 10–13:   Compute the aggregate cumulative subsidies by educational attainment and income group by multiplying the data in columns 2–5 with the corresponding data in columns 6–9.
- Column 14:   Compute the total cumulative subsidies for each income group by summing over all levels of educational attainment.
- Column 15:   Compute the entries as a percentage share of the cumulative subsidies summed for all income groups.

Step 3   Use your results to relate the share of public subsidies received by the children in each income group relative to their share of the population. For this purpose use the data in the last column of tables 7.A.3.8 and 7.A.3.9. Enter your results in table 7.A.3.11, and comment on them briefly.

Comment: _____

_____

_____

_____

Step 4   Go now to worksheet 4. Complete the working template tables there using your results from table 7.A.3.10. Then plot Lorenz

7

Table 7.A.3.11: Comparing the Distribution of Subsidies and the Distribution of the Population

Income group	Share of school-age population (%)	Share of subsidies (%)	Share of subsidies relative to share of population	
			Absolute	Relative to Q1
Q1				1.00
Q2				
Q3				
Q4				
All groups	100.0	100.0	1.00	n.a.

n.a. Not applicable.

curves to show the distribution of subsidies, by income group (using the box labeled figure 7.A.4.3 in the CD-ROM) and by educational attainment (in the box labeled figure 7.A.4.4). Comment briefly on the graphs.

Comment: _____

_____

_____

_____

Simulating the Impact of Policy Changes

Policy changes in education typically alter at least one of the following features of the system: enrollments rates, unit costs, and the extent of public subsidization of the costs. Even when the changes are implemented at only one level of education, their effects may spill over to other levels. For example, raising fees in lower secondary education may reduce enrollments at this level, thereby reducing the pool of potential candidates for the next level. Primary school enrollments also may drop if parents take into consideration the availability of subsidized places in lower secondary education when making decisions to enroll a child in primary school. When policy changes favor particular population groups, they also modify the composition of the student population. In general, therefore, policy changes in education almost always affect the distribution of public spending on education.

In assessing the impact of a policy change on equity, we can focus only on the impact at the level of education immediately affected by the change, or broaden the perspective to consider also the global impact for the whole education system. The latter treatment is more appropriate in view of the fact that all education systems operate under budget constraints, which implies that tradeoffs exist in the allocation of subsidies across levels of education. For example, using public subsidies to expand access to upper secondary education may improve equity at this level of education. But the policy may worsen equity for the system as a whole if the expansion in access is achieved at the cost of reducing access to primary education, a decline in subsidies per student at this level, or a combination of both effects. The problem below illustrates how to simulate the impact of policy changes on equity in education, assessed from the global perspective.

Problem 4

Retrieve the data for this problem from worksheet 1 of the Excel file "Equity_Subsidy4" and continue reading for further instructions. The data, shown in table 7.A.4.12 below, are the same as those for problem 1. Treating these data as those for the base case, you are asked to asses the impact on overall equity in education under a proposed policy to halve the average level of public subsidies per student in higher education. Assume that the remaining subsidies for higher education are targeted to ensure that overall enrollment at this level and its composition by income group remain unaffected. Students receiving smaller subsidies would finance the extra private costs through student loans or other arrangements.

Assume further that the public resources thus freed from higher education are reallocated to primary education and used as follows:

- *Scenario A*: to expand enrollments at existing levels of subsidies per pupil.
- *Scenario B*: to increase public subsidies per pupil to improve the schooling conditions, with no increase in coverage.

Step 1   Calculate the new enrollment ratios and the new levels of subsidies per student implied by the proposed policy under scenarios A and B, using your results to complete table 7.A.4.13.

Table 7.A.4.12: Enrollment Rates and Public Subsidies per Student under the Base Case

Level of education	Length of cycle (years)	Public subsidy per student per year (US$)	Enrollment rate (%)	School-age population
Primary	6	200	45	3,000,000
Lower secondary	4	400	20	1,600,000
Upper secondary	3	700	8	1,400,000
Higher	4	2,400	3	1,360,000

Table 7.A.4.13: Enrollment Rates and Public Subsidies per Student Year under Alternative Policy Options

Level of education	Base case		Scenario A		Scenario B	
	Subsidy per student (US$)	Enrollment rate (%)	Subsidy per student (US$)	Enrollment rate (%)	Subsidy per student (US$)	Enrollment rate (%)
Primary	200	45				
Lower secondary	400	20				
Upper secondary	700	8				
Higher	2,400	3				

Table 7.A.4.14: Cumulative Distribution of Cohort Population and Aggregate Public Subsidies Corresponding to Selected Policies in Education (percent)

Indicator	Base case		Scenario A		Scenario B	
	Cohort population (%)	Aggregate subsidies (%)	Cohort population (%)	Aggregate subsidies (%)	Cohort population (%)	Aggregate subsidies (%)
Education attainment						
No schooling						
Primary						
Lower secondary						
Upper secondary						
Higher						
Gini coefficient						

Step 2 Calculate the distribution of public spending on education as well as the corresponding Gini coefficients under scenarios A and B. To facilitate your calculations, use the working templates in worksheet 2 (for scenario A) and in worksheet 3 (for scenario B) in the Excel file "Equity_Subsidy4." Summarize your results in table 7.A.4.14 above or in worksheet 4. For your convenience, the results for the base case have been linked from the worksheets you completed in problem 1 above. Draw three Lorenz curves in the same graph (in the box labeled figure 7.A.4.5 in the CD-ROM) to show the distribution of public subsidies under the base case and the two scenarios. Comment briefly on your results.

Comment on results: _____

_____

_____

_____

Part B: Disparities in Learning

Beyond issues relating to access to schooling and the incidence of public subsidies, equity in education also encompasses disparities in student learning itself. Such disparities matter because they have implications for students' schooling careers and subsequent labor market performance.

We elaborate here on two separate influences on disparities in learning across students:

1. The first has to do with differences in students' initial learning or ability. Disparities in learning can widen over time if the education process is geared more to the learning needs of high achievers than to other students. But other processes may be more helpful to the weaker students, thereby causing the disparities in learning to narrow over time.

2. The second influence on disparities has to do with the fact that students' social backgrounds affect their academic performance. Because children from certain social groups may benefit more or less than others from a given pedagogical process, the initial disparities in learning across social groups may grow or decline over time.

These two influences operate in all schooling environments and combine to produce observed disparities in learning across students.

These disparities may motivate new policies or investments. It is obviously desirable that the new interventions promote efficiency in the learning process, so that students achieve, on average, the maximum possible gains during the school year per dollar of investment. But policymakers also care about disparities in learning, probably preferring that they not widen over time. Given these objectives, how can policy choices be analyzed?[4]

A first step in the analysis is to recognize that education essentially involves a process of transformation: it transforms what students know at the beginning of the school year or cycle into what they know by the end. Our analytical task is thus to examine the relationship between students' initial and final achievements in different learning contexts or under different policies. The discussion below elaborates on a conceptual framework for this purpose, followed by hands-on exercises on two specific topics to illustrate the analysis.

Determinants of Student Learning: A Conceptual Framework

A student's academic performance observed over a given period of time reflects the impact of various factors: prior learning, personal and family background, and conditions in the classroom and school. Using test scores as a measure of learning, we can express a student's achievement at the end of a school year, OUTSCORE (measured as scores observed at year end), as a function of his or her initial learning, INSCORE (measured through test scores at the beginning of the school year), and the other variables indicated above:

$$OUTSCORE = f(INSCORE, PERSONAL, FAMILY, CLASS, SCHOOL)$$

The expression generally is referred to in the literature as an education production function. Combined with information on costs, estimates of the function's parameters typically are used to assess the cost-effectiveness of alternative school inputs. Each variable in the expression can be represented using a vector of measurable indicators—for example, parental education, ownership of household assets, and distance from home to the school for FAMILY; the child's age, gender, and ownership of textbooks for PERSONAL; class size, teacher's qualification and training, and availability of pedagogical materials for CLASS; school size, school-head's age and gender, and his or her management style, and the location of the school by region or locality (urban or rural) for SCHOOL. Because we are interested in policy options, it is especially important to define carefully the indicators for CLASS and SCHOOL.

In most production function analysis we focus on the *average* impact of the various factors on learning outcomes. The focus is valid as long as the main policy concern relates to the choice of policies with the most efficient *overall* impact for the student population as a whole. However, if the concern also encompasses inequities in learning outcomes, focusing on averages is unlikely to yield sufficient information to guide policy. The foregoing framework therefore needs to be adapted for this purpose. The two problems below show how we can proceed in this regard.

Achievement across Students Differing in Initial Learning

The analysis is best conducted using data for individual students. Often, however, such data may not be available—a constraint that would necessitate the use of less desirable, although still serviceable data, such as achievement scores aggregated at the school level. Because many factors may influence student learning, the analysis typically involves the application of regression techniques. To focus attention on the main ideas, we specify regression equations that are highly simplified in the choice of variables.

Problem 1

Suppose two pedagogical methods have been used for teaching the same curriculum to pupils in a certain grade. Method A is a new approach that educators consider particularly helpful for students who find it difficult to understand abstract concepts; method B consists of traditional techniques. You are asked in this problem to analyze the impact of the two methods on student achievement at the end of the school year, in terms of both the average impact as well as its distribution across students.

Retrieve the data in worksheet 1 in the Excel file labeled "Equity_ Learn1." They relate to 100 pupils in fourth grade for whom there is

7

Table 7.B.1.15: Variables in the Data Set for Problem 1

Variable name	Definition
endscore	Test score at the beginning of grade four
inscore	Test score at the end of grade two
rich	Dummy variable with a value of 1 if the child is from a rich family; 0 otherwise

information on the variables defined in table 7.B.1.15. Follow the steps below to analyze the data.

Step 1   Make a scatter plot in the box labeled figure 7.B.1.16 in the CD-ROM, using the data on "endscore" and "inscore," with the former variable on the y-axis and the latter on the x-axis. Use Excel's regression facility to estimate the relationship between endscore as the dependent variable and inscore and "rich" as regressors. Report the regression coefficients and the corresponding t-statistics in the spaces below (showing accuracy to only two decimal places), and comment on your findings.

endscore = _____ + _____ inscore + _____ rich R^2 = _____

Comment on the regression results: _____

_____

_____

_____

Use the estimated regression equation to simulate the endscore of students from poor families with an inscore of 75 and those with an inscore of 125; and calculate the difference in endscore between the two groups. Fill in columns 2 and 3 of table 7.B.1.16.

Step 2   Stay in worksheet 1 in the Excel file, "Equity_Learn1." The worksheet includes the same data as in the previous worksheet, with the addition of a new variable, "methodA." This new item is a dummy variable that takes on the value of one if a child has been taught using method A during the year, and a value of zero if he or she has been taught using method B.

Table 7.B.1.16: Predicted Endscore Values Based on Regression Results from Step 1

Value of inscore	Predicted endscore	Difference in predicted values of endscore
75		
125		

Use the data to estimate a regression with endscore as the dependent variable, and inscore, rich, and methodA as explanatory variables. Report the coefficient estimates and the corresponding *t*-statistics below. Comment on the results, paying particular attention to the coefficient on methodA.

endscore = _____ + _____ inscore + _____ rich + methodA R^2 = _____

Comment on regression results: _____

_____

_____

_____

Step 3   Go to worksheet 2. Consider a new specification of the regression equation to allow for the possibility that method A differs from method B in its impact on students with high and low entering scores. We need to disaggregate the impact of inscore on endscore according to pedagogical method. The specification therefore should allow for a difference in the slopes of the relationship between the two variables. For this purpose, specify two new regressors in the worksheet as follows:

insA = inscore if the student has been exposed to method A; otherwise 0

insB = inscore if the student has been exposed to method B; otherwise 0

Step 4   Estimate a new regression function linking endscore to rich, methodA, insA, and insB. Report the coefficient estimates and the corresponding *t*-statistics below. Comment on the results, noting in particular the magnitude of the coefficients on the two new variables.

endscore = ____ + ____ insA + ____ insB + ____ rich + ____ methodA

R^2 = ____

Comment on regression results: _____

_____

_____

_____

Step 5   Go now to worksheet 3. Use the regression equation you have just estimated to simulate endscore for children from poor families, the values of endscore corresponding to the inscore values shown in table

7

Table 7.B.1.17: Simulations of Endscore According to Inscore and Pedagogical Method for Children from Poor Families

	Simulated endscore	
Value of inscore	Method A	Method B
70		
80		
90		
100		
110		
120		
130		

7.B.1.17. Recall the definitions of methodA, insA, and insB above. Enter your simulations in columns 2 and 3, and use the results to plot a graph (in the Excel file box labeled figure 7.B.1.7) of the predicted endscore against the corresponding inscore values.

Step 6 For a student from a poor family with an inscore of 80, calculate the difference in endscore under the two pedagogical methods. Repeat the calculation for the same student if she or he had an inscore of 120. Enter your results in table 7.B.1.18, and comment on the conclusions you might draw from the analysis thus far.

Step 7 So far we have seen that the coefficients on insA and insB differ, but we have not tested that the difference between them is statistically significant. In order to perform this test, go now to worksheet 4 in the Excel file "Equity_Learn1," which repeats the relevant data from the previous steps, and run a regression linking endscore to the following variables: inscore, insA, rich, and methodA. Report the coefficient estimates and the corresponding t-statistics results below.

endscore = _____ + _____ inscore + _____ insA + _____ rich + _____ methodA

$$R^2 = \underline{\hspace{1cm}}$$

The above specification can be understood as follows. Because the regression equation includes both inscore and insA, the impact of

Table 7.B.1.18: Simulated Differences in Endscore for Selected Students from Poor Families

	Value of inscore		
Pedagogical method	80	120	Difference in endscore
A			
B			

method B is in fact captured by the coefficient on inscore. This is because when a student is taught under method B, insA is zero, leaving only inscore in the regression. When a student is taught under method A, the impact of incoming achievement is captured by the sum of inscore and insA. Therefore, the coefficient on insA represents the additional impact of method A over that of method B. Bearing these properties of the specification in mind, comment on your regression results regarding the impact of the two pedagogical methods on equity in learning.

Comment on regression results: _____

_____

_____

_____

Learning Outcomes across Population Groups

We turn now to consider the influence of social selectivity in learning outcomes. As before, we apply regression techniques to data on individual pupils, using a highly simplified equation to focus on the main ideas.

Problem 2

Suppose policymakers in a hypothetical country are concerned about the lagging academic performance of first graders from disadvantaged families. Various interventions might redress the situation. For simplicity you are asked to consider only two options: investing in preschool education or in a reduction in class sizes in schools serving children from low-income families.

The data can be found in worksheet 1 of the Excel file "Equity_Learn2." They relate to a sample of 100 pupils in first grade for whom there is information on the variables listed and defined in table 7.B.2.19. Only the gender of the child and a dichotomous variable indicating the wealth of his or her family are included as proxies for personal and family background. There is no information on initial test scores; you may assume that they are randomly distributed in the sample.[5] Follow the steps below to analyze the data.

Step 1 Perform a regression linking endscore to the four other variables in the working table above, and report the coefficient estimates and the corresponding t-statistics below:

endscore = _____ + _____ boy + _____ rich + _____ csize + _____ pschool

$$R^2 = \text{\_\_\_\_\_}$$

Table 7.B.2.19: Variables in the Data Set for Problem 2

Variable name	Definition
endscore	Test score at the end of first grade
boy	Dummy variable with a value of 1 for a boy, and a value of 0 for a girl
rich	Dummy variable with a value of 1 if child is from rich family, and a value of 0 otherwise
csize	Number of pupils taught in the classroom in which the child is taught
pschool	Dummy variable with a value of 1 if the child has attended preschool, and a value of 0 otherwise

Comment on the results:

_____

_____

_____

_____

_____

Step 2   The previous equation suggests that preschool has a positive impact on endscore. Recall that the estimated impact refers to the average in the population. To allow for possible differences in impact across children from rich and poor families, consider a new regression specification in which the "pschool" variable is split into two, one for measuring the impact of preschool on children from rich families, the other measuring the impact on children from poor families. You are asked to create these variables as follows:

psrich = pschool × rich,   that is, psrich = pschool if child is from a rich family; and psrich = 0 if child is from a poor family.

pspoor = pschool × (1-rich)   that is, pspoor = pschool if child is from a poor family; and pspoor = 0 if child is from a rich family.

Step 3   Perform a new regression using the two new variables you have just created to replace the pschool variable in the regression specification in step 1. Report your results here:

endscore = ____ + ____ boy + ____ rich + ____ csize + ____ psrich

+ ____ pspoor $R^2 =$ ____

7

Comment on the implications of these results regarding the impact on equity of investing in preschool education for children from low-income families. How would you compare this investment with that of reducing class size in schools primarily serving children who come from such families?

_____

_____

_____

_____

Endnotes

1. All of these approaches involve the use of various operational measures of equity. None of them is perfect, which reflects the difficulty of constructing indicators that capture all dimensions of the concept. But the lack of a comprehensive indicator does not limit us necessarily to a vague and general discussion of the subject. The use of specific, although admittedly flawed, measures often can offer persuasive and useful insights for policy analysis.

2. See the hands-on learning module "Analyzing Costs in Education," by Jean-Pierre Jarousse, Alain Mingat, Stella Tamayo, and Jee-Peng Tan, for an elaboration of methods for estimating unit costs and public subsidies, and the module "Diagnosing Structural Weaknesses in Education," by Alain Mingat and Jee-Peng Tan, for details on constructing the enrollment rate.

3. The Gini coefficient is useful for tracking changes through time or across space. Although no comparisons are involved here, the results will be used in a subsequent problem below.

4. A full analysis of this question requires consideration of both the impact of interventions and their costs. The material below focuses only on the impact side of the analysis, which provides a vital although incomplete ingredient for policy or project design.

5. Data on incoming test scores for children in first grade are typically unavailable, in part because of the difficulty and expense of test design and administration.

7

Addressing Policy Issues in Girls' Schooling

A Three-Part Module

Alain Mingat and Jee-Peng Tan, with Esin Sile

In many developing countries girls have fewer opportunities for schooling than boys have, and where education systems are poorly developed only a tiny proportion of girls receive any schooling at all. These patterns are both inequitable and inefficient. Wide gaps in the opportunities for schooling mean that most girls will grow up without the personal human capital advantage that most boys will have. They also imply efficiency losses to the extent that poorly educated girls will be less effective than other girls in their future roles as caregivers and managers at home, and as workers in the labor force.

The issue of girls' education has attracted much debate. A wide range of opinions exists regarding the role, scope, and nature of public intervention to address the issue. At the risk of exaggeration, the extreme positions can be characterized as follows:

- *The do-nothing-specific position.* The often implicit arguments used to support this position range from reservation in the face of what is perceived as a passing fad fueled by feminist activism to the belief that schooling opportunities for girls will improve "naturally" as the education system develops and economic conditions improve. A related argument is that gender differences in schooling reflect cultural attitudes that probably cannot be changed, at least in the short to medium run, by explicit government intervention.

- *The do-everything-possible position.* This proactive position stems from a strongly held belief that improving girls' education is a social, if not economic, priority; any activity to this end is therefore worth implementing. Those holding this view try to show detractors how wrong—or more accurately, how politically incorrect—they are. At the same time they get on with the task of actually implementing activities to promote schooling for girls.

These extreme attitudes regarding girls' schooling are surprisingly common in the education sector. But as with most extreme positions, neither is completely convincing because both rely heavily, or perhaps even solely, on ready-made normative opinions. The do-nothing-specific position is too pessimistic in failing to acknowledge that even when country circumstances are dismal there often remains some scope, albeit limited in some settings, for public intervention to improve the status quo. The do-everything-possible position, on the other hand, is too indiscriminate in entirely ignoring issues of costs and benefits in the choice of interventions.

This chapter offers some methods for reaching a more rational perspective on girls' schooling. It focuses on three specific analytical issues: (a) diagnosis of the problem, including its locus in the education system; (b) assessment of potential options to address the problem; and (c) translation of the analysis into a well-justified and locally appropriate implementation strategy. As will become clear below, the intention is not to showcase sophisticated quantitative techniques, but to show how relatively simple approaches can yield reasonably persuasive inputs for policy design. The data needs are not uniformly demanding: some of the data are available from the administrative records kept by national data collection agencies; other data may require specific surveys which need to be incorporated into a systematic program of analytical work.

This training package contains the module write-up and the corresponding Excel files on the CD-ROM, and instructions for two Excel functions that you will need in the exercises (instructions for drawing graphs and doing array sums in appendixes B and C). The best way to use the materials is to scan the write-up quickly, and then follow the step-by-step instructions. Following the steps in sequence is recommended because many of the problems build on material or information presented in earlier steps.

Part A: Diagnosis of the Problem

8

There are two issues involved in the diagnosis. First we need to establish that girls' education is indeed a problem that warrants specific attention in the context of a particular country. Beyond that we also need to discover the actual locus of the problem in the education system. Both steps in the analysis are essential to prepare the way for subsequent analysis on the choice of policy options.

Determining that a Problem Exists

Is there a problem? The question can be answered in many ways. One approach, for example, is to compute the social returns to education for boys and girls. Briefly, this approach involves estimating the benefits of expanding girls' schooling, with benefits defined to include productivity in economic and noneconomic (that is, household) activity; and comparing the benefits to the corresponding costs of expansion. A high return would suggest that the country is currently underinvesting in girls' education, with the implication that increased investment would be worthwhile. Without elaborating, it is clear that this approach would require an enormous amount of data that are often difficult, if not impossible, to collect. For this reason it is rarely used in practice.

A more practicable approach is to compare girls' education in country X to girls' education in other countries. Because no country's achievement provides a truly normative yardstick by which to judge performance, the comparative approach has obvious limitations. Yet it offers a relatively simple way to identify outliers and fulfills a useful function in signaling *possible* shortfalls in performance. We therefore elaborate on this approach below, using exercises based on readily available data to illustrate its implementation.

As context, note that the approach requires a judicious choice of comparators relative to the country under consideration. Two sets of comparators, not necessarily mutually exclusive, appear to be particularly useful for this purpose: (a) countries with a similar cultural, social, or geographic context; and (b) countries at similar levels of per capita gross domestic product (GDP). In using these countries as comparators the implicit line of reasoning is as follows: if girls in country X receive fewer opportunities for schooling than do girls in countries in the comparator groups, there is reason to believe that public policy in the country is probably insufficiently supportive of girls' schooling. Therefore, there probably is scope for policy intervention to address the issue.

Problem 1

Consider the hypothetical data in table 8.A.1.1 showing enrollment ratios in primary and secondary education in country A, in three countries from the same region as A, and in three countries with a per capita GDP similar to A (with country C appearing in both sets of comparators). Use these data to assess the extent to which girls' schooling at the primary and secondary levels is an issue in country A. Take a moment now to scan the data to form a casual understanding of the education in country A from a comparative perspective.

To facilitate analysis of the data it is helpful to plot a graph showing the relationship between the gross enrollment ratio and girls' share of enrollments. Load the Excel file "Girls_Schooling_Ex1" now and check that you are in the worksheet titled "problem 1." There you will find a

Table 8.A.1.1: Gross Enrollment Ratio and Girls' Share of Enrollment in Country A and Comparator Countries (percent)

Country	Primary		Lower secondary		Upper secondary	
	GER (%)	Girls (%)	GER (%)	Girls (%)	GER (%)	Girls (%)
Country A	52	42	21	39	10	23
Countries in same region as country A						
B	47	48	14	44	8	40
C	76	51	34	49	20	43
D	63	41	36	40	22	39
Countries with similar per capita GDP as country A						
C	76	51	34	49	20	47
F	54	46	30	44	18	43
G	71	46	32	46	24	38

GER Gross enrollment ratio.

copy of table 8.A.1.1 as well as the graph, with the data for each of the seven countries drawn in a different color. Country A is depicted in red.

Comment briefly on the patterns in the graph in terms of (a) the global relationship between enrollment ratios and girls' share of enrollments, and (b) the specific performance of individual countries in comparative perspective. On the basis of the comparative data, would you consider girls' schooling to be an issue in country A?

Comment: _____

_____

_____

_____

8

Problem 2

Now focus more closely on the data for country A. Based on data for this country in table 8.A.1.1, compute the gross enrollment ratio separately for girls and boys, and the ratio of boys to girls enrolled, using the results to complete table 8.A.2.2. The calculations are relatively simple, but if you would like to follow the detailed instructions skip now to the next paragraph. Otherwise tab over now to the worksheet titled "problem 2" and complete the exercise; then skip to problem 2, paragraph 2.

Suppose girls' share of enrollment is g percent (which implies that enrollment share of boys is $100 - g$), and the overall gross enrollment ratio is E percent. Assuming equal population sizes for boys and girls, the gross enrollment ratio would then be $[(g/50) \times E]$ for girls; and

Table 8.A.2.2: Gross Enrollment Ratio among Boys and Girls by Level of Education (percent)

	Primary	Lower secondary	Upper secondary
Both sexes	52	21	10
• Boys			
• Girls			
Ratio of boys to girls enrolled			

$\{[(100 - g)/50] \times E\}$ for boys. The ratio of boys to girls enrolled is simply the ratio of boys' gross enrollment to that of girls.

Comment on your results, noting any implications they may have regarding the ranking of priority sectors for addressing issues in girls' schooling. Are your conclusions, based as they are on the data available so far, sufficiently convincing? In what ways might they be open to criticism?

Comment:

_____

_____

_____

_____

Locating the Source of the Problem

When you have identified that a problem in girls' schooling exists, an immediate question arises regarding its location in the education system. Answering this question is important to ensure an appropriate *placement* of interventions to improve girls' schooling. The answer also has implications for specifying a suitable analytical work program to inform policy and project design.

As hinted at in problem 2, gross enrollment ratios are an unreliable guide in this regard. Even so, they are often used and the results can be disastrous, as the experience in one World Bank–financed project shows. The data for the country in question (called country Y here) appear in table 8.A.2.3, showing gross enrollment ratios for boys and girls in urban and rural areas.

The data imply that at the primary level there are, for each girl enrolled, 1.03 boys (= 73.7/71.7) in urban areas, and 1.25 boys in rural areas. At the lower secondary level, the corresponding ratios are 1.75 in urban areas, and 4.40 in rural areas. These data were used in the project document to justify building more lower secondary schools in rural areas and equipping some of them with boarding facilities. The argument is

8

Table 8.A.2.3: Gross Enrollment Ratios by Level of Education for Urban and Rural Boys and Girls, Country Y

Indicator	Boys (%)			Girls (%)			Boys-to-girls ratio	
	Urban	Rural	Overall	Urban	Rural	Overall	Urban	Rural
Primary	95	75	80	92	60	71	1.03	1.25
Lower secondary	70	40	50	66	18	33	1.75	4.40
Lower secondary/ Primary	73.7	53.3	62.5	71.7	30.0	46.5	—	—

— Not applicable.

that girls are especially underrepresented at the lower secondary level, most schools at this level are currently located some distance from students' homes, and none of them offers boarding facilities.

Although the argument looks persuasive at first sight, it is deeply flawed. A main problem is that it is based on data which refer to the *average* for the entire cycle of study. Such data have their uses but are inadequate for diagnosing the locus of the problem at hand. In particular, they tend to hide important grade-to-grade transition patterns; and they may misrepresent these patterns if grade repetition is common. In the specific example here, more detailed analyses have subsequently revealed that most girls fail to reach the end of primary education and therefore were never even eligible for lower secondary school. In this context, building more lower secondary schools in rural areas and offering boarding facilities would hardly help to improve the situation—an expectation now confirmed by the fact that many of the schools financed by the project in question sit empty for want of students.

To avoid the serious mistakes that may arise from using gross enrollment ratios for assessing the placement of interventions, we need to analyze the grade-to-grade student flow profile for the population in question. Depending on the data at hand, there are two main ways to accomplish the computation:

1. *Administrative data* on the number of pupils (separately for repeaters and nonrepeaters) by grade and data on (or estimates of) the population by single years of age in the relevant age groups. If data are available for two consecutive years the calculations can proceed using what is known as the reconstructed cohort method; if they are available only for one year the calculations can still be accomplished using what can be described as the direct method.

2. *Survey data* of recent vintage and nationally representative in coverage. With such data it is often possible to compute overall student

8

flow profiles as well as group-specific profiles (for example, by income, socioeconomic status, or residence).

In problem 3 below we illustrate the use of the direct method based on administrative data for one year.

Problem 3

Your task is to construct and analyze the grade-to-grade student flow profiles for boys and girls in urban and rural areas in country Y, using the data in table 8.A.3.4. The data show the school population by grade (non-repeaters only), and the estimated total population in the one-year age group corresponding to the average age of the students at each grade.[1] Briefly scan the table and then proceed to the next paragraph.

The ratio between the school population and the total population at each grade can be interpreted as the enrollment rate at that grade. Repeaters are excluded from the calculation to avoid double counting. Consolidating the ratios thus calculated for all the grades would then yield a full picture of student flow or grade-to-grade progression in the education system. The instructions below guide you in calculating and analyzing the data.

Table 8.A.3.4: Basic Data for Estimating the Student Flow Profile in Country Y

	Boys				Girls			
	School population		Total population		School population		Total population	
	Urban	Rural	Urban	Rural	Urban	Rural	Urban	Rural
Grade 1	100,940	167,500	103,000	209,400	98,100	141,600	102,200	208,300
Grade 2	94,520	150,500	99,400	203,400	91,400	117,100	98,300	202,100
Grade 3	88,540	141,400	95,200	199,200	87,600	103,300	96,300	198,700
Grade 4	82,170	126,700	91,300	192,000	81,300	88,300	92,400	192,000
Grade 5	77,000	116,400	87,500	184,700	75,000	72,200	88,200	185,100
Form 1	56,840	74,130	83,600	176,500	56,100	42,500	85,000	177,000
Form 2	52,650	67,800	81,000	169,400	51,700	32,500	83,400	171,200
Form 3	48,670	58,300	78,500	161,900	46,300	26,200	79,900	163,600
Form 4	45,600	53,100	76,000	156,200	42,100	22,000	78,000	157,200
Form 5	23,700	18,130	74,100	151,100	18,200	9,200	75,900	153,000
Form 6	21,800	14,600	72,800	146,300	15,500	7,400	74,000	148,400

Note: The school population refers to nonrepeaters only. The total population refers to the number of children in the one-year age group corresponding to the average age of the children in the indicated grade. Although such data rarely are available directly, they can be estimated by applying standard techniques in demography to population data typically found in published sources.

8

Step 1 Tab over now to the worksheet titled "problem 3," where you will find a copy of table 8.A.3.4. Compute the grade-specific enrollment rates for grades one through five among urban boys and enter your results in the cells colored yellow in table 8.A.3.5. To save time the other calculations in the table have been completed for you.

Step 2 Use the age-specific enrollment rates to make a line graph in the designated box showing the student flow profiles for boys and girls in urban and rural areas. If you wish you may skip this step and simply use the graph. Take a few moments here to review the graph and proceed to the next step.

Step 3 The results in table 8.A.3.5 can be summarized to reflect the pattern of children's schooling careers at key points: entry to first grade, survival to the end of the primary cycle, and transition between the last grade of primary school (grade five) and the first grade of secondary school (form one). Compute these indicators for urban boys and enter your results in the yellow cells in table 8.A.3.6. As before, the calculations

Table 8.A.3.5: Grade-Specific Enrollment Rates by Gender and Geographic Location

| | Boys (%) | | Girls (%) | |
	Urban	Rural	Urban	Rural
Grade 1		80	96	68
Grade 2		74	93	58
Grade 3		71	91	52
Grade 4		66	88	46
Grade 5		63	85	39
Form 1	68	42	66	24
Form 2	65	40	62	19
Form 3	62	36	58	16
Form 4	60	34	54	14
Form 5	32	12	24	6
Form 6	30	10	21	5

Table 8.A.3.6: Summary Indicators of the Schooling Careers of Boys and Girls in Urban and Rural Areas in Country Y

| Summary indicator | Boys (%) | | Girls (%) | |
	Urban	Rural	Urban	Rural
Entry rate to grade one		80.0	96.0	68.0
Survival rate from grade one to grade five		78.8	88.6	57.4
Transition rate between grade five and form one		66.6	77.5	61.6

8

for the other population groups have been completed for you. Comment on the patterns in the tables and briefly note potential sources of the differences in entry, survival, and transition rates across population groups.

Comment: _____

_____

_____

_____

_____

Step 4   To exploit the results in tables 8.A.3.5 and 8.A.3.6 to full advantage you are asked to perform and evaluate some simple simulations of rural girls' enrollment rates in form one under various assumptions about their rates of entry to grade one, survival between grades one and five, and transition from grade five to form one. Table 8.A.3.7 has been organized to facilitate the simulations. Scroll down the worksheet to locate the table, take a moment to scan it briefly, and then read below for further instructions.

Table 8.A.3.7: Simulations of Rural Girls' Enrollment Rates in Form One

		Assumptions about rural girls' rates of entry, survival, and transition			
Simulation	Rate	Rises to level of urban girls	Remains unchanged	Rural girls' form one enrollment rate	Gain in form one enrollment rate relative to actual rate of 24 percent (%)
A	Entry rate	—	68.0		
	Survival rate	—	57.4	30.2	6.2
	Transition rate	77.5	—		
B	Entry rate	—	68.0		
	Survival rate	88.6	—		
	Transition rate	—	61.5		
C	Entry rate	96.0	—		
	Survival rate	—	57.4	33.9	9.9
	Transition rate	—	61.5		

— Not applicable.

Note: According to data in table 8.A.3.5, among rural girls the current enrollment rate is 68 percent in grade one, 39 percent in grade five, and 24 percent in form one.

8

Table 8.A.3.7 shows three alternative simulations corresponding to the following assumptions:

1. *Simulation A* (already completed) assumes that the transition rate between grade five and form one among rural girls rises to the same level as for urban girls, whereas the entry rate to grade one and the survival rate from grades one to five remain unchanged.

2. *Simulation B* (to be completed by you) assumes that the survival rate rises to the same level as for urban girls, whereas the entry rate and transition rate remain unchanged.

3. *Simulation C* (already completed) assumes that the entry rate rises to the same level as for urban girls, while the survival and transition rates remain unchanged.

The calculation for simulation A proceeds as follows: with the rates of entry and survival unchanged at 68 percent and 57.4 percent, respectively, the enrollment rate in grade five remains at 39 percent. With the transition rate raised to 77.5 percent, the enrollment rate in form one rises to 30.2 (= 39 × 0.775) percent, representing a gain of 6.2 percentage points over the current rate of 24 percent. The computation for simulation C is as follows: with the entry rate raised to 96 percent, and the survival and transition rates maintained at 57.4 percent and 61.5 percent, respectively, the enrollment rate in form one would be 33.9 (= 96 × 0.574 × 0.615) percent—a gain of 9.9 percentage points.

Follow a similar procedure to complete the calculations for simulation B. After completing the exercise take a moment to scan your results briefly and then go on to the next step.

Step 5 Look over your results from all the preceding steps and summarize their implications for project or policy development to improve girls' access to schooling. Comment in particular on their implications for the placement of interventions to improve girls' representation in secondary education, noting any assumptions you make in your evaluation. On the basis of the results so far, can you say anything about the specific choice of interventions that might be helpful in this regard?

8

Comment on overall results: _____

_____

_____

_____

Problem 4

The student flow profile in the foregoing problem is only one among many conceivable patterns. In this problem you are given a set of seven other possible patterns, in all of which girls are underrepresented in secondary education. Tab over now to the worksheet titled "problem 4," where you will find the seven patterns. Enter a descriptive title (in the cell colored yellow) corresponding to each figure to reflect the source or sources of the observed underrepresentation of girls in secondary education. As an example, the first figure is titled "pure transition problem."

Part B: Identification of Possible Solutions

After diagnosing the problem we turn to identifying possible solutions. The task is to assess which among the range of potential interventions would make most sense to include in a program of action. Specifically we need to identify those that are likely to produce the greatest improvement in girls' schooling at least cost.

As before, ready-made opinions shed little light on this issue and may even point to erroneous and wasteful solutions. Because all interventions need to be tailored to country- or project-specific conditions, evaluation results that pertain to other contexts probably are helpful but typically insufficient as a guide. The collection and analysis of context-specific data is unavoidable for good project or policy design. Although the task is demanding and time consuming, it often can be accomplished as part of a systematic program of analytical work.

As context for the analytical techniques, we begin below by elaborating on the data issues, followed by examples to illustrate the techniques. If you are familiar with household and school-based surveys you may want to skip now to the first problem below (problem 1); otherwise simply continue reading until you reach that problem.

Deciding on the Data to Collect

Depending on the results from the diagnosis of the problem, three generic problems may warrant further analysis: (a) low entry rates to first grade; (b) low survival rates (or equivalently, high dropout rates) within cycles of education; and (c) low transition rates between one cycle of education and the next. Because grade repetition often is associated with high dropout propensities, it often is included as part of the analysis on dropout behavior.

Analysis of all of these outcomes involves a common two-step strategy: relating observed patterns of schooling across individual children to their personal characteristics, family background, and school environment; and using the estimated relationship to determine the impact of potential interventions. From a policy perspective the impact of supply-side factors is particularly relevant because they are the ones most amenable to public intervention in the short run. These supply-side factors need not reside exclusively in the education sector; for example, the

8

availability of tap water may be important in some settings because of its influence on the opportunity cost of time for girls. While focusing on the supply-side factors we obviously cannot ignore the role of family background and other demand-side influences. Typically the latter enter as control variables in the analysis.

The data for analyzing any of the three generic issues center on two blocks of information: personal and family background of the children and their schooling environment. There basically are two sources for these data: household surveys and school-based surveys. Although both types of surveys can be used to generate the requisite data, they each have their strengths and weaknesses. Household surveys are superior for collecting data on personal and family background, in part because the respondents are typically adults in the family who are in a position to offer the most accurate information. School-based surveys, on the other hand, are superior for collecting information on the schooling environment, particularly on such policy-relevant and child-specific variables as teacher qualification, classroom conditions, textbook supply, and so on. School-based surveys probably also are easier to implement when collecting data for relatively sizable groups of students who have been exposed to a common (or even identical) schooling environment.

Problem 1

On the basis of the foregoing discussion and your own knowledge about household and school-based surveys, rate their suitability as sources of data for analyzing the issues shown in table 8.B.1.8. For this purpose use a varying number of check marks to indicate the degree of suitability, and leave the cell blank if you consider the data source to be inappropriate. You may enter your answers by hand on the table below or type them into the worksheet titled "problem 1" in the Excel file "Girls_Schooling_Ex2."

Problem 2

Suppose that your analysis of student flow profiles identifies low entry rates to grade one among rural girls as an issue for further scrutiny. The

8

Table 8.B.1.8: Suitability of Household and School-Based Survey Data for Analyzing Selected Issues in Education

Indicator	Household survey	School-based survey
Entry rates to grade one		
Survival patterns within cycles of education		
Grade repetition		
Dropout behavior		
Transition between cycles of education		

task then is to identify potential interventions to raise entry rates. For this purpose we need to estimate the relationship between enrollment and supply-side factors while controlling for the personal and family characteristics of children. Suppose that the requisite data do not exist and you proceed by first embarking on a household survey. In the spaces below, or in the worksheet titled "problem 2," briefly indicate your thoughts regarding the broad design of the survey in terms of the type of households you would include in the sample, as well as the information you would collect from the sample households and the community in which they live.

Before proceeding, recall that your analysis is intended to provide guidance on policy interventions to improve girls' schooling. The policy focus of your analysis implies that your sample would need to capture a diversity of supply-side conditions. In addition, the survey instruments would need to generate data that correspond explicitly to potential policy levers.

(i) Your thoughts on sampling criteria:
     (Comment on the selection of regions to sample, as well as the selection of localities within the regions and households within the sample localities.)

_____

_____

_____

(ii) Your thoughts on the data to be collected regarding:
     The household and its composition of members

_____

_____

_____

     The adult members of the household

_____

_____

_____

     The school-age children in the household

_____

_____

_____

8

iv) Schools in the household's neighborhood

_____

_____

_____

v) The household's community

_____

_____

_____

Implementing and Interpreting the Analysis

To continue with the example of analyzing low entry rates to grade one among rural girls suppose the available data are for a sample of children aged 8 to 10 years, some of whom have been to school (and indeed may still be enrolled) and some of whom have never enrolled. Our task is to relate the observed enrollment status to the children's personal and family background as well as to the characteristics of schooling supply in the community. In view of the multivariate nature of the relationship we would need multiple regression analysis to estimate the desired relationship. In the exercises below we will focus on interpreting the regression results for their policy implications, rather than on details of the techniques for obtaining the regression estimates.

Nonetheless, it is important to understand a few technical details before proceeding. Because the dependent variable here is dichotomous (ever enrolled or never enrolled) it is common to specify a logistic functional form for the regression equation:

$$p = \frac{1}{1 + e^{-bX}}$$

where p is the probability that a child has ever entered grade one, e is the exponent, X is a vector of independent variables, and b is the corresponding set of regression coefficients. This functional form ensures that the estimated regression is consistent with enrollment probabilities that are bounded by zero and one. The regression equation is easily implemented using any of the standard software packages (for example, STATA, SPSS, and SAS).

Problem 3

Suppose the regression analysis yields the results shown in table 8.B.3.9. Most of the regression variables are dichotomous variables (for example,

8

"father is a farmer"); such variables have a value of one when the indicated condition is satisfied and a value of zero when it is not. The regression variables are grouped under three rubrics: characteristics of the school nearest to child's home, child's family background, and indicators of constraints on child's time for school. They are context specific; those shown in the table are chosen merely for illustration.

Table 8.B.3.9: Regression Estimates of the Probability of Ever Being Enrolled in Grade One, Rural Girls and Boys in Country Y

	Boys		Girls	
	Coefficient	*Statistical significance*	*Coefficient*	*Statistical significance*
Characteristics of the school nearest to child's home				
Free meal at school:				
Not offered (omitted category)	—	—	—	—
Offered and school is less than 2 km from home	−0.01	n.s.	+0.03	n.s.
Offered and school is more than 2 km from home	+0.22	*	+0.57	***
School has toilet facilities	−0.14	n.s.	+0.55	**
School uses multigrade teaching	−0.07	n.s.	+0.09	n.s.
School offers all grades of instruction in primary cycle	+0.38	***	+0.03	n.s.
Distance between the school and child's home:				
Less than 0.5 km (omitted category)	—	—	—	—
Between 0.5 km and 2 km	−0.08	n.s.	−0.43	***
Between 2 km and 4 km	−0.23	n.s.	−0.91	***
More than 4 km	−0.51	**	−1.15	***
School is in district with publicity campaign for girls' schooling	+0.19	n.s.	+0.45	***
First-grade teacher in the school is female	−0.12	n.s.	−0.11	n.s.
Child's family background variables				
Father is a farmer	+0.03	n.s.	−0.37	***
Father has at least primary education	+0.31	*	+0.37	***
Mother is literate	−0.03	n.s.	+0.44	**
Number of adult women in the household	+0.08	n.s.	+0.12	*
Number of children under six years of age	−0.04	n.s.	−0.32	***

Table continued on next page

177

Table 8.B.3.9 (continued)

	Boys		Girls	
	Coefficient	Statistical significance	Coefficient	Statistical significance
Indicators of constraints on child's time for school				
Family relies on collected fuelwood	+0.04	n.s.	–0.31	*
Distance from home to source of water (km)	+0.07	n.s.	–0.03	*
Index of household reliance on home-based economic activities	0.12	**	–0.14	**
Constant		0.985		1.305
Number of observations		1,621		1,465
Sommer's D[a]		0.44		0.49
Average probability of ever enrolling in grade one		0.787		0.658

— Not applicable.

n.s. Not statistically significant.

*Statistically significant at the 10 percent level.

**Statistically significant at the 5 percent level.

***Statistically significant at the 1 percent level.

a. Sommer's D is an index of the overall goodness-of-fit of the regression equation, ranging between zero (no fit) and one (perfect fit).

Review the regression coefficients and briefly summarize what they suggest about the impact of the supply- and demand-side variables on enrollment probabilities, noting any differences between boys and girls. For this purpose note the magnitude as well as the statistical significance of the coefficient estimates. Write your answers in the spaces below or on the worksheet named "problem 3."

Comment on impact of (a) the supply-side factors and (b) the demand-side factors:

_____

_____

_____

_____

Problem 4

To make a more systematic comparison we can use the coefficient estimates to calculate the marginal impact of the various factors on enroll-

8

ment probabilities. By convention, the impacts are evaluated at the sample mean of the dependent variable. The precise formula for computing the marginal impact of factor i (MI_i) is as follows:

$$MI_i = b_i \times p \times (1 - p) \times 100$$

where b_i is the corresponding coefficient estimate, and p is the mean probability of ever being enrolled for children in the sample; in the present data set, the value of p is 0.787 for boys and 0.658 for girls. The result thus calculated shows the percentage point increase or decrease in enrollment probability corresponding to a unit change in the indicated variable. For dichotomous variables it shows the difference in enrollment probability between the two groups defined by the indicated criteria (for example, between a child whose father is a farmer and one whose father is not a farmer).

On the basis of the coefficient estimates in table 8.B.3.9, compute the marginal impact of the three supply conditions listed in table 8.B.4.10. Tab over to the worksheet titled "problem 4" where you will find a copy of the table; for convenience, table 8.B.4.10 (which contains the coefficient estimate) also is reproduced there. As an example, the cells for boys have been completed for you, so you need only make the corresponding computations for girls. Confining yourself to only the three variables in the table, comment on their relative impact on enrollment probabilities among boys and girls.

Comment:

_____

_____

_____

_____

Table 8.B.4.10: Marginal Impact of Selected Variables on Enrollment Probabilities among Rural Boys and Girls, Country Y (percentage point change)

Variable	Boys	Girls
School offers free meal and school is more than 2 km from child's home[a]	3.7	
School is more than 4 km from home[b]	−8.5	
Child's father has at least primary education[c]	5.2	

a. Relative to school that does not offer free meals.
b. Relative to school that is less than 0.5 km from home.
c. Relative to child whose father has no schooling.

8

Problem 5

Simulations based on the regression results are another approach for comparing the impact of the various factors on enrollment probabilities. One advantage of simulations is that they allow us to evaluate the combined influence of several variables; in contrast, calculating marginal impacts allows us only to assess the individual influence of each variable. Simulation results often are more easily understood than raw data by policymakers.

In this problem you are asked to consider simulations of the global influence of supply- and demand-side conditions. Because it is important to understand the underlying assumptions for the simulations, you are asked in step 1 below to go through the calculations for one of the simulations—for girls under "all unfavorable" supply-side conditions (that is, schooling conditions), with demand-side variables maintained at the sample mean. The full set of simulation results for similar extreme combinations of supply- and demand-side conditions then are presented for you to evaluate for their policy implications.

Step 1 Retrieve the file named "Girls_Schooling_Ex2" and check that you are in worksheet "problem 5," where you will find a copy of table 8.B.5.11. Skip now to the next paragraph if you wish to follow the detailed instructions on how to proceed; otherwise, read the rest of this paragraph to complete the simulations. Enter the appropriate data for the X_is in the cells colored yellow. Note that for the two supply-side variables— use of multigrade teaching and presence of a female teacher—with statistically insignificant coefficients in the regression analysis, we have set their values of the sample mean for the purpose of this simulation; these values already have been entered for you. After completing your entries proceed to evaluate the predicted entry rate in two steps: compute the sum of the product of the X_is and the b_is by invoking Excel's array sum function (see the Excel instructions in appendix C), and then plug the resulting sum into equation (1) in the Excel worksheet to obtain the desired result. Then proceed directly to step 2 below.

This and the following paragraphs provide detailed instructions on the mechanics of the simulations. The calculations involve evaluating equation (1) in the Excel worksheet at the relevant values of X_i and b_i. Recall that X_i refers to the vector of regression variables and b_i refers to the corresponding estimated coefficients. Table 8.B.5.11 is a convenient format for setting up the simulation; it is on the worksheet you have just retrieved from the file named "Girls_Schooling_Ex2." Scan the table quickly and continue reading below.

In the table we have listed all the regression variables (that is, the X_is), the coefficients estimates (that is, the b_is), the sample means, and a column to enter the assumed values of X_is for the simulation. Because we

8

Table 8.B.5.11: Data for Simulating Girls' Entry Rate to Grade 1 in Country Y under Selected Supply- and Demand-Side Conditions

Regression variables X_i	Regression coefficient	Sample mean	Value of X_i assumed for simulation
Characteristics of the school nearest to child's home			
Free meal at school:	0	0.6	
No free meal offered	+0.03	0.2	
Offered and school is less than 2 km from home	+0.57	0.2	
Offered and school is more than 2 km from home	+0.55	0.4	
School has toilet facilities	+0.09	0.3	
School uses multigrade teaching	+0.03	0.6	0.3
School offers all grades of instruction in primary cycle			
Distance between the school and child's home:			
Less than 0.5 km	0	0.4	
Between 0.5 km and 2 km	−0.43	0.3	
Between 2 km and 4 km	−0.91	0.2	
More than 4 km	−1.15	0.1	
School is in district with publicity campaign for girls' schooling	+0.45	0.3	
First-grade teacher in the school is female	−0.11	0.2	0.2
Child's family background variables			
Father is a farmer	−0.37	0.8	0.8
Father has at least primary education	+0.37	0.7	0.7
Mother is literate	+0.44	0.3	0.3
Number of adult women in the household	+0.12	1.6	1.6
Number of children under six years of age	−0.32	1.8	1.8
Indicators of constraints on child's time for school			
Family relies on collected fuelwood	−0.31	0.6	0.6
Distance of home to source of water (km)	−0.03	1.2	1.2
Index of household reliance on home-based economic activities	−0.14	1.5	1.5
Constant	1.305	1.0	1.0
Simulated entry rate to grade one[a]			

a. Corresponding to assumed values of X_is in last column and evaluated using equation (1) in the Excel worksheet.

8

are looking only at the supply-side variables in this simulation, the values of the demand-side variables have been set to the sample mean. In addition, we also set to the sample mean the values for the two supply-side variables with statistically insignificant coefficient estimates; they relate to the use of multigrade teaching and the presence of a female teacher.

Your task is to enter the appropriate values to reflect all unfavorable supply-side conditions for the X_is in the cells colored yellow in the worksheet. Specifically, the values of the X_is should correspond to the following assumptions: the school in question is more than 4 kilometers from the girl's home, it does not offer free meals, it does not have toilet facilities, it does not offer instruction in all of the primary school grades, and it is not in a district with a campaign to promote girls' schooling. To illustrate, the value for the first two variables listed in the table would be zero, indicating that free meals are not offered, whereas the value of the first three distance variables would be zero, and the value for the last distance variable would be one. Continue in this manner until all of the yellow cells have been filled.

The predicted entry rate corresponding to the foregoing assumptions can then be calculated in two steps: compute the sum of the product of the X_is and the b_is by invoking Excel's array sum function (see appendix C for array functions); and then plug the resulting sum into equation (1) in the Excel worksheet to obtain the desired result.

Step 2 In this step you are provided with all the simulation results— including the one you have just completed—and asked to comment on the results for their policy implications. Recall that in this problem we are focusing on the impact of extreme combinations of the supply- and demand-side conditions (table 8.B.5.12). Scroll down the worksheet until you locate the table titled "Working Table for Calculations in Table

8

Table 8.B.5.12: Simulation of Boys' and Girls' Grade-One Enrollment Probabilities under the Combined Influence of Various Supply- and Demand-Side Conditions (percent)

Simulation	Supply-side conditions	Demand-side conditions	Boys	Girls
Base case (that is, under initial conditions)	At sample mean	At sample mean	78.7	65.8
S.1a	All favorable	At sample mean	82.8	83.9
S.1b	All unfavorable		65.6	
D.1a	At sample mean	All favorable	83.3	92.7
D.1b		All unfavorable	71.1	34.9
SD.1a	All favorable	All favorable	86.7	97.2
SD.1b	All unfavorable	All unfavorable	55.9	13.7

8.B.5.12." Your work from the previous step corresponds to simulation S.1b in the table. Take a moment to understand the entries for the values of X_is corresponding to the various simulations. Your calculation from step 1 is linked to this worksheet and is shown in the cells colored yellow.

Examine the results in table 8.B.5.12 and comment on their implications for policy or project design.

Comment on results: _____

_____

_____

_____

Problem 6

Beyond assessing the global impact of supply- and demand-side conditions it is often useful, particularly in policy or project design, to examine the impact of individual factors. As before, we focus on the supply-side variables with statistically significant coefficient estimates in the regression analysis. Each one of them is set, in turn, to values corresponding to various assumptions, whereas all of the other regression variables are set to the sample mean. To understand the mechanics of the simulation you are asked in the first step below to simulate the entry rate to grade one for rural girls when the school is equipped with toilet facilities. You then are presented with the full set of simulation results for you to evaluate their policy implications.

Step 1   Tab over to the worksheet named "problem 6," where you will find a copy of table 8.B.6.13. You have only one number to enter, corresponding to the simulation assumption that the school is equipped with toilet facilities. All the other regression variables have been set to the sample mean. After entering the number, compute the predicted entry rate to grade one, following the same two-step procedure as in the previous problem: calculate the sum of the product of the X_is and the b_is by invoking Excel's array sum function; and then plug the resulting sum into equation (1) in the Excel worksheet to obtain the desired result.

Step 2   You now are given the full set of simulation results in the format of table 8.B.6.14. Scroll down the worksheet until you locate a table titled "Working Table for Calculations in Table 8.B.6.14," which contains the assumptions underlying the simulations. The values of the X_is have been set to correspond to the simulation listed in table 8.B.6.14. Take a moment now to scan the entries in the working table; your calculation from the previous step has been linked to this table and is colored yellow.

8

Table 8.B.6.13: Data for Simulating Girls' Entry Rate to Grade One in Country Y When the School Is Equipped with Toilet Facilities

Regression variables X_i	Regression coefficient	Sample mean	Value of X_i assumed for simulation
Characteristics of the school nearest to child's home			
Free meal at school:			
No free meal offered	0	0.6	0.6
Offered and school is less than 2 km from home	+0.03	0.2	0.2
Offered and school is more than 2 km from home	+0.57	0.2	0.2
School has toilet facilities	+0.55	0.4	
School uses multigrade teaching	+0.09	0.3	0.3
School offers all grades of instruction in primary cycle	+0.03	0.6	0.6
Distance between the school and child's home:			
Less than 0.5 km	0	0.4	0.4
Between 0.5 km and 2 km	−0.43	0.3	0.3
Between 2 km and 4 km	−0.91	0.2	0.2
More than 4 km	−1.15	0.1	0.1
School is in district with publicity campaign for girls' schooling	+0.45	0.3	0.3
First-grade teacher in the school is female	−0.11	0.2	0.2
Child's family background variables			
Father is a farmer	−0.37	0.8	0.8
Father has at least primary education	+0.37	0.7	0.7
Mother is literate	+0.44	0.3	0.3
Number of adult women in the household	+0.12	1.6	1.6
Number of children under six years of age	−0.32	1.8	1.8
Indicators of constraints on child's time for school			
Family relies on collected fuelwood	−0.31	0.6	0.6
Distance from home to source of water (km)	−0.03	1.2	1.2
Index of household reliance on home-based economic activities	−0.14	1.5	1.5
Constant	1.305	1.0	1.0
Simulated entry rate to grade one[a]			

a. Corresponding to assumed values of X_is in last column and evaluated using equation (1) in the Excel worksheet.

Table 8.B.6.14: Predicted Probability of Ever Being Enrolled in Grade One under Various Supply-Side Conditions

Simulation	*Assumptions about supply-side factors (with demand-side factors set at sample mean)*					*Probability of entering grade one*	
	Free meal	*Latrines*	*Complete*	*Campaign*	*Distance to school (km)*	*Boys*	*Girls*
Base case (that is, under initial conditions)	average					0.787	0.658
Extreme cases (from table 8.B.5.12 above)							
S.1a: least favorable	no	no	no	no	5.0	0.656	0.363
S.1b: most favorable	yes	yes	yes	yes	0.2	0.828	0.839
Varying distance to school with no school meal							
S.2a	no		average		0.2	0.799	0.724
S.2b	no		average		1.0	0.786	0.630
S.2c	no		average		3.0	0.760	0.513
S.2d	no		average		5.0	0.705	0.453
Varying distance to school with school meal							
S.3a	yes		average		0.2	0.798	0.729
S.3b	yes		average		1.0	0.785	0.637
S.3c	yes		average		3.0	0.798	0.651
S.3d	yes		average		5.0	0.749	0.594
Varying availability of toilets							
S.4a	average	yes	average			0.772	
S.4b	average	no	average			0.796	0.607
Varying completeness of instruction offered							
S.5a	average		yes	average		0.811	0.661
S.5b	average		no	average		0.746	0.654
Varying the use of publicity campaigns							
S.6a	average			yes	average	0.808	0.725
S.6b	average			no	average	0.777	0.627

8

Then comment on the simulation results, noting in particular gender differences in the impact of the various supply-side factors on enrollment probabilities.

Comment: _____

_____

_____

_____

_____

_____

_____

Problem 7

In this problem you are asked to take a closer look at the impact of the demand-side factors. In the interest of time all the simulations have been completed for you, and you need only examine the results for their policy implications. Tab over to the worksheet titled "problem 7," where you will find a working table titled "Working Table for Table 8.B.7.15" (pp. 188–9 of the text). The table is set up in the same format as before, showing entries for the X_is corresponding to the various assumptions in table 8.B.7.15. As before, take a moment to examine one or two of the columns of entries to make sure you understand the underlying assumptions. Then scroll down to the table (or use the table printed here) showing the completed calculations. Comment on what the results reveal about the influence of the various demand-side factors on enrollment probabilities among girls and boys. What implications do these results have for policy and project design to improve girls' schooling?

Comment on results: _____

_____

_____

_____

_____

_____

8

Part C: Consolidation of the Analysis for Policy or Project Design

In the first two parts of this module we have focused on diagnosing the problem and assessing its response to various potential interventions. These steps build a good understanding of the issues and point to possible directions for intervention. To bring the analysis even closer to policy and project design, two additional issues need to be addressed:
1. Appropriate targeting of interventions across localities
2. Maximization of cost-effectiveness and impact across interventions

The exercises below elaborate on these issues and show how the analysis might be accomplished.

Customizing Locally Responsive Intervention Packages

Continuing with the example of girls' access to grade one, we have so far ignored possible disparities in entry rates across localities. Because the disparities may arise for different reasons, it is important to select interventions that relieve the *effective* constraints on girls' schooling in each locality. Suppose, for example, that in province X schools are generally well placed to address girls' educational needs (that is, they are plentiful and relatively close to pupils' homes, equipped with toilets, and so on), but parents are reluctant for various reasons to send their daughters to school. In this province, publicity campaigns to change social attitudes to girls' schooling may be more effective for expanding girls' participation in schooling than improvements to the already favorable conditions in schooling supply. In some other provinces, however, the operating constraint may be on the supply side, implying that such publicity campaigns would be relatively ineffective. The problems below offer guidance for systematic analysis of such targeting issues.

Problem 1

In this problem your task is simply to examine regional data on entry rates to grade one and make some simple comparisons. Follow the steps below to complete the exercise.

Step 1 Locate the file titled "Girls_Schooling_Ex3" on the CD-ROM and retrieve the worksheet named "problem 1," where you will find a copy of table 8.C.1.16 showing entry rates to grade one for girls in the four geographic regions of country Y (column 2). Compute the deviation of each region's entry rate relative to the country average and enter your results in column 3 of the table.

8

Table 8.B.7.15: Simulated Probability of Ever Being Enrolled under Various Demand-Side Conditions

| Simulation | Assumptions about demand-side factors (with supply-side factors set at sample mean) | | | | | Indicators of constraints on children's time for school | | | Probability of entering grade one | |
| | Father | | Mother | | | | | | | |
	Farmer	Primary	Literate	No. of women at home	No. of children under six	Fuel-wood	Water	Production	Boys	Girls
Base case (that is, under initial conditions)	average								0.787	0.658
Extreme cases (from table 8.B.5.12 above)										
D.1a: Least favorable	yes	no	no	1	3	yes	2.0	3.0	0.711	0.349
D.1b: Most favorable	no	yes	yes	3	0	no	0	0	0.833	0.927
Varying father's job										
D.2a	yes			average	average				0.788	0.642
D.2b	no			average	average				0.782	0.724
Varying father's education										
D.3a	average	yes		average	average				0.802	0.683
D.3b	average	no		average	average				0.748	0.598
Varying mother's literacy										
D.4a	average	average	yes	average	average				0.783	0.724
D.4b	average	average	no	average	average				0.788	0.628

8

Varying no. of women at home					
D.5a	1	average		0.778	0.642
D.5b	3	average		0.805	0.695
Varying no. of children under six at home					
D.6a	average	0	average	0.798	0.774
D.6b	average	1	average	0.792	0.713
D.6c	average	3	average	0.778	0.568
Varying dependence on fuelwood					
D.7a	average	yes	average	0.789	0.630
D.7b	average	no	average	0.782	0.699
Varying distance to water source					
D.8a	average	0	average	0.772	0.666
D.8b	average	1	average	0.784	0.660
D.8c	average	2	average	0.796	0.653
Varying children's involvement in production					
D.9a	average		0	0.815	0.704
D.9b	average		1.5	0.787	0.658
D.9c	average		3.0	0.755	0.610

8

Table 8.C.1.16: Entry Rates across Localities in Country Y

Region	Grade one entry rate (%)	Deviation from country average (percentage points)
North	40.2	
South	30.7	
East	37.8	
West	25.5	
Country average	35.8	

Step 2   Drawing on the analysis in part B above as well as your own ideas, suggest possible reasons for the observed differences in entry rates across the four regions. Comment also on any implications the data might have regarding the targeting of interventions to expand girls' schooling.

Possible reasons for the regional differences in entry rates:

_____

_____

_____

Implications for intervention:

_____

_____

_____

Problem 2

In the previous problem you probably have identified three types of factors accounting for the observed disparities in entry rates to grade one: (a) differences in the distribution of schooling supply across regions; (b) differences in the household characteristics of the population across regions; and (c) differences in culture, religion, or tradition across regions that affect social attitudes toward schooling for girls. Evaluating how much each of these sets of factors contributes to the existing regional disparities in girls' schooling is important because it provides guidance regarding the domains in which intervention is likely to be effective in each region.

Toward this end you are asked here to disaggregate into three parts each region's deviation in entry rates from the country average (that is, the data in column 3 in table 8.C.1.16), with each part corresponding to the three broad factors indicated above. Follow the steps below to accomplish the analysis.

Step 1   To isolate the influence of the three factors the basic technique involves comparison of the regional entry rates to grade one under various conditions. For this purpose we use the actual data on entry rates as currently observed, as well as entry rates simulated from regressions. Earlier, in part B, our regression specification of entry rates to grade one included a set of regressors for demand-side factors (to the extent captured by variables describing household characteristics) and another set for supply-side factors. For the present purpose we modify the specification to include regional dummy variables. The coefficient estimate on these variables in this specification can be interpreted as capturing the influence of region-specific social attitudes to girls' schooling, controlling for supply- and demand-side conditions. In a second specification we include only the demand-side regressors and the regional dummy variables. The coefficient on the regional variables can be interpreted as capturing the combined influence of region-specific social attitudes and supply-side conditions.

The mechanics of the simulations are the same as those done in part B, problems 3 to 6 above. To recall, they basically involve evaluation of equation (1) in the Excel worksheet using the estimated regression coefficients, with the values of the regressors set to reflect the assumptions in each simulation. For our purpose here we will set the values of the regressors to the country mean. To save time the simulations needed for this exercise have already been completed for you and the results appear in table 8.C.2.17. Entries in the table are defined as follows:

1. $ER_{i,a}$ refers to region i's actual entry rate as currently observed.
2. $ER_{i,s1}$ refers to region i's entry rate simulated using coefficient estimates from the regression specification with regional dummy variables as well as the demand- and supply-side variables as regressors, and setting the values of all of these variables to the country mean.
3. $ER_{i,s2}$ refers to region i's entry rate simulated using coefficient estimates from the regression specification with regional dummy

8

Table 8.C.2.17: Actual and Simulated Entry Rates to Grade One (percent)

Region	Actual entry rate $ER_{i,a}$	Simulated entry rates[a]	
		$ER_{i,s1}$	$ER_{i,s2}$
North	40.2	50.1	57.0
South	30.7	21.0	28.5
East	37.8	37.4	29.4
West	25.5	36.3	27.2
Country average	35.8	35.8	35.8

a. See part C, problem 2, step 1, for details on the simulation assumptions.

variables and only the demand-side variables as regressors, and setting the values of all of these variables to the country mean.

Your task in this step is simply to understand how the simulations are done. Take a moment now to examine the results and then proceed to the next step.

Step 2   The task here is to use the results in table 8.C.2.17 to decompose region i's entry rate deviated from the country average, $DER_{i, all\ factors}$, into three components representing regional deviations from the country mean in social attitudes to girls' schooling ($DER_{i, social\ attitudes}$); in the household characteristics of the population ($DER_{i, household\ factors}$); and in the characteristics of the supply of schooling ($DER_{i, school\ factors}$).

Given the definitions of $ER_{i,a}$, $ER_{i,s1}$, and $ER_{i,s2}$ above, and annotating the country mean in entry rates as $ER_{country\ mean}$, the following relationships hold:

$$DER_{i, all\ factors} = DER_{i, social\ factors} + DER_{i, household\ factors} + DER_{i, school\ factors}$$

$$= ER_{i,a} - ER_{country\ mean}$$

$$DER_{i, social\ attitudes} = ER_{i,s1} - ER_{country\ mean}$$

$$DER_{i, household\ factors} = ER_{i,a} - ER_{i,s2}$$

$$DER_{i, school\ factors} = ER_{i,s2} - ER_{i,s1}$$

Take a moment now to understand the relationships in the foregoing equations.

Tab over to the worksheet named "problem 2," where you will find a copy of table 8.C.2.18. Using the relationships defined in the foregoing equations you are asked to complete the table. To minimize the Excel manipulations you need only do the calculation for one region, the north.

Step 3   Review the decomposition results obtained in the previous step, making a note of what they reveal regarding the source or sources of variation in the observed entry rates to grade one among girls across the four regions. Based on your assessment, indicate with a check mark in table 8.C.2.19 the domain or domains of policy interventions that appear to be appropriate in each of the four regions.

Maximizing Impact at Least Cost

After identifying the appropriate domains for action across localities, the question arises as to the choice of specific interventions within the iden-

Table 8.C.2.18: Decomposition of Observed Regional Deviations in Entry Rates to Grade One Relative to the Country Average

| | Entry rate to grade one (%) | | | Deviation from country average attributed to various factors (percentage points) | | | |
| | | Simulated | | | | | |
Region	Actual $ER_{i,a}$	$ER_{i,s1}$	$ER_{i,s2}$	All factors	Social attitudes	Household factors	School factors
North	40.2	50.1	57.0	+4.4			
South	30.7	21.0	28.5	−5.1	−14.8	+2.2	+7.5
East	37.8	37.4	29.4	+2.0	+1.6	+8.4	−8.0
West	25.5	36.3	27.2	−10.3	+0.5	−1.7	−9.1
Country mean	35.8	35.8	35.8	0.0	0.0	0.0	0.0

Note: See the text discussion for an explanation of the mechanics of the calculation.

Table 8.C.2.19: Identifying Appropriate Domains of Intervention across Localities

| | Target domain to be addressed by intervention | | |
Region	Social attitudes	Household factors	School factors
North			
South			
East			
West			

tified domain or domains. To ensure that the choice produces the largest educational impact at least cost requires additional assessment of the following issues:

- *The scope for intervention.* Broadly, this refers to how far a particular option can be pushed before reaching limits on its effectiveness that arise from its intrinsic nature or from the characteristics of the context. Offering free textbooks may attract many girls to attend school, but the effectiveness of this option is likely to decline (or even vanish altogether) as the number of free books continues to increase beyond a certain point. Similarly, building more schools to improve accessibility has limited effectiveness if only a small proportion of the out-of-school girls in the target population currently lives a long way from existing schools. In both examples the scope for action encounters natural limits either because diminishing returns in the intervention itself set in or because the potential pool of beneficiaries is small.

8

193

- *The cost-effectiveness of potential interventions.* Within each domain for action a range of options exists, each of which typically entails different costs—capital as well as recurrent costs—and produces different impacts on entry rates to grade one. The choice of specific interventions needs to be informed by a comparison of their relative costs and effectiveness.

- *The impact of the interventions on other schooling outcomes.* Besides entry rates to grade one, the interventions also may affect such outcomes as students' regular class attendance, academic performance, repetition and dropout behavior, persistence to the end of the cycle, transition probabilities between cycles of schooling, and so on. How much these other outcomes matter in ranking the options depends on the presence and magnitude of the problem in the target population. If, for example, prior analysis of student flow patterns reveals that high repetition rates or dropout rates are serious problems in the system, then the impact of the potential options on these outcomes clearly deserves explicit consideration in selecting the interventions.

Ideally we would prefer policy or project designs to rely on interventions with the following features: (a) they allow a large scope for action; (b) they produce, for any given investment of resources, larger gains than alternative options in terms of the immediate policy objective; and (c) they generate substantial positive effects on other schooling outcomes relevant in the policy or project context.

Time constraints and lack of data often prevent a detailed assessment, but even a comparison based on rough orders of magnitude for costs and impacts can help clarify the choices.[2] Such information is often good enough to steer policy and project design in the right direction. The exercises below illustrate a possible approach to the analysis; they are intended more as a guide than as a recipe for doing the analysis. Indeed, diversity in the available data and their quality often mean that the analyst's own judgment is a key ingredient in the analysis. Three problems follow below, with the first two providing the building blocks for the last problem, which involves making an overall assessment of the choice of interventions.

Problem 3

Continuing with the issue of girls' entry rates to grade one, suppose the government decides to improve supply-side conditions in the east or the west, the two regions where our earlier analysis suggest that supply-side intervention is appropriate. Your task here is to assess the scope for intervention through the two options listed in table 8.C.3.20. For this purpose you are given some relevant information on the project context (column

8

Table 8.C.3.20: Assessing the Scope for Action through Selected Supply-Side Interventions

			Scope for action	
Option	*Current supply conditions in target locality*		*Estimated percentage of target population benefiting[a]*	*Ranking*
Build more schools to improve accessibility	*Distance to school (km)*	*Percentage of target population[a]*		
	0.0–0.5	40	45	Moderate
	0.5–2	30		
	2–4	20		
	> 4	10		
Offer daily free school meal	*Distance to school (km)*	*Percentage of schools with no free meal*		
	< 2	80		
	≥ 2	80		

a. In this example the target population is girls of primary-school-entry age who are out of school.

2 in the table). Take a moment now to scan the table and then proceed to the next paragraph for further instructions.

There is no standard method for quantifying the scope for action. One approach might be to estimate the size of the target population that is likely to benefit from the proposed option; another might be to estimate the share of schools lacking a selected feature that have proved effective in attracting girls to attend school. Rough estimates are all that we need for the present purposes and we can obtain them using the sort of information presented in the table above, along with some simplifying assumptions.

As an example, consider the intervention to build more schools to improve accessibility. Suppose all of the girls living more than 2 kilometers from an existing school would benefit from having a school built near them, and that only half of those living between 0.5 and 2 kilometers from an existing school would benefit.[3] Given the distribution of the target population in the table, the proportion of the target population that would benefit from the intervention would amount to about 45 percent ($10 + 20 + 0.5 \times 30$). To emphasize that the calculation is rough we can convert the result into a three-category qualitative assessment of the scope for action: modest, moderate, and large. This is done in the last column of the table.

As you can see, the calculations are simple enough to accomplish by hand, but if you prefer to do them electronically you can tab over now to

8

the worksheet titled "problem 3," where a copy of the table can be found. Your task is to evaluate the scope for action through the option of offering free school meals. Consider how you might use the two pieces of information in the table—distribution of the out-of-school population by distance from nearest school and share of schools not currently offering free meals—for this purpose. Recall that in the earlier regression analysis it was found that for children living within 2 kilometers of a school the offer of a free school meal does not affect entry rates to grade one. Enter your result in the second row of the table and annotate your calculation and assumptions as appropriate.

Comment/notes: _____

_____

_____

_____

Problem 4

Continuing with the two interventions in the previous problem, we now need to rank them in terms of their costliness and impact on entry to grade one. Assembling the underlying data for the rankings requires prior work. On cost estimates, the work involved is beyond the scope of this module to discuss; on impact on learning, prior work in part B offers some guidance.[4] For example, we can take the difference in simulated entry rates to grade one corresponding to the most- and least-favorable situations as a measure of the impact of each intervention. For the present purpose, suppose that we have done the work and obtained the data indicated in table 8.C.4.21. As before, to emphasize that the estimates are rough we translate the quantitative data into a qualitative ranking, using a trichotomous scale (low/modest, moderate, and high). The rankings for the first intervention have been completed for you. Your task is to rank the second intervention using a similar qualitative scale.

Tab over to the worksheet titled "problem 4," where you will find a copy of table 8.C.4.21, and complete the assignment.

Problem 5

Your task here is make a judgment about overall policy or project design in the target region to promote girls' education, using information for the full range of potential supply-side interventions identified in the regression analysis discussed earlier. To focus attention on policy formulation, only the processed qualitative rankings of the interventions are provided

8

Table 8.C.4.21: Selected Information about the Costliness and Impact of Two Potential Interventions

Intervention	Estimated annual cost per student[a]	Impact on entry rate to grade one[b]	
		Boys	Girls
Build more schools to improve accessibility	$120	9.4%	27.1%
	High	Modest	Large
Offer daily free school meal	$80	4.4%	14.1%

a. For comparison, the annual cost to build toilet facilities amounts to an average of US$15 per pupil.

b. The impact is measured in terms of the percentage rise in entry rates between an unfavorable supply situation with respect to the indicated intervention and a more favorable situation. The data are based on the simulation results in table 8.B.6.14 above. For the first intervention, the relevant simulations are S1.2a and S1.2d; for the second simulation they are S1.2d and S1.3d.

here; you are assumed to have previously assembled and analyzed the underlying quantitative data using the same procedure as in the previous two problems. The relevant information appears in table 8.C.5.22. For completeness, the table also includes a column indicating the impact of the interventions on schooling outcomes other than entry rates to grade one; to mimic reality, rankings in that column deliberately are left as

Table 8.C.5.22: Qualitative Rankings of Selected Aspects of Potential Policy Options

Intervention	Scope for action	Costliness	Impact on entry rate to grade one		Impact on other primary school outcomes
			Boys	Girls	
Reducing distance to school	Moderate	High	Modest	Large	?
Providing free school meal	Modest	High	Modest	Moderate	?
Adding toilet facilities	Large	Low	None	Large	?
Offering all grades at the school	Moderate	Moderate	Moderate	None	?
Expanding use of multigrade teaching	Modest	Low	None	None	?
Hiring more female teachers	Modest	High	None	None	?
Increasing coverage of publicity campaigns	Large	Low	Modest	Large	?

8

question marks to indicate that the underlying quantitative data are lacking for the project context. Take a moment now to scan the table and then follow the steps below to accomplish your analysis.

Step 1   Your work can be accomplished using either the paper or electronic version of table 8.C.5.22. If you wish to use the latter, tab over now to the worksheet titled "problem 5." Review the table with an eye to eliminating interventions that you would not consider including in your policy or project design to expand girls' entry rates to grade one in the region under analysis, commenting briefly on your decision.

Options to eliminate: _____

_____

_____

_____

Reasons for decision: _____

_____

_____

_____

_____

Step 2   Identify the options that are clear winners, and comment briefly on your choices.

Clear winners: _____

_____

_____

_____

Comments on choices: _____

_____

_____

_____

_____

Step 3 Elaborate on how you would decide on the remaining options. Would you consider their impact on boys' entry rates to grade one as an additional input? How about their unknown impact on other schooling outcomes besides entry to grade one? What knowledge from the broader literature can you mobilize to inform your decision? What would be your overall strategy regarding these ambivalent options?

Description of overall strategy: _____

_____

_____

_____

_____

_____

_____

Endnotes

1. Demographic data typically are not available by single years of age, but rather by five-year age groups. Various techniques are available to disaggregate the data, as discussed in the hands-on module "Diagnosing Structural Weaknesses in Education," by Alain Mingat and Jee-Peng Tan.

2. Estimation of the relationship between interventions and other schooling outcomes often requires explicit work that may not be feasible in the project context. In such situations it may be necessary to use the estimates based on data from other contexts as a guide.

3. The other half of the population already has a school within close range from home so the availability of another nearby school would not alter the supply condition for them.

4. For a more elaborate and general discussion of cost analysis, see the hands-on module "Analyzing Costs in Education," by Jean-Pierre Jarousse, Alain Mingat, Stella Tamayo, and Jee-Peng Tan.

8

Performing Economic Analysis of Educational Technology

A Two-Part Module

Alain Mingat and Jee-Peng Tan, with Stella Tamayo

Educators and others have long recognized the potential of computers and other advanced technology to transform education. Most education systems currently rely on labor-intensive pedagogical processes, typically involving teachers in face-to-face interaction with their students in classroom settings. The process may include textbooks, workbooks, chalk, blackboards, and other pedagogical materials as additional inputs, but the classroom teacher invariably plays a central role. What students learn depends to a large extent on the teacher's personal knowledge of the subject matter, expository technique, and skill in arranging the lessons and exercises.

Electronic media create opportunities for reshaping education in important ways. At their most passive they make it possible to expand the sheer volume of intellectual resources readily available to students in the classroom or at home. But the technology also allows for more focused learning—for example, through educational radio or television broadcasts and computer software which open the way for students to receive lessons from off-site expert teachers. As a conduit for information flow the new educational technology is akin to the printing press in an earlier era. But it can pack far more content in the same space as printed matter and transmit the material faster and in forms that can be customized to each student's learning needs.

The new educational technology entails logistical arrangements that distinguish it from traditional classroom teaching, with important cost implications. In the latter setting, recurrent costs in the form of teacher salaries typically exceed the cost of all other inputs, including that of the physical infrastructure (that is, school buildings, classroom equipment, and furniture). Because teachers can be hired incrementally to match enrollment trends, the resource requirements of traditional classroom teaching generally bear a close relationship to the size of enrollments. The pedagogical process thus involves investments that are relatively divisible. In contrast, the use of educational technology typically requires lumpy initial investments to create the systemwide physical infrastructure (such as transmission and communication networks and computers) and pedagogical software to support it. And often the investment must be made in anticipation of an expanding clientele for the services to be offered.

By its very nature the electronic media is feasible only in contexts with a reliable source of electricity and adequate telephone lines. But technical feasibility alone is not sufficient to justify an investment. At issue is a classic economic problem: Are its costs, including both the initial investment and subsequent recurrent costs, worth the benefits in education outcomes? The purpose of this chapter is to illustrate the methods for addressing the question, using two applications of the new educational technology: computer-assisted instruction in primary or secondary education (part A), and distance learning in higher education (part B). The exercises rely on hypothetical data because such data allow a sharper focus on the overall analytical concepts. In actual project- or country-specific contexts the analysis obviously would need to be adapted to the explicit policy choices involved as well as to the scope of the available data.

Before proceeding it is useful to note some additional data issues. Data on the costs of educational technology often can be compiled using information from the market for the relevant goods and services. In contrast, it is much more difficult to gather data on the benefits side. Ex ante information on the impact of new technologies is by definition nonexistent. Although experiences with similar interventions in other contexts may offer some insights, implementation practices and local conditions (including composition of the target student population) are likely to differ, thereby diluting the applicability of the information. For this reason, ex post assessments using data from pilot interventions in the intended context are more relevant. Such assessments are indeed imperative to justify expanding the use of the new technologies. Ex post evaluation is also appropriate because the actual costs of the intervention may diverge from those anticipated prior to implementation. Indeed, given the volatility of prices for the goods and services associated with educational technology, the divergence may be quite substantial.

This module includes the write-up and Excel files on the CD-ROM corresponding to the exercises in the two parts: "Ed_Technology_tci_cost_Ex1," "Ed_Technology_cai_cost_Ex2," "Ed_Technology_Simulate," and "Ed_Technology_Learn_Ex3" for part A; and "Ed_Technology_

9

distance_Ex4" for part B. Although some of the calculations can be accomplished with a handheld calculator, it is most convenient to do them all on the computer using Excel software.[1]

Part A: Assessing Delivery Options Using Student Learning as an Outcome Measure

Educational technology widens the options for delivering services at all levels of education. To compare the various options we need first to specify an outcome measure. At the lower levels of education, student learning is particularly relevant for two reasons: first, because policymakers everywhere consider it a key measure of success; and second, because the use of educational technology is often geared toward enhancing pedagogical effectiveness. (It should also be noted that other performance measures, such as dropout and repetition rates, may be used if data on student learning are unavailable.) Below we use student learning as an outcome measure to exemplify an evaluation of two delivery modes: traditional classroom instruction (TCI) and computer-assisted instruction (CAI). The exercises elaborate separately on the analysis of the costs and benefits, and then consider both elements jointly to assess the economic basis for choosing between the two options.

Analyzing the Costs of the Delivery Options

For our purpose we begin by noting that the usual setup in TCI involves a single teacher giving lessons in front of a group of students; the classroom teacher is thus the main input in this delivery mode. Because there often is a close link between teacher qualification and pay, the bulk of the costs associated with this method of instruction depend on the qualifications of the classroom teacher. On a per-student basis, recurrent costs depend also on the class size, the provision of pedagogical materials to each student, and minor administrative overheads. Capital costs are limited to the use of classrooms and other school facilities.

With CAI, students spend only a part of their class time interacting directly with the classroom teacher, using the remaining time to work with computers. The cost of computer-assisted instruction reflects the components of traditional classroom instruction, but it differs in its composition across the various components. The approach typically involves more capital-intensive inputs and substantial spending on systemwide inputs. These overheads arise at various levels in the school system—for example, at the center, in the form of development costs for computer software, and costs to train teachers to use the software; at each school that offers computer-assisted instruction, in the form of costs to install

9

and maintain the communication and computer networks; and in each classroom equipped for computer-assisted instruction, in the form of the costs of computer hardware and related supplies (such as diskettes and paper) as well as those of the services of a technology facilitator.

Below, we consider the costs of TCI and CAI in turn. We begin with computations using explicit data. The exercises then are followed by a discussion of the general cost functions that describe how costs vary according to the input characteristics of the two delivery modes. These functions form the basis of the cost simulations that are used later in the module for policy evaluation.

Traditional Classroom Instruction

Consider the hypothetical data for primary education in table 9.A.1.1. For the purpose of this exercise, we assume that teaching is not specialized by subject, so that each classroom teacher is responsible for teaching only one group of students. The arrangement implies that the pupil–teacher

Table 9.A.1.1: Cost-Related Data for Traditional Classroom Instruction

Item	Variable[a]	Amount
Number of students (millions)	S	1.25
Average class size (or pupil–teacher ratio)	CSIZE	27.1
Average ratio of students to nonteaching staff	SNTR	120.0
Distribution of teachers by qualification (%)		
Credential A	n.a.	34.1
Credential B	n.a.	40.4
Credential C	n.a.	25.5
Average annual salary of school personnel (Kwachas)		
Teachers with credential A	TS	50,000
Teachers with credential B	TS	80,000
Teachers with credential C	TS	100,000
Nonteaching staff	NTS	60,000
Other recurrent spending (millions of Kwachas a year)		
Administrative overheads	ADM	500
Pedagogical supplies	PED	300
Cost of physical facilities (Kwachas)		
Classroom structure for 40 pupils	n.a.	100,000
Related classroom furniture and equipment	n.a.	20,000

n.a. Not applicable.

a. Corresponds to the variables in equation (1).

ratio is the same as the class size.[2] In problems 1 and 2 below you are asked to compute the per-student recurrent and capital costs of traditional classroom instruction. Take a moment now to review the data in table 9.A.1.1 and then proceed to problem 1.

Problem 1: Compute TCI's Average Recurrent Cost per Student

The average recurrent unit cost (RUC_{tci}) is defined simply as follows:

$$(1) \qquad RUC_{tci} = \frac{TS}{CSIZE} + \frac{NTS}{SNTR} + \frac{ADM}{S} + \frac{PED}{S}$$

where TS is the average annual salary of a teacher; $CSIZE$ is the class size; NTS is the average annual salary of a nonteaching staff; $SNTR$ is the ratio of pupils to nonteaching staff; ADM and PED are, respectively, the total annual spending on administrative overheads and pedagogical materials for primary education; and S is the total number of primary school pupils in the system.

Retrieve the Excel file titled "Ed_Technology_tci_cost_Ex1," where you will find a copy of table 9.A.1.2 in the worksheet labeled "recurrent." The table shows the average recurrent cost per student corresponding to situations in which the class size is 20, 30, and 40 students, and teachers hold one of the three types of credentials; the cell in the last row and column corresponds to system averages in class size and teacher qualification. Use equation (1) to complete the table.

Problem 2: Compute TCI's Annualized Capital Cost

Capital costs refer to the costs of using school or classroom facilities and equipment over a given time period. Conceptually they are the same as rental for the facilities and equipment. Because recurrent costs typically

Table 9.A.1.2: Recurrent Cost per Pupil of Traditional Classroom Instruction (Kwachas)

Teacher qualification	Class size			System average (= 27.1)
	20	30	40	
A	3,640			
B	5,140			—
C	6,140			—
System average[a]	—	—	—	

— Not applicable.

a. Refers to the distribution of teachers by qualification shown in table 9.A.1.1.

9

refer to annual amounts, it is appropriate to render the capital costs in annual terms too. Adding the two components together then would yield the overall annual cost of schooling.

Before proceeding with the exercise below it is important to note that capital costs are not the same as investment spending per se. Investment spending tends to be volatile from year to year, reflecting the timing of additions to the existing stock of facilities or equipment. In contrast, capital costs generally are stable over time and correspond to the value of the services generated during a given time period by the total stock of facilities and equipment.

There are three potential methods for computing capital costs: (a) use accounting procedures to amortize the investment cost of the school property at the time it was purchased or built; (b) annualize the current value of the school property on the basis of prevailing market interest rates; and (c) evaluate the (pseudo) market rental for the school property. The first method is suitable for assessing the tax liability of a private investment but is inappropriate for assessing the economic implications of public policy choices. The second method takes explicit account of the opportunity cost of funds in that the computation incorporates the market interest rate. It also uses the current value of the property as opposed to its value at the time of purchase or construction. These features make it appropriate for assessing the economic cost of an investment. The third method, in the context of markets for school buildings and equipment that functions perfectly, should yield the same answer as the second method. This condition is seldom met, however, especially in rural areas, and little information exists on the rental value of school buildings or equipment.[3] In practical terms, therefore, annualized capital costs typically are estimated using the second method.

The formula for annualizing capital costs is the following:

$$(2) \qquad ACC = \frac{CV \bullet k(1 + k)^n}{(1 + k)^n - 1}$$

where ACC is the annualized capital costs—for classroom facilities as well as for equipment and furniture; CV is the current value of these durable school inputs; k is the opportunity cost of funds or, equivalently, the market interest rate; and n is the useful lifetime of the durable school inputs.

Assuming that the market interest rate is 10 percent a year, you are asked to use equation (2) to annualize the cost of capital shown in table 9.A.2.3. The table may be retrieved from the worksheet "capital" in the same Excel file (that is, "Ed_Technology_tci_cost_Ex1"). Enter your answers in the last column of the table.[4]

Dividing the annualized cost by the number of pupils yields the capital unit cost of traditional classroom instruction (CUC_{tci}). Adding the

9

Table 9.A.2.3: Capital Cost of Classroom Facilities

Item	Current investment cost (Kwachas)	Useful lifetime (years)	Annualized capital cost (Kwachas)
Classroom structure	100,000	25	
Equipment and furniture	20,000	10	

Note: Assume that the market interest rate is 10 percent a year.

result to the recurrent costs per pupil yields the overall unit cost of traditional classroom instruction. The overall unit cost thus depends on the number of pupils assigned to each classroom, as well as on the distribution of teachers by qualification. Under the prevailing TCI conditions shown in table 9.A.2.1 above, compute the average capital cost per pupil, as well as the overall cost per pupil, filling in the blanks below:

Capital unit cost = _____ Kwachas a year

Recurrent unit cost = _____ Kwachas a year

Overall unit cost = _____ Kwachas a year

Computer-Assisted Instruction

For the purpose of the exercise, consider a program—offered in a subset of schools in the education system—in which a part of children's instructional time is set aside for them to work with computers. In each participating school several classrooms are fitted with the equipment and the computer-assisted lessons are facilitated by the classroom teacher with the help of a technology assistant. The program represents an enriched instructional approach involving incremental costs beyond those of traditional classroom instruction. The exercises below focus on the magnitude of the incremental costs and the relationship between these costs and the number of schools participating in the CAI program.

Problem 3: Compute CAI's Annual Incremental Costs

Retrieve table 9.A.3.4 from the worksheet titled "costdata" in the Excel file labeled "Ed_Technology_cai_cost_Ex2," and continue reading for further explanation of the data.

The program involves a three-tier arrangement: (a) a center that creates the educational software for computer-assisted instruction, trains teachers in the participating schools in the use of the software, provides technical support, and operates a communications network linking it to the participating schools; (b) participating schools, which interact with the center; and (c) classrooms in each school that are equipped and staffed for computer-assisted instruction. For the purpose of this exer-

9

Table 9.A.3.4: Investment and Operating Costs of a Three-Tier Structure of Computer-Assisted Instruction (Kwachas)

Cost item	Center	School	Classroom equipped for CAI (full-time use)
Building facilities	6,000,000	50,000	100,000
Lifetime (years)	(25)	(25)	(25)
Equipment	80,000,000	60,000	140,000
Lifetime (years)	(8)	(5)	(4)
Annual operating cost	10,000,000	75,000	75,000
Personnel	8,800,000	70,000	60,000
Of which for training[a]	(2,800,000)		
Supplies/Maintenance	1,200,000	5,000	25,000
Of which for training[a]	(200,000)		

a. Figures refer to the costs associated with training teachers in computer-assisted instruction.

Note: Figures in parentheses in the first two rows refer to the useful lifetime of the building and equipment.

cise assume that each school has four such classrooms. The table shows the investment cost of facilities and equipment at all three levels in the structure, as well as recurrent spending on staff, training, and supplies.

You are asked to annualize the capital costs of the facilities and equipment at each level in the structure, using the formula in equation (2) above. Enter your answers in table 9.A.3.5. Add the result to the annual operating costs to obtain the total annual costs for the center, for each school, and for each classroom outfitted for CAI. As an example, the calculations for the costs at the center have been completed for you.

Problem 4: Compute CAI's Annual Incremental Cost per Pupil

As in any investment-intensive setup, the per-pupil cost of computer-assisted instruction depends on the number of participating schools in the system, as well as their characteristics. For the purpose of this exercise we assume that each participating school has, on average, four classrooms that are equipped for CAI. Each of the 4 classrooms serves 3 groups of pupils, for an average of 12 groups of pupils per school. The average class size is 26.3 pupils. These assumptions allow us to compute the number of pupils in the CAI program according to the number of participating schools. For example there would be 6,312 pupils in systems serving only 20 schools (= 26.3 × 12 × 20) compared with 315,600 pupils in systems with 1,000 participating schools (= 26.3 × 12 × 1,000).

To compute the cost per pupil we need also to assemble the data on the aggregate costs of the system. These costs include both the capital and recurrent components. At the center the recurrent costs include fixed overheads as well as costs that vary with the number of teachers being trained.

Table 9.A.3.5: Incremental Annual Capital and Recurrent Costs of Computer-Assisted Instruction (Kwachas)

Cost item	Center	School	Classroom equipped for CAI (full-time use)
Annualized capital cost			
Building	661,008		
Equipment	14,995,521		
Subtotal[a]	15,656,530		
Annual operating costs			
Training-related[b]	3,000,000	n.a.	n.a.
Other	7,000,000	n.a.	n.a.
Subtotal[a]	10,000,000	75,000	75,000
Total annual cost per unit[c]	25,656,530		

n.a. Not applicable.

a. Subtotal may not add up because of rounding.

b. As indicated in the text, the cost refers to training for 1,000 teachers. The assumed lifetime of the training is about three years, which implies an annual training cost per teacher of approximately K1,000.

c. The unit corresponds to the center, individual participating schools, or individual classrooms equipped for CAI.

The cost of teacher training itself has two components: the direct costs and the opportunity cost of teachers' time spent in training. For the purpose of this exercise we will focus only on the direct costs, leaving the treatment of opportunity costs to a later step. The direct costs of teacher training amount to 3,000 Kwachas (K3,000) per teacher. Because the training is expected to equip the teachers for three years, the annual direct costs of the training amount to an average of K1,000 per teacher.[5] For the present purpose we assume that all teachers—averaging 12 per participating school—receive the training.

Using as a basis the foregoing assumptions and your calculations in table 9.A.3.5, complete table 9.A.4.6. Retrieve the table from the

Table 9.A.4.6: Simulation of the Incremental Direct Cost per Student Associated with Computer-Assisted Instruction[a]

Number of schools in the system	20	50	100	300	500	1,000
Number of pupils	6,312	15,780	31,560	94,680	157,800	315,600
Aggregate direct costs[b]						
Cost per student						

a. Assume for these simulations that all teachers receive training to deliver computer-assisted instruction.

b. Includes capital and recurrent costs, but excludes the opportunity cost of teachers' time spent to receive training in CAI.

worksheet titled "unit cost" in the Excel file labeled "Ed_Technology_cai_cost_Ex2." As needed, follow the instructions below to complete the table.

As a further guide, note that under the assumptions elaborated earlier the incremental direct unit cost of computer-assisted instruction ($IDUC_{cai}$), including both the recurrent and capital components, may be expressed and then simplified as:

$$(3) \quad IDUC_{cai} = \frac{(25,656,530 - 3,000,000) + (3,000 / 3 \times NTT) + (96,336 \times NS) + (130,183 \times NS \times 4)}{26.3 \times 12 \times NS}$$

$$= \frac{(22,656,530) + (1,000 \times 12 \times NS) + (96,336 \times NS) + (520,732 \times NS)}{315.6 \times NS}$$

$$= \frac{22,656,530 + 629,068 \times NS}{315.6 \times NS}$$

where NTT is the number of teachers who have received training in computer-assisted instruction, and NS is the number of participating schools. Because there are, on average, 12 teachers per participating school we can simplify the equation as a function of the number of schools in the CAI system. This expression can be used to simulate the unit costs of the system as its size varies from 20 participating schools to 1,000.

After completing table 9.A.4.6, plot a graph in the space indicated in the worksheet showing the relationship between the direct cost per student and the number of schools offering computer-assisted instruction. By casual inspection, comment on the pattern of returns to scale. At which point do diminishing returns appear to set in?

Answer:

_____

_____

_____

_____

Generalizing the Cost Functions for TCI and CAI

To anticipate the policy analysis that will be addressed later in the module, it is useful at this point to develop general expressions for the annual cost per student (that is, unit cost) of TCI and CAI. These expressions define the costs as functions of potential policy options. For TCI we assume the following variables to be amenable to policy action: class size, the distribution of teachers by qualification, and the amount of pedagogical materials available to each student. For CAI additional options include whether teachers receive training to deliver CAI, and the propor-

9

tion of instructional time devoted to CAI.[6] You may wish to pause here to consider how these expressions might be developed and then continue below for the answers.

Cost Functions for TCI

Consistent with the basic data in table 9.A.1.1, the annual recurrent unit cost of traditional classroom instruction (RUC_{tci}) is given by:

$$(4) \qquad RUC_{tci} = \frac{(P_a \times 50{,}000 + P_b \times 80{,}000 + P_c \times 100{,}000)}{CSIZE}$$

$$+ \frac{60{,}000}{120} + 70.6 \times IPED + \frac{500}{1.25}$$

$$= \frac{(P_a \times 50{,}000 + P_b \times 80{,}000 + P_c \times 100{,}000)}{CSIZE}$$

$$+ 500 + 70.6 \times IPED$$

$$= \frac{(P_a \times 50{,}000 + P_b \times 80{,}000 + P_c \times 100{,}000)}{CSIZE}$$

$$+ 70.6 \times IPED + 900$$

where P_a is the proportion of teachers with qualification A; P_b is the proportion with qualification B; and P_c is the proportion with qualification C; $CSIZE$ is the class size; and $IPED$ is an index of pedagogical material input per pupil, ranging from one to six. Each point on the index corresponds to an annual cost of K70.6.[7]

Consistent with the results reported in table 9.A.2.3, the annual capital unit cost (CUC_{tci}) is given by:

$$(5) \qquad CUC_{tci} = \frac{11{,}017 + 3{,}255}{CSIZE} = \frac{14{,}272}{CSIZE}$$

The annual overall cost per pupil of TCI is simply the sum of equations (4) and (5).

Cost Functions for CAI

Recall that under the specific arrangements considered here, computer-assisted instruction represents an additional cost beyond that of traditional classroom instruction. The total recurrent unit cost of CAI (RUC_{cai}) is therefore the sum of the incremental recurrent unit cost of CAI ($IRUC_{cai}$) and the recurrent unit cost of traditional classroom instruction (RUC_{tci}).[8] The incremental costs of computer-assisted instruction arise at each of the three tiers of the system: at the center for teacher training and overheads, as well as at the school and classroom levels. Denoting the

9

costs associated with each tier by the index i, we can express RUC_{cai} and CUC_{cai} as follows:

$$(6) \qquad RUC_{cai} = RUC_{tci} + IRUC_{cai} = RUC_{tci} + \sum_{t=1}^{3} IRUC_{cai,i}$$

$$(7) \qquad CUC_{cai} = ICUC_{tci} + CUC_{cai} + \sum_{t=1}^{3} ICUC_{cai,i}$$

We proceed below to develop the desired incremental recurrent and capital unit cost functions at each of the three tiers.

(a) Incremental recurrent unit costs at the center ($IRUC_{cai}$). There are two components of incremental recurrent unit costs at this level: one for teacher training in computer-assisted instruction ($RUCTT_{cai}$) and the other for central operations ($RUCCO_{cai}$):

$$(8) \qquad IRUC_{cai,1} = RUCTT_{tci} + RUCCO_{cai}$$

The first item, $RUCTT_{cai}$, is the sum of the opportunity cost of a teacher's time spent in training, and the direct cost of the training, both divided by the class size ($CSIZE$). The magnitude of opportunity costs depends on the duration of the training (assumed here to be two months) and its expected duration of effectiveness (assumed here to be three years), as well as the qualification of the teacher. Because the training is effective for three years, the opportunity cost per training episode needs to be divided by three—ignoring discounting here for simplicity— to obtain the annual opportunity cost of the training. The direct costs amount to K3,000 per teacher per episode of training. Again, the figure needs to be divided by three to obtain the annual direct cost of training. Thus, given the prevailing salary structure assumed in the exercise (see table 9.A.1.1), $RUCTT_{cai}$ can be written as follows:

$$(9) \quad RUCTT_{cai} = \frac{[2 / (12 \times 3)] \times (P_a \times 50{,}000 + P_b \times 80{,}000 + P_c \times 100{,}000) + (3{,}000 / 3)}{CSIZE}$$

$$= \frac{(0.0556)(P_a \times 50{,}000 + P_b \times 80{,}000 + P_c \times 100{,}000) + 1{,}000}{CSIZE}$$

where P_a, P_b, and P_c are, respectively, the proportions of teachers in the three different qualification groups.

The above equation applies only to teachers who receive the training; for other teachers there is no training cost. We need to generalize $RUCTT_{cai}$ to include all teachers, whether or not they receive training. To do so we define a new variable ($TRAIN$), which is the proportion of teachers who have received training in CAI. If we multiply $TRAIN$ by the expression on the right-hand side of equation (7), we obtain the desired generalization of $RUCTT_{cai}$:

$$(9') \quad RUCTT_{tci} = \frac{(0.0556)(P_a \times 50{,}000 + P_b \times 80{,}000 + P_c \times 100{,}000) + 1{,}000}{CSIZE}$$

$$\times TRAIN$$

Consider next the recurrent unit cost for central operations. These are fixed costs incurred at the center, net of teacher training costs. $RUCCO_{cai}$ depends on the total number of students in the CAI program. In our example we assume there are 500 participating schools, each of which has, on average, 12 groups of pupils exposed to the CAI program. The total number of schools in the program would then depend on the size of each group of pupils ($CSIZE$). Given that the annual operating costs at the center amount to K7,000,000 (from table 9.A.3.5), $RUCCO_{cai}$ is given by:

$$(10) \quad RUCCO_{cai} = \frac{7{,}000{,}000}{500 \times 12 \times CSIZE} = \frac{7{,}000{,}000}{6{,}000 \times CSIZE}$$

(b) Incremental recurrent unit costs at the school level ($IRUC_{cai,2}$). According to table 9.A.3.5, the total recurrent costs associated with CAI incurred by each participating school amount to K75,000. The recurrent cost per pupil at the school level is therefore K75,000 divided by the number of students receiving CAI in each school, that is:

$$(11) \quad IRUC_{cai,2} = \frac{75{,}000}{12 \times CSIZE}$$

For our exercise there are, on average, 12 classes per school. At the current average of 26.3 pupils per class, the incremental recurrent unit cost at the school level amounts to K237.64.

(c) Incremental recurrent unit costs at the classroom level ($IRUC_{cai,3}$). Again, according to table 9.A.3.5, the total recurrent costs associated with CAI arising at the classroom level amount to K75,000 per classroom. The recurrent unit cost at the classroom level is therefore K75,000 divided by the class size. Because several groups of pupils use the computer-equipped classroom, the total cost needs to be apportioned according to the proportion of instructional time ($COMPTIME$) spent by the class in computer-assisted instruction. The desired expression for $IRUC_{cai,3}$ is then given by:

$$(12) \quad IRUC_{cai,3} = \frac{75{,}000}{CSIZE} \times COMPTIME$$

9

(d) Overall recurrent unit cost. Summing up all of the relevant components of costs, we may express the overall recurrent unit cost of CAI as follows:[9]

$$(13) \quad RUC_{cai} = RUC_{tci} + IRUC_{cai} = RUC_{tci} + \sum_{t=1}^{3} RUC_{cai,1}$$

$$= \frac{(P_a 50,000 + P_b 80,000 + P_c 100,000)}{CSIZE} + 70.6 \, IPED + 900$$

$$+ \frac{75,000}{12 \times CSIZE} + \frac{75,000}{CSIZE} \times COMPTIME$$

(e) Overall capital unit cost. Following the same procedure of computing the capital costs at each tier, we obtain the following expression for the capital cost per pupil associated with computer-assisted instruction. According to the data in table 9.A.3.5, the aggregate capital cost at the center amounts to K15,656,530 (K661,008 for facilities and K14,995,521 for equipment); costs incurred at the school level amount to K21,336 (K5,508 for facilities and K15,828 for equipment); and those at the classroom level amount to K55,183 (K11,017 for facilities and K44,166 for equipment).[10] The overall capital cost per pupil is therefore as follows:

$$(14) \quad CUC_{cai} = CUC_{tci} + ICUC_{cai}$$

$$= \frac{14,272}{CSIZE} + \frac{15,656,520}{6,000 \times CSIZE} + \frac{21,336}{12 \times CSIZE} + \frac{55,185}{CSIZE} \times COMPTIME$$

Problem 5 (Optional): Simulate the Unit Costs of TCI and CAI

The per-pupil cost of TCI and CAI depends on the underlying arrangements with regard to teacher qualification, teacher training, allocation of time for computer work, and so on. Retrieve table 9.A.5.7 now from the worksheet titled "sim cost" in the Excel file labeled "Ed_Technology_Simulate." Complete the table by applying the general unit cost functions developed above to the specific input options indicated in the table. The relevant equations are: (4), (5), (13), and (14).[11] Later in this module, we will consider many other combinations of inputs. The exercise here is intended to help you understand the cost simulations, so you may wish to skip over it and continue to the next paragraph.

The above simulations confirm that computer-assisted instruction involves extra costs and that the magnitude of the increase is sensitive to the specific choices in inputs in terms of teacher qualification, allocation of instructional time, and teacher training. Are the additional costs justified on pedagogical and economic grounds? To address this question we

9

Table 9.A.5.7: Simulation of the Unit Cost of TCI and CAI under Various Input Options

Input Options	Traditional classroom instruction		Computer-assisted instruction	
	Option 1	Option 2	Option 3	Option 4
Teacher qualification	B	A	B	A
Teacher training in CAI	n.a.	n.a.	yes	no
Instructional materials (IPED)	3	6	3	6
Class size	40	20	40	20
CAI allotment of instructional time	n.a.	n.a.	30	60
Unit cost (Kwachas)				

n.a. Not applicable.

IPED Index of availability of pedagogical materials.

need also to analyze the benefits associated with the delivery modes. We turn to this problem below.

Comparing the Learning Outcomes

Recall that the context here concerns the application of educational technology in primary and secondary education. At these levels it is appropriate and feasible to use student learning and schooling careers (for example, incidence of dropping out or repetition) as measures of benefits: these outcomes are of immediate interest to educators and policymakers alike, and are indeed tracked from year to year in a growing number of countries. Labor market performance, another possibly appealing outcome measure, is much less feasible to track because the relatively young ages of primary and secondary pupils imply that most of them will enter the labor force only after a very long lag. For the purpose of this module we focus on student learning as the outcome measure. The issues then become whether pupils learn better under CAI compared with TCI, and, if so, by how much.

The Pedagogical Environment and Learning

To compare the two delivery modes we begin with a simple framework linking the pedagogical environment to learning outcomes. We note that student learning is the product of a cumulative process that takes place over a period of time—for example, between the beginning and end of the school year. Using test scores as a proxy for learning we can express scores observed at year end (*OUTSCORE*) as a function of scores at the start of the school year (*INSCORE*), personal and family factors (*PERSONAL* and *FAMILY*, respectively), and characteristics of the learning environment as reflected by conditions in the classroom (*CLASS*)

9

and the school (*SCHOOL*), including exposure to computer-assisted instruction:

$$OUTSCORE = f\,(INSCORE, PERSONAL, FAMILY, CLASS, SCHOOL)$$

In the literature the foregoing expression is generally referred to as an education production function. The function is commonly estimated using data for individual pupils. Each variable in the expression can be represented by a vector of explicitly measurable indicators: for example, the age and sex of pupils for *PERSONAL;* their parents' education and income for *FAMILY;* teacher qualification, class size, and availability of pedagogical materials for *CLASS;* and school size, location, and school-head's management style for *SCHOOL.* Because many influences affect learning, the analysis inevitably involves the application of regression techniques.

Problem 6: Estimate and Analyze the Production Function

Using a hypothetical data set to be described below, compare the impact on learning of computer-assisted instruction with that of traditional classroom instruction. Compare their average impacts, as well as their impacts on students with different initial capabilities. Follow the step-by-step instructions below to accomplish the analysis.

Retrieve the data in the worksheet titled "learn data" in the Excel file labeled "Ed_Technology_learn_Ex3." They relate to 607 hypothetical pupils in grade four. To keep the exposition simple and the analysis manageable we use a highly limited set of variables, defined in table 9.A.6.8; the table also shows the sample mean and standard deviation of these variables. (Note that although *INSCORE* and *OUTSCORE* are measured in the same units, it is invalid to compare them directly because the tests were different at the beginning and end of the school year.)

Step 1   Make a scatter plot of the relationship between *OUTSCORE* (*y*-axis) and *INSCORE* (*x*-axis), and estimate a regression equation relating the dependent variable *OUTSCORE* to *INSCORE, TEACHR_B, TEACHR_C, CSIZE, IPED,* and *TCI.* To economize on time these tasks have been completed for you and the results can be found in the worksheet titled "regress1" of the Excel file "Ed_Technology_learn_Ex3."[12] Examine the regression results and comment on them. By how much less does the average pupil score when exposed to TCI instead of CAI?[13] Do the results support the claim that CAI is more efficient than TCI?

Answer: **points**

9

Table 9.A.6.8: Variables in the Hypothetical Data Set for Part A, Problem 6

Variable	Definition	Mean	Standard deviation
OUTSCORE	Test score at the end of the school year	103.97	10.8
INSCORE	Test score at the beginning of the school year	101.38	17.8
TEACHR_B[a]	Dummy variable with a value of 1 if teacher has qualification B; 0 otherwise	0.35	0.48
TEACHR_C	Dummy variable with a value of 1 if teacher has qualification C; 0 otherwise	0.30	0.46
CSIZE	Number of pupils in the class	26.61	6.7
IPED	Index of availability of pedagogical materials	3.40	1.5
TCI[b]	Dummy variable with a value of 1 if the pupil is exposed to traditional classroom instruction; 0 otherwise	0.39	0.49
TRAIN	Dummy variable if the teacher has received training in computer-assisted instruction; 0 otherwise	0.40	0.49
COMPTIME	Percentage of instructional time devoted to CAI.	17.2	16.2

a. Because a teacher may hold qualification A, B, or C, one of the three dummy variables relating to teacher qualification—that is, *TEACHR_A, TEACHR_B,* or *TEACHR_C*— must serve as the omitted category in the regression analysis. We chose to omit category A in the exercise below.

b. A value of zero for *TCI* implies that a pupil has been exposed to computer-assisted instruction; there is thus no need to include a separate variable for CAI.

Step 2 Consider now a new specification of the regression equation to assess possible differences in the impact of CAI and TCI on students with low and high entering scores. If such differences exist they would affect the slope of the relationship between *OUTSCORE* and *INSCORE* for pupils exposed to the two pedagogical approaches. To allow for the possible slope differences we modify the regression specification by including an interaction term in the regression, *INS_TCI,* defined as the product of *INSCORE* and *TCI.* Thus, for pupils exposed to TCI the value of *INS_TCI* would be *INSCORE,* although for pupils exposed to CAI, the variable simply would be zero (because TCI would be zero). The coefficient on the new variable can thus be interpreted as the amount by which the slope of the relationship between *OUTSCORE* and *INSCORE* changes when a pupil is exposed to TCI instead of CAI.

Again, to economize on time the regression has been performed for you and the results can be found in the worksheet titled "regress2" of "Ed_Technology_learn_Ex3." Take a moment to reflect on the regression estimates. Use the coefficient estimates to predict the *OUTSCORE* under TCI and CAI, respectively, for pupils with an *INSCORE* of 70, and enter your answers in the appropriate columns in table 9.A.6.9 (in the same worksheet). For each of these simulations set the values of the other regression variables at their

9

Table 9.A.6.9: Predicted OUTSCORE Values for Various INSCORE Values for Pupils Exposed to TCI and CAI

	INSCORE values			
Pedagogical approach	70	100	130	$OUTSCORE_{130} - OUTSCORE_{70}$
Traditional classroom instruction		100.5	107.1	
Computer-assisted instruction		105.6	116.6	

Note: $OUTSCORE_{130}$ and $OUTSCORE_{70}$ refer to the predicted OUTSCORE corresponding, respectively, to INSCORE values of 130 and 70.

sample means; for convenience, the sample means are reproduced in the worksheet. The columns corresponding to *INSCORE* values of 100 and 130 involve the same computations and have already been completed for you. Fill in the last column of the table and comment on the results.

Step 3 Turn now to examine the impact of the other policy variables on student learning. For this purpose it is easier to analyze the data separately for the two pedagogical approaches. Retrieve the worksheet titled "regress3" from the Excel file labeled "Ed_Technology_learn_Ex3," which contains data only for the 235 pupils exposed to TCI. Based on these data we estimate a regression with *OUTSCORE* as the dependent variable and *INSCORE, TEACHR_B, TEACHR_C, CSIZE,* and *IPED* as the regressors. As before, the regression has been performed for you to save time. Examine the results in the worksheet, think about their implications, then comment on them.

Comment on the regression results: _____

_____

_____

Step 4 Retrieve the worksheet titled "regress4" from the same Excel file, "Ed_Technology_learn_Ex3"; it contains data only for the 372 pupils exposed to CAI. In addition to the regressors used to analyze student learning under TCI, we add two more variables that apply to CAI: *TRAIN* (whether the teacher has received training in CAI) and *COMPTIME* (percentage of instructional time allocated for CAI). We also include an interaction term, *INS_TIME,* defined below, to capture possible differences in the impact of *INSCORE* on *OUTSCORE* according to the amount of instructional time allocated to CAI:

INS_TIME = INSCORE if *COMPTIME* exceeds the sample average (that is, 28 percent)

INS_TIME = 0 if *COMPTIME* is at or below the sample average

9

Notice that the new variable is conceptually the same as *INS_CAI* (see part A, problem 6, step 2), in that *INSCORE* is interacted with a dummy variable. The coefficient on the new variable therefore has a parallel interpretation: it is the extent to which the slope of the relationship between *OUTSCORE* and *INSCORE* changes according to the amount of instructional time allocated to CAI.

Invoke Excel's regression function to perform the regression now. If you lack time for this step, simply skip it and use the completed regression output. Examine the results and comment on them, comparing them with the results for TCI as appropriate.

Comment on the regression results:

_____

_____

_____

_____

Evaluating the Policy Options

The analysis of learning outcomes accomplished above may suggest such options for improvement as the following:
- Retain TCI but reduce class size.
- Retain TCI but alter composition of teachers by qualification.
- Retain TCI but increase availability of pedagogical materials.
- Shift from TCI to CAI as currently organized.
- Expand CAI and increase class size.
- Expand CAI and increase instructional time for computer work.
- Expand CAI and alter composition of teachers by qualification.

Each of these options entails specific implications for unit costs, and it is unclear which of them would be most efficient. To inform the choice of intervention we need to compare the benefits against the costs for both TCI and CAI. You are asked in the problems and steps that follow to perform this analysis.[14]

Simulating Learning Outcomes and the Unit Costs

Using the regressions in part A, problem 6, steps 3 and 4, we can simulate *OUTSCORE* for pupils with a given initial level of learning under various learning conditions. We also can use the generalized cost functions developed in equations (4), (5), (13), and (14) to simulate the corresponding unit costs. Because we wish to illustrate the effects of alternative options for the full spectrum of pupils, we will use simulations of *OUTSCORE* for *INSCORE* values of 70, 100, and 130, respectively, to represent pupils of low, average, and high initial learning. In the first exercise

9

below you are asked to perform only a few simulations to appreciate the underlying mechanics of the analysis. You are then given a full set of simulation results to analyze for their policy implications. If you wish, you may skip the illustrative simulations and go to the next problem involving policy interpretation.

Problem 7: Simulate Illustrations

Consider the two options regarding the learning environment shown in table 9.A.7.10. The unit costs corresponding to these conditions are reproduced from your results in problem 5 above. Your task is to use the regression results in part A, problem 6, step 4, to simulate *OUTSCORE*, focusing only on pupils with an *INSCORE* of 100. To do so, retrieve the Excel file labeled "Ed_Technology_Simulate" and go to the worksheet titled "sim_e.g." to complete the table. To save time the simulations for options 3 and 4 have been completed for you. After you have completed your work take a moment to reflect on the results, commenting on the tradeoffs in costs and benefits that they reveal.

Problem 8: Consolidate Simulations for Policy Evaluation

If you are short of time, read the next two paragraphs rapidly and then proceed with the instructions thereafter.

Step 1 In the worksheet titled "sim tci 100" in the Excel file "Ed_Technology_Simulate" you will find a set of simulations of *OUTSCORE* under traditional classroom instruction for pupils with *INSCORE* values of 100, as well as the unit costs corresponding to the specified combinations of school inputs that affect the learning environment. The data have been generated following the procedure illustrated in part A, problem 7. Use the data to plot a graph showing the relationship between *OUTSCORE* (*y*-axis)

Table 9.A.7.10: Simulation of the Unit Costs of TCI and CAI under Various Input Options

Input Options	Traditional classroom instruction		Computer-assisted instruction	
	Option 1	Option 2	Option 3	Option 4
Teacher qualification	B	A	B	A
Teacher training in CAI	n.a.	n.a.	yes	no
Instructional materials	3	6	3	6
Class size	40	20	40	20
CAI allotment of instructional time	n.a.	n.a.	30	60
Unit cost				
OUTSCORE				

n.a. Not applicable.

9

and the corresponding unit cost (*x*-axis). In the adjacent worksheet titled "sim cai 100" is a similar set of simulations but this time the delivery mode is computer-assisted instruction. Use the data to plot a similar graph.

On each of the two graphs relating to pupils with *INSCORE* values of 100, draw by hand a "production frontier" showing the maximum *OUTSCORE* for each level of unit cost. Align the graphs on the two sheets of paper, with the TCI graph on top. Then trace the production frontier for CAI onto the same sheet as TCI, labeling the two graphs accordingly. Mark on the figure the current average unit costs and *OUTSCORE* for TCI and CAI, using the data in table 9.A.8.11. How would you interpret the results so far? Comment briefly here.

Comment on results: _____

_____

_____

_____

Step 2   Recall that the simulations so far relate to pupils with average levels of initial learning. As a complement it might be useful to repeat the simulations for pupils with low and high initial levels of learning. The results would make it possible to assess the impact of computer-assisted instruction on equity and the scope for using this delivery mode to address the learning needs of low achievers (for example, by increasing the time for CAI in specific population groups). To save time, however,

Table 9.A.8.11: Simulated Average Unit Costs and OUTSCORE under TCI and CAI for Pupils with an INSCORE of 100

System characteristic	TCI	CAI
Distribution of teachers by qualification		
TEACHR_A	0.340	0.355
TEACHR_B	0.404	0.312
TEACHR_C	0.255	0.333
CSIZE	3.340	3.441
IPED	27.106	26.290
TRAIN	n.a.	28.086
COMPTIME	n.a.	0.645
Average OUTSCORE	100.9	105.9
Average unit costs (Kwachas)	4,425	6,545

n.a. Not applicable.

Note: OUTSCORE simulations are based on regression results discussed in part A, problem 6, and unit cost simulations are based on equations (4), (5), (13), and (14) discussed in the text.

9

we proceed below using only the simulations for the average pupil (that is, for *INSCORE* = 100).

Tab over now to the worksheet titled "frontier" where you will find a copy of table 9.A.8.12, which shows the various combinations of school inputs corresponding to points on the combined production frontiers for TCI and CAI; these combinations are a subset of those simulated above and used to plot the graphs. Plot *OUTSCORE* (*y*-axis) against *UNIT COST* (*x*-axis) to show the combined frontier. Then use the information in the table to summarize your recommendations regarding efficient arrangements for improving student learning. How can you apply the methodology covered in this module to evaluate other project and policy issues in education?

Summary:

_____

_____

_____

_____

Table 9.A.8.12: Unit Costs and OUTSCORE Corresponding to Input Mixes on the Combined Production Frontiers of TCI and CAI for Pupils with an INSCORE of 100

	OUTSCORE	Unit cost	A	B	C	CSIZE	IPED	TRAIN	COMPTIME
			\multicolumn{3}{Teacher qualification}				
TCI options									
Equation (1)	96.7	2,648	1	0	0	40	2	n.a.	n.a.
Equation (2)	98.3	2,789	1	0	0	40	4	n.a.	n.a.
Equation (3)	99.4	2,930	1	0	0	40	6	n.a.	n.a.
Equation (5)	101.6	3,466	1	0	0	30	6	n.a.	n.a.
CAI options									
Equation (4)	100.9	3,363	1	0	0	40	2	1	10
Equation (6)	101.3	3,504	1	0	0	40	4	1	10
Equation (7)	105.1	3,830	1	0	0	40	4	1	20
Equation (8)	108.5	4,014	1	0	0	40	2	1	30
Equation (9)	108.9	4,155	1	0	0	40	4	1	30
Equation (10)	112.3	4,339	1	0	0	40	2	1	40
Equation (11)	112.7	4,481	1	0	0	40	4	1	40
Equation (12)	116.1	4,665	1	0	0	40	2	1	50
Equation (13)	116.5	4,806	1	0	0	40	4	1	50
Equation (14)	116.8	4,947	1	0	0	40	6	1	50

Part B: Assessing Delivery Options Using Labor Market Performance as an Outcome Measure

As the level of education rises and the student population matures, the scope for exploiting educational technology widens. Many options exist besides traditional on-site instruction in classroom settings. They range from distance education based entirely on electronic media, to correspondence courses involving mixes of face-to-face interaction and lessons by mail and television or radio broadcasts. To evaluate the various delivery options the basic principle of comparing the costs of alternatives against their benefits remains valid. Analysis of the direct costs can be approached in the same way as in part A: it basically involves the identification of investment and recurrent costs at various levels in the delivery system, and appropriate treatment to annualize the investment costs. Because older students are involved, opportunity costs—that is, forgone earnings while the students are in training—also matter. On the benefit side, student learning remains a valid measure of outcomes, but given that most students soon will enter the labor market, performance at work provides a more direct measure of the economic value of the delivery modes being evaluated. The sections below show how to proceed with the analysis.

Specifying the Delivery Options and Their Costs

For our purpose consider a specific application of educational technology in higher education: the use of distance education in the training of accountants. We focus on three options for training these professionals: a traditional two-year polytechnic course, a two-year full-time course by distance education, and a four-year part-time course by distance education. The methods elaborated below are sufficiently general for use in evaluating other applications of technology in education where the outcome measure of interest is labor market performance.

Direct Costs Associated with the Three Options

As in part A, the direct costs of the three delivery modes may arise at various levels in the system. Consider the data in table 9.B.1.13, which shows the costs associated with the three options. Retrieve the table from the worksheet titled "costs" in the Excel file labeled "Ed_Technology_distance_Ex4," and continue reading below for further instructions. To avoid repetition, the table shows processed cost data: the capital costs are already expressed in annualized amounts (using the procedures discussed in detail in part A), and the recurrent costs for administration and operations have been attributed properly across the three types of

9

Table 9.B.1.13: Hypothetical Cost Data for Polytechnic and Distance Courses in Accountancy

| | | Course by distance education | |
Item	Two-year polytechnic course	Two-year full-time	Four-year part-time
Annual administrative overheads (millions of Kwachas)	50	36	3
Annual operating costs (millions of Kwachas)	100	16	2
Annualized capital costs of facilities (millions of Kwachas)	350	8	1
Overall annual costs (millions of Kwachas)	500	60	6
Number of students enrolled	20,000	10,000	2,000
Annual direct cost per student (Kwachas)	25,000	6,000	3,000
Annual fees per student (Kwachas)	2,000	0	0
Annual other course-related private costs (Kwachas)	750	600	300

courses. In addition to the direct institutional costs students also incur private costs in the form of fees and other course-related expenses. Take a moment now to assimilate the data and then continue to the next step in this exercise.

Impact on Costs of Repetition and Dropping Out

If students progress on schedule through their training, the cost of the full course of study simply will be the annual cost shown in the table above, multiplied by the corresponding duration of the course. But students may drop out or repeat and graduate later than expected. Where these problems are significant and differ substantially in magnitude across the three modes of study, it is important to take account of them in the cost analysis. The exercise below shows how to incorporate the effects of repetition and dropping out in the cost estimates.

Problem 1: Compute the Effective Duration of Study

Consider the data in table 9.B.1.14, which shows the distribution of each cohort of students by repetition and dropout status. The table may be retrieved from the worksheet titled "student flow" in the "Ed_Technology_distance_Ex4" Excel file. Use the data to compute (a) the average number of years invested to produce an accountancy graduate (Y_a) via each of the three modes of study and (b) the number of years that a graduate takes, on average, to complete the course (Y_b). Enter your results in the table. For the last row, simply compute the ratio between Y_a and Y_b. Because Y_a incorporates the influence of both repetition and dropping out—whereas Y_b incorporates only that of repetition—the ratio of Y_a to Y_b can be used to adjust costs upward to reflect the burden associated with

Table 9.B.1.14: Student Flow Characteristics Associated with the Three Options for Accountancy Training

Item	Two-year polytechnic course	Course by distance education	
		Two-year full-time	Four-year part-time
Percentage graduating on time	80	40	30
Percentage graduating late by:			
One year	5	15	15
Two years	0	10	10
Three years	0	0	5
Percentage dropping out after:			
One year	10	20	20
Two years	5	10	10
Three years	0	5	5
Four years	0	0	5
Average number of years invested per graduate (Y_a)			
Average number of years for graduates to complete course (Y_b)			
Loading factor to adjust for dropping out (Y_a/Y_b)			

dropping out.[15] The burden associated with repetition is accounted for by the increased time that graduates take to complete the course.

Problem 2: Adjust and Organize the Data on Direct Costs

As preparation for the cost-benefit analysis below, you are asked here to incorporate the impact of repetition and dropping out on the cost of training; and to organize the data in the format of table 9.B.2.15. Tab over to the worksheet titled "cost stream," where you will find the blank table

Table 9.B.2.15: Direct Social and Private Costs of Accountancy Training via Three Delivery Modes (Kwachas)

Year	Polytechnic course		Full-time distance course		Part-time distance course	
	Social	Private	Social	Private	Social	Private
1			8,800	800	4,153	378
2			8,800	800	4,153	378
3			4,738	431	4,153	378
4	—	—	—	—	4,153	378
5	—	—	—	—	3,461	315
Total for the course			22,338	2,301	20,075	1,825

— Not applicable.

and a copy of the relevant calculations from tables 9.B.1.13 and 9.B.1.14 to help with your work. Take a moment to consider how you might approach the problem, then follow the more detailed instructions below as needed.

There are two perspectives for computing the cost streams: society's and individual students'. In the table you are asked to compute both streams. Social costs refer to all costs, regardless of who bears them. For the purpose of this exercise social costs include those borne by the government as well as those borne by individual students. Note that fees should not be included because they are a transfer between students and the government. Private costs include only those borne by the students, that is, fees and other course-related private spending.

To adjust the cost streams for the burden of dropping out and repetition consider as an example the polytechnic course. Graduates take an average of 2.06 years to complete the two-year course. Thus in years one and two the cost would be the full annual amount, whereas in year three the cost would be only 0.06 of the full annual amount. The cost in all three years should be multiplied by the ratio of Y_a to Y_b, which in this example is 1.11 (refer to the introduction to this module for the definition of these variables). As preparation for a later exercise, add up the direct costs for the duration of each course to obtain the total direct costs for the entire course of training (for simplicity you may ignore discounting the cost streams). To save time the calculations for the courses by distance learning have been completed for you.

Assessing the Labor Market Outcomes

We turn now to analyze the benefit side of the equation. We use labor market performance to quantify the benefits. It is both an appropriate and a desirable measure here because the investments being evaluated concern professional training. Earnings are a common measure of performance, but there are other nonpecuniary indicators—such as quantity of output, percentage of defective goods, number of contracts approved—which also may be appropriate in some situations. The choice of indicator depends on conditions in the relevant labor markets.

In markets where wages tend to be shielded from competitive influences, quantitative measures of work performance may be better to use than earnings. For example, in evaluating the benefits of alternative modes for teacher training, the learning outcomes of the graduates' own pupils may be more appropriate as an outcome measure. This is because teacher salaries, particularly in the public sector, tend to be set by administrative rules and therefore may be linked only tenuously to teaching effectiveness. There are also situations where the training

9

courses under evaluation produce a limited number of graduates for a highly specialized market. Here again, nonmonetary measures of work performance may be more appropriate than earnings as an outcome measure, in part because such factors as temporary mismatches between the supply and demand for specialized workers or idiosyncratic institutional factors may exert substantial influence over fresh graduates' earnings.

For the exercise below we assume that the market for accountants is sufficiently competitive for earnings to be a valid indicator of labor market performance.

Earnings Related to Graduates' Training

Following common practice in the economics literature, we relate graduates' observed earnings to such factors as experience and type of training. The estimated earnings equation provides the basis for simulating earnings profiles according to the different sources of training and duration of experience. These profiles are an input for computing the rates of return that would facilitate comparison of the three options of accountancy training.

Problem 3: Estimate and Analyze the Wage Equation

Use the hypothetical data set described below to estimate a wage equation, and use the results to compare the impact of accountancy training delivered via the polytechnic course and through distance education. For lack of data, no distinction will be made between the part-time and full-time distance course. Follow the instructions below to perform the analysis.

Tab over to the next worksheet titled "earnings" (in the "Ed_Technology_distance_Ex4" Excel file) and continue reading for further information. Definitions of the variables in the data set appear in table 9.B.3.16 below.

The data relate to a cross-sectional sample of 198 men with at least a high school education and between 1 to 10 years of experience in a service or management-related professional job, including accountancy.[16] The reason for using a broader data set than just accountants is that some of the benefits of training derive from increased job mobility, which makes it important to capture this aspect of benefits in assessing the impact of alternative training modes. The data set also includes men with no more than a high school education, which makes it possible to assess the advantage of having had accountancy training beyond secondary school, whether through the polytechnic course or via distance education.[17] Finally, to keep our focus on assessing the benefits of

9

Table 9.B.3.16: Variables in the Hypothetical Data Set for Part B, Problem 2

Variable	Definition	Mean	Standard deviation
WAGE	Annual earnings (Kwachas)	28,281	10,627
EXP	Years of work experience	5.06	2.47
HS_SCORE	Score on examination when leaving high school	48.80	6.97
RICH	Dummy variable with a value of 1 if the worker is from a rich family; 0 otherwise	0.30	0.46
ACNTANT	Dummy variable with a value of 1 if the worker is employed as an accountant; 0 otherwise	0.56	0.50
POLY	Dummy variable with a value of 1 if the worker received accountancy training through the polytechnic course; 0 otherwise	0.38	0.49
DISTANCE	Dummy variable with a value of 1 if the worker received accountancy training through distance education; 0 otherwise	0.30	0.46
HI_SCH	Dummy variable with a value of 1 if the worker has only a high school education; 0 otherwise	0.32	0.47

Note: POLY, DISTANCE, and HI_SCH are mutually exclusive dummy variables. In the regression analysis only two of them can be included. In the analysis below you are asked to exclude HI_SCH. Thus the coefficients on the other two variables indicate the magnitude of the wage advantage for having accountancy training relative to having only a high school education.

accountancy training, the data exclude workers with post-secondary education or training in other fields.

Step 1   If you have time, use the data in the worksheet titled "earnings" to estimate a regression relating *WAGE* to *EXP, HS_SCORE, RICH, ACNTANT, POLY,* and *DISTANCE;* otherwise, simply examine the completed regression results that appear on the right-hand side of the worksheet. Note that in wage equations the *WAGE* variable is commonly expressed in logarithmic units, so that the coefficients on the regressors can be interpreted as percentage changes in wages associated with a unit change in the relevant regressor. Because our intention is to simulate wage profiles later on in this exercise, we use the wage variable directly without performing the logarithmic transformation. Another common practice is to include the square of experience as an additional regressor to allow for possible diminishing returns to experience. We exclude the squared term here, however, because the sample consists of people with no more than 10 years of experience—a range over which diminishing returns are unlikely to be a strong feature.[18] Examine the results and comment on them, noting differences in the wage advantage conferred by accountancy training via the polytechnic course and through distance education.

Comment on regression results:

_____

_____

_____

Average wage advantage over high school graduates:

Polytechnic course:

Distance education:

How would you interpret the magnitude of the wage gap indicated by the estimated coefficient on *POLY* and *DISTANCE*? To what extent do the estimates reflect the true earnings advantage of accountancy training relative to a high school diploma?

Step 2   Simulate the earnings of people with the various qualifications. As context for the calculation, note that because part of the benefits of the training accrues through enhanced chances of obtaining higher-paying jobs (such as accountancy), differences in the probability of working as an accountant must be taken into account in simulating the earnings of people with the various qualifications. Note from the regression that the earnings of accountants in this example are indeed higher, on average, than those for people in other jobs. Thus, to assess the wage advantage of accountancy training it is better to make the calculation from simulated wage profiles rather than to rely on the regression coefficients directly. For the simulations for each subsample, the values of *RICH*, *HS_SCORE*, and *EXP* are set at the mean for the whole sample, but the value of *ACNTANT* (which denotes the probability of getting a job as an accountant) is set at the subsample mean. In the current data set, recall that *ACNTANT* has a mean of 0.72 in the *POLY* group, 0.70 in the *DISTANCE* group, but only 0.22 in the *HI_SCH* group).

Tab over now to the next worksheet titled "wage_sim." Use the regression results from the previous step to simulate the wages for the three groups: (a) high school graduates, (b) accountancy degree holders who received training via the polytechnic course, and (c) accountancy degree holders who received training via distance learning. Enter your results in table 9.B.3.17. To save time these simulations have been completed for you. They have been computed assuming sample mean values for all the regressors except for two variables: *EXP* has been assigned values ranging from 1 year to 10 years, and *ACNTANT* takes on the sample means of the three population groups. What is the earnings advantage relative to high school graduates (year 10)? Enter your data in table 9.B.3.17.

9

Table 9.B.3.17: Simulated Annual Earnings of Graduates by Years of Experience (Kwachas)

Years of experience	High school graduates	Accountancy degree holder	
		Polytechnic course	Distance education
1	18,674	27,233	25,770
2	19,711	28,271	26,808
3	20,749	29,309	27,845
4	21,787	30,347	28,883
5	22,825	31,384	29,921
6	23,862	32,422	30,959
7	24,900	33,460	31,996
8	25,938	34,498	33,034
9	26,976	35,535	34,072
10	28,013	36,573	35,109

Note: Earnings advantage relative to high school graduates.

Making the Cost-Benefit Evaluation

To compare the three delivery modes for accountancy training we can use standard techniques in cost-benefit analysis. These techniques essentially permit a joint consideration of the relevant costs and benefits.

As context for the exercise below, note that three related indicators are commonly used to summarize the data: net present value (*NPV*), cost-benefit ratio (*CBR*), and rate of return (*ROR*). The standard formula for computing the *NPV* of an investment which costs C_t in year t and generates benefits B_t in year t, for n years, at a discount rate of i percent a year, is given by:

$$(15) \qquad NPV = \sum_{t=0}^{n} \frac{Bt - Ct}{(1 + i)^t}$$

The *NPV* is the discounted sum of the net benefits (that is, benefits minus costs). The *CBR* is the discounted stream of costs divided by the discounted stream of benefits; it is equivalent to $(1 - NPV/$ discounted sum of benefits). The ROR is the value of i corresponding to an *NPV* value of zero. An *ROR* of 15 percent, for example, says that the future stream of income from an investment is the same as that of putting the money in the bank to earn interest at a rate of 15 percent a year. Because of data limitations, the exercise below focuses on calculating the *ROR*.

The desired rates of return can be computed using either the elaborate method or the short-cut method. The former involves setting up a complete net benefit stream over the working lifetime of graduates, based on data on direct costs and graduates' earnings profiles. However,

9

230

because our data relate only to the first 10 years of the graduates' working lifetime, the regression on earnings is valid mainly for wage simulations in the vicinity of this experience range. Beyond that range the simulations become less reliable and it is unclear that the quality of the data is sufficiently high to warrant using the elaborate method.

Given the incompleteness of the data we will use the short-cut method to compute the relevant *ROR*. It requires only two pieces of information: (a) the sum of the direct costs (*DC*) and opportunity costs (*OC*)[19] and (b) the average gap in annual earnings between accountancy graduates and high school graduates (*EGAP*) over the working lifetime of the graduates. The desired rate of return would then be:

(16)
$$ROR = \frac{EGAP}{DC + OC}$$

Problem 4: Compute the Full Costs of Accountancy Training

These costs comprise two components: the direct costs as calculated in table 9.B.1.14 and the opportunity costs. The latter stem from the fact that while students are enrolled (even though they may drop out before completing their studies) they forgo income. These costs are incurred both by the individual student and by society at large. Follow the steps below to prepare a table showing the full costs associated with accountancy training via the polytechnic course and through distance learning.

Step 1   Tab over to the worksheet titled "Opportunity cost" (in the "Ed_Technology_distance_Ex4" Excel file) where you will find a copy of table 9.B.4.18. Complete it, basing your answers on the wage simulations from table 9.B.3.17; to save time the columns for distance education have been completed for you. There are three items to remember in making your calculations. First, graduates take longer than the official length of the course to complete their studies (which implies that graduates' earn-

Table 9.B.4.18: Opportunity Costs of Accountancy Training (Kwachas)

Year	Polytechnic course	Distance education	
		Full-time	*Part-time*
1		24,898	11,752
2		26,282	12,405
3		14,897	13,058
4		0	13,711
5		0	11,970
Sum total of opportunity costs		66,077	62,895

9

ings in the first year of work should be adjusted for the portion of the year they are effectively in the labor market, ignoring in this exercise the possibility of unemployment); second, the impact on costs of dropping out must be taken into account in the same way that it was in computing the direct costs (that is, apply the loading factor from table 9.B.1.13 to adjust the costs upward); and third, that part-timers incur only half of the relevant opportunity costs over the duration of their studies.

Step 2 Tab over to the worksheet titled "full costs," (in the "Ed_Technology_distance_Ex4" Excel file) where you will find a partially completed copy of table 9.B.4.19. Fill in the cells for the polytechnic course using data from tables 9.B.2.15 and 9.B.4.18.

Problem 5: Compute and Assess the Rates of Return to the Three Options

As indicated above, we have no information on the entire earnings profile. We can make the simplifying assumption, however, that the average is close to the gap observed at about 10 years from the start of the graduates' working lifetime. Based on this assumption, compute the social and private returns to the various modes of accountancy training and enter your results in table 9.B.5.20. Comment on the policy implications of the results.

Table 9.B.4.19: Full Costs of Accountancy Training via Three Delivery Modes (Kwachas)

Item	Polytechnic course		Full-time distance course		Part-time distance course	
	Social	Private	Social	Private	Social	Private
Total direct costs			22,338	2,031	20,075	1,825
Total opportunity costs			66,077	66,077	62,895	62,895
Full costs			88,416	68,108	82,970	64,720

Table 9.B.5.20: Estimates of Rates of Return to Accountancy Training via Three Delivery Modes

Item	Polytechnic course		Full-time distance course		Part-time distance course	
	Social	Private	Social	Private	Social	Private
Full costs (Kwachas)	59,074	6,309	88,416	68,108	82,970	64,720
Annual earnings gap (Kwachas)						
Estimated rate of return (percent per annum)						

Endnotes

1. The instructions in the exercises are consistent with Excel's specific features. Participants also may use other software to accomplish the analysis after making the appropriate data conversion.

2. We make the assumption here in order to focus attention on the main elements of cost-benefit analysis. Where subject specialization by teachers is the practice, the cost analysis obviously must be adjusted accordingly. Details of cost analysis in such situations may be found in the hands-on training module "Analyzing Costs in Education," by Jean-Pierre Jarousse, Alain Mingat, Stella Tamayo, and Jee-Peng Tan.

3. Note, however, that in urban areas where public and private schools may exist in close proximity, the private school may be renting its facilities, in which case the rental it pays would provide a good proxy for the capital cost of the public school.

4. In the example here, we specify the data for a single classroom to facilitate subsequent cost simulations. The total investment cost includes a portion of the cost of shared school facilities, such as administrative buildings, assembly halls, physical education facilities, and so on.

5. The amount, strictly, should be annualized using the same procedure as those used earlier to annualize capital costs. However, because the lifetime of training is only three years, we simply have divided the training costs per teacher by three.

6. The number of participating schools in the CAI system is also a policy variable, but it is best addressed separately along the lines of the exercise just completed.

7. We specify the amount of pedagogical materials per pupil as an index to simplify the calculations. The index ranges from 1 to 6, with an average of about 3.4 for the school system as a whole. For simplicity we assume that spending on pedagogical materials increases at a constant rate of K70.6 per point on the index.

8. Note that throughout this module the term "unit costs" refers to the cost per pupil. It is not to be confused with the cost per episode of teacher training, nor with the cost of investment spending per school or per classroom to provide computer-assisted instruction.

9. Note that the second line in the equation refers to the cost of traditional classroom instruction; the third line refers to the incremental costs of computer-assisted instruction incurred at the center; the fourth line refers to the incremental costs of computer-assisted instruction incurred at the school and classroom levels.

10. As noted earlier, the sums may not add up exactly due to rounding.

11. Because the input option for teachers is specified here for a single teacher, the distribution of teachers by qualification and the proportion trained in CAI simplify to variables that take on the values of zero or one, according to whether or not the teachers is in the indicated category. Thus, for a teacher with qualification B, the value of P_a and P_c would be equal to zero, whereas that of P_b would be equal to one. Similarly, for teachers who have been trained in CAI, the variable *TRAIN* takes on the value of one.

12. Participants who wish to attempt the regression estimation themselves may do so in a new worksheet.

9

13. For those unfamiliar with regression analysis, you can do a simple calculation to answer this question. Simply use the estimated regression equation in worksheet 2 to predict *ENDSCORE* for two pupils with average characteristics (that is, with sample means as the values for the regression variables). The value of CAI would be one for those exposed to CAI and zero for those exposed to TCI. You will notice that your answer is exactly the same as the estimated coefficient on the CAI variable.

14. Because of their intuitive appeal we will use simulations to perform the analysis. An alternative is to compare marginal benefits with marginal costs for each of the policy-sensitive variables. The regression coefficients are an estimate of the marginal benefits, whereas the cost functions developed earlier in the module can be differentiated to obtain the corresponding marginal costs.

15. Other procedures probably exist for incorporating the cost of dropping out, but the procedure used here is both simple and intuitively appealing.

16. Because we are interested in fresh graduates' earnings profiles earlier rather than later in their careers the sample includes only relatively young men. We focus on men because analysis of women's labor market participation tends to be more complex in view of their child-bearing and -raising roles within households.

17. For those trained as accountants via distance education, additional information is unavailable regarding their earnings according to whether they pursued the two-year full-time course or the four-year part-time course. In the analysis here we assume that their earnings are the same.

18. If you have time, you may wish to perform the regression including the square of experience as an additional regressor. You will find that the coefficients on both the experience and experience-squared terms are statistically insignificant, which suggests a linear relationship between wages and experience in this data set.

19. For simplicity we will use the undiscounted stream of costs.

9

Conducting Comparative Policy Analysis in Education

A Three-Part Module

Alain Mingat and Jee-Peng Tan, with Shobhana Sosale

Comparative policy analysis offers a simple yet surprisingly insightful approach for gauging the performance of education systems across countries as well as across regions within a country. Although data issues—some of which are elaborated in the annex to this chapter—do place limitations on the analysis, the results often remain relevant for policy development. The purpose of this chapter is to illustrate some approaches for accomplishing the analysis.[1]

This chapter has three parts. Part A focuses on simple comparisons of education indicators. Part B goes beyond simple comparisons, notably to adjust the comparisons for differences in economic context across comparators, to incorporate structural aspects of education in the comparisons, and to consider the use of comparative analysis in assessing the relationship between education resources and outcomes. Part C shows how to consolidate the various pieces of analysis to form an overall assessment of education in the country or region of interest.

The module includes this write-up and Excel data files on the CD-ROM. The Excel files have names that correspond to each of the three parts, and individual exercises within each part are placed in worksheets identified with a name corresponding to the exercise. For example, the file "Comparative_Policy_Analysis_Ex1" refers to the exercises in part A of the module, and the worksheet "problem 1" in that file refers to the first exercise.

The write-up contains all the information you need to understand and accomplish the exercises. The first few problems deliberately are kept simple in order to acclimatize users to the hands-on pedagogical method. Excel procedures are invoked in the exercises but are kept to a minimum so as to focus attention on the substance. Because the exercises are arranged in sequence it is best to proceed systematically from problem to problem. You are strongly encouraged to read the text relating to each exercise before attempting the computations.

Part A: Making Simple Comparisons of Education Indicators

The analysis here consists of a straightforward comparison of the values of selected education indicators. For each indicator the comparison involves two complementary (and very simple) operations. The first is to arrange countries in the relevant sample in ascending (or descending) order according to the value of the indicator, and then to locate the position of the country of interest in that ranking. The second is to compute a relative index for each of the indicators, the simplest index being the ratio between the indicator for the country of interest and the corresponding average for the country group to which it belongs.[2]

For this part of the module we consider indicators relating to four distinct dimensions: (a) the financing of education, (b) the operational characteristics of the education system, (c) schooling outcomes for the population as a whole, and (d) the distribution of schooling outcomes by population groups. These dimensions have obvious interest for policy analysis: the first two items relate to investment of resources in education and how those resources are used, and the last two relate to the system's output performance. For the exercises, we select one explicit indicator for each of the four dimensions (table 10.A.1.1).

The data on these indicators for a sample of 28 countries appear in table 10.A.1.2. Although the data refer to actual countries, we use codes to identify the countries simply to focus attention on the analysis rather than on the data for particular countries. All three problems in part A of the module involve the use of these data. Take a moment now to scan them quickly before proceeding to problem 1 below.

Table 10.A.1.1: Education Indicators Corresponding to Four Selected Dimensions of Education

Dimension	Indicator
Education finance	Public spending on education as a percentage of GNP
Operational characteristics of the education system	Pupil–teacher ratio in primary schooling
Aggregate schooling outcomes	Percentage of first graders who reach grade four
Distribution of the schooling outcomes	Ratio of girls to boys enrolled in primary school

GNP Gross national product.

10

Table 10.A.1.2: Data on Selected Education Indicators for a Sample of Countries

				Primary education indicators		
Country code	Region	Per capita GNP (US$)	Public spending on education as percentage of GNP	Number of pupils per teacher	Percentage of first graders who reach grade four	Ratio of girls to boys in school
C1	LAC	6,050	3.1	16	80	99.1
C2	Asia	220	2.3	63	52	101.8
C3	LAC	2,770	4.6	23	72	96.5
C4	LAC	2,730	2.9	25	95	99.0
C5	Asia	380	2.0	22	88	94.4
C6	LAC	1,290	3.1	28	59	100.9
C7	AFR	670	7.8	37	73	71.6
C8	LAC	1,070	2.7	31	68	98.4
C9	MENA	630	5.0	22	98	84.8
C10	AFR	450	3.1	29	80	84.3
C11	LAC	980	1.5	32	43	87.6
C12	Asia	310	3.7	48	62	79.5
C13	Asia	670	2.2	23	86	96.6
C14	LAC	1,340	4.7	37	96	100.9
C15	MENA	1,120	6.5	22	98	101.1
C16	AFR	330	5.4	31	77	97.8
C17	Asia	6,790	4.2	33	99	101.0
C18	Asia	250	2.3	29	53	72.4
C19	Asia	2,790	5.5	20	98	101.1
C20	LAC	3,470	4.9	30	84	99.1
C21	MENA	1,040	5.8	28	80	70.6
C22	Asia	410	2.7	41	48	52.6
C23	Asia	770	2.9	34	75	96.5
C24	AFR	780	4.2	59	88	74.6
C25	Asia	540	3.3	29	92	98.1
C26	Asia	1,840	4.0	17	88	98.0
C27	MENA	1,740	6.1	26	90	90.2
C28	AFR	570	9.1	38	76	97.5

LAC Latin America and the Caribbean.
AFR Africa.
MENA Middle East and North Africa.
GNP Gross national product.

10

Problem 1

Insert the CD-ROM into the computer and retrieve the file "Comparative_Policy_Analysis_Ex1." Check the bottom of the screen to make sure that you are in the worksheet titled "problem 1." The screen should contain table 10.A.1.2. Assume for this exercise that countries of interest are C3 and C22, and that we are interested in comparing them with other countries in terms of public spending on education as a percentage of grosss national product (GNP). Follow the steps below to complete the task.

Step 1

The first step is to decide on the appropriate comparator groups for the two countries. For this purpose, regional affiliation is an obvious criterion, but per capita income is equally valid. In most comparative analysis, country groups based on these criteria are commonly used.

Consider, for example, country C3. In table 10.A.1.3 we have indicated the specific criteria we believe are appropriate for choosing C3's comparators. To elaborate, because C3 is a Latin American country we suggest including all Latin American countries in the sample to form one comparator group. The per capita GNP of C3 is US$2,770, so we propose an income band of US$1,200 to US$5,000 to define a second comparator group. A smaller range obviously would be better but, given the limited number of countries in the sample, its use would result in a comparator group with too few countries. Under the criteria defined here there happen to be eight countries in both the comparator groups; the sample size is noted in the table by the figure in parentheses.

Your task now is to complete the last column of table 10.A.1.3 following the same line of reasoning as above. Enter your proposed criteria in the table here or in the Excel worksheet.

Step 2

This step involves creating a new table from the data in table 10.A.1.2 in order to facilitate comparison of C3 and C22 with their respective com-

Table 10.A.1.3: Choice of Appropriate Comparator Groups for Countries C3 and C22

Criteria for choosing countries in comparator group	Country C3	Country C22
Regional affiliation	All Latin American countries in the sample (8)	
Per capita income	All countries with per capita income from US$1,200 to US$5,000 (8)	

parators. The new table thus would contain data only for the countries identified by the criteria specified in step 1, with the observations sorted by level of public spending on education, and a summary index computed to relate C3's and C22's levels of spending on education to average spending in the relevant comparator countries. The desired table would thus look like table 10.A.1.4.

The data relating to the comparative analysis for C3 have been prepared for you; so has part of the data for C22's analysis. The entries for both countries are colored as a visual aid to locate their position in the Excel worksheet. Your task is simply to complete the last column of the table. Take note of the selection criteria for the comparator countries for C22. They may differ from those you suggested in step 1 above, but should be used here in order to produce results that are consistent with subsequent sections of the module.

If you would like more detailed instructions, skip now to the next paragraph. Otherwise simply read on in this paragraph. In your Excel worksheet (still in "problem 1") locate table 10.A.1.4 by scrolling down

Table 10.A.1.4: Comparative Data for Evaluating C3's and C22's Public Spending on Education as a Percentage of GNP

Comparative analysis for C3				Comparative analysis for C22		
Compare C3 with other Latin American countries		Compare C3 with countries with per capita incomes from US$1,200 to US$5,000		Compare C22 with other Asian countries		Compare C22 with countries with per capita GNP <US$600
C11	1.5	C4	2.9	C5	2.0	
C8	2.7	C6	3.1	C13	2.2	
C4	2.9	C26	4.0	C2	2.3	
C1	3.1	C3	4.6	C18	2.3	
C6	3.1	C14	4.7	C22	2.7	
C3	4.6	C20	4.9	C23	2.9	
C14	4.7	C19	5.5	C25	3.3	
C20	4.9	C27	6.1	C12	3.7	
				C26	4.0	
				C17	4.2	
				C19	5.5	
Group average	3.4	n.a.	4.5	n.a.	3.2	
Ratio of country's indicator to the group average	1.33	n.a.	1.03	n.a.	0.85	

n.a. Not applicable.

the sheet. Complete it using any working area for managing your data. Then proceed to step 3 below.

To complete the last column of table 10.A.1.4, you need to apply a few Excel procedures to the data in the mauve-colored working table in the worksheet. Scroll down the sheet now to locate this working table. The table contains data copied from the first four columns of table 10.A.1.2. First, sort the data by per capita income and by spending on education; then block the set of countries with per capita GNP below US$600. Next invoke Excel's "copy-paste special-values" sequence to populate the last column of table 10.A.1.4. Then complete the calculation at the bottom of the table.

Step 3

Review the completed table and briefly comment on the levels of public spending on education in C3 and C22 relative to their comparators. Confirm that for each country its position in the distribution of the relevant group of countries is consistent with the ratio between its spending indicator and the country group average for that indicator. For example, if the ratio exceeds unity, the country should be ranked in the upper half of the sample of countries.

Comment: _____

_____

_____

_____

Problem 2

Earlier in the discussion we identified four education indicators for our comparative analysis of education in C3 and C22. Aside from overall public spending on education, they include indicators relating to primary schooling: (a) pupil–teacher ratio, (b) proportion of first graders reaching grade five, and (c) ratio of girls to boys in school. For each of these indicators we can perform the same comparative analysis as in problem 1. To save time the task has been accomplished and you are asked in this problem simply to review and comment on the results.

Tab over now to the worksheet titled "problem 2," where you will find a copy of table 10.A.2.5 containing the ratios of C3's and C22's indicators to the corresponding averages of the relevant comparator groups.[3] Briefly look at the data in the table and then proceed to the next paragraph.

10

Table 10.A.2.5: Selected Education Indicators for C3 and C22 Relative to the Relevant Country Group Averages

| Indicator | C3's indicators | | C22's indicators | |
	Relative to Latin American countries	Relative to countries with per capita income from US$1,200 to US$5,000	Relative to Asian countries	Relative to countries with per capita income at or below US$600
Public spending on education as a percentage of GNP	1.34	1.03	0.85	0.72
Pupils per teacher, primary schooling	0.83	0.89	1.26	1.12
Share of first graders reaching grade five	0.96	0.84	0.63	0.69
Ratio of girls to boys in primary school	0.99	0.98	0.58	0.61

As a visual aid, the data in the table have been depicted in the form of "development diamonds," one for each of the two countries. Scroll down the worksheet to locate the diamonds. The four arms in each diamond correspond to the four indicators listed in the table. The diamond is formed by connecting the ratios marked off on the four arms. The pink diamond depicts comparisons relative to countries in the same region; the green diamond depicts comparisons relative to countries at comparable levels of per capita GNP.

Take a moment now to review the results in the table and graphs and comment briefly on their implications regarding educational development in C3 and C22. In addition you are asked to reflect on possible limitations of simple comparisons in policy analysis, such as the one you have just completed.

Comment on education in C3 and C22:
_____

_____

_____

_____

General comment on the limitations of simple comparisons:
_____

_____

_____

10

Part B: Going beyond Simple Comparisons

Various ways exist to expand the analysis beyond simple comparisons. Here we consider three possible approaches: (a) bringing out structural aspects of education in the comparative analysis, (b) adjusting the comparisons for differences in economic context across comparators, and (c) evaluating the relationship between resources and schooling outcomes in comparative perspective.

Comparing Structural Aspects of Education

By "structural aspects" we mean the relationship across levels of education within a given system. Comparative analysis of education structures can be performed using various indicators, including those relating to financial quantities as well as those relating to physical attributes of the education system (such as enrollment ratios and pupil–teacher ratios). In the problem below, the comparative analysis is illustrated using public spending per pupil as the indicator of interest.

Problem 1

Your task in this problem is to compute several indicators for comparative analysis of the structure of education costs in four countries (C5, C10, C21, and C26) selected from the 28-country sample presented in part A. Follow the steps below to accomplish the analysis.

Step 1   Retrieve now the Excel file "Comparative_Policy_Analysis_Ex2," making sure that you are in the worksheet titled "problem 1." The worksheet shows data on public spending per pupil as a percentage of per capita GNP by level of education for the four countries (see table 10.B.1.6). One column in the table—relating to country C5—is blank. Complete it by expressing the public spending per pupil at each level as a ratio of the spending in primary education. To save time similar calculations for the other three countries have already been completed for you. Take a moment now to review the data in the completed table and comment on the structure of per pupil spending across levels of education in the four countries.

Comment on structure of costs: _____

_____

_____

_____

_____

10

Table 10.B.1.6: Public Spending per Pupil by Level of Education in C5, C10, C21, and C26

Level of education	C5[a] Percentage of per capita GNP	C5[a] Ratio to primary education	C10[b] Percentage of per capita GNP	C10[b] Ratio to primary education	C21[c] Percentage of per capita GNP	C21[c] Ratio to primary education	C26[d] Percentage of per capita GNP	C26[d] Ratio to primary education
Primary	8	1.0	26	1.0	18	1.0	12	1.0
Secondary	11		16	0.6	54	3.0	14	1.2
Higher	140		234	9.0	92	5.1	26	2.2

a. Per capita GNP = US$380.
b. Per capita GNP = US$450.
c. Per capita GNP = US$1,040.
d. Per capita GNP = US$1,840.

Step 2 To bring a systematic international perspective to the comparisons, we need to relate the structure of spending in each of the four countries to that in countries with comparable per capita incomes. For this purpose we define the comparator countries as follows: C5's and C10's comparators include countries with per capita incomes at or below US$600, C21's comparators include countries with per capita incomes between US$600 and US$2,000, and C26's comparators include countries with per capita incomes between US$1,200 and US$5,000. The average per pupil public spending on education for countries in these per capita income ranges appears in table 10.B.1.7, based on the data in the 28-country sample used in this module. Take a moment now to scan the table and then go on to the next paragraph.

Using the data in the preceding two tables, compute the ratio between per pupil spending at each level of education in the four countries and the corresponding averages for their respective comparators. Use table 10.B.1.8 below to enter your results (in your Excel worksheet you can find it by scrolling down the page). As an example, consider the calculation for C5: for primary education the desired ratio is 0.65 (= 8/12.3); for secondary education it is 0.50 (= 11/21.8); and for higher education it is 1.29 (= 140/108.9). The bottom row of the table shows an index of overall costliness, calculated as the average of the ratios for the three levels of education.[4] For C5, the index is 0.81 [= (0.65 + 0.50 + 1.28)/3]. The index is below 1 here, which implies that public spending per pupil in C5 is generally lower than in countries with comparable per capita incomes.

Table 10.B.1.7: Average Public Spending per Pupil by Level of Education in Countries with per Capita Incomes Comparable to C5, C10, C21, and C26 (percentage of per capita GNP)

Level of education	C5's comparators	C10's comparators	C21's comparators	C26's comparators
Primary	12.3	12.3	13.8	9.9
Secondary	21.8	21.8	25.0	16.6
Higher	108.9	108.9	130.6	75.8

Table 10.B.1.8: Public Spending per Pupil as a Multiple of the Corresponding Average for the Relevant Comparator Group

Level of education	C5	C10	C21	C26
Primary	0.65		1.30	1.22
Secondary	0.50		2.16	0.84
Higher	1.28		0.70	0.35
Index of overall costliness	0.81		1.39	0.80

10

Following the same procedure as above, complete the calculation for C10. To save time, the entries for the remaining two countries—C21 and C26—have been completed for you. Take a moment now to review the results in the table, comparing the four countries in terms of (a) the overall level of public spending per pupil, and (b) the structure of spending across levels of schooling.

Comment on level and structure of per pupil spending: _____

_____

_____

_____

_____

Adjusting for Differences in Countries' Economic Contexts

The problems encountered so far recognize the importance of taking account of countries' economic contexts in comparative analysis simply by limiting the comparisons across countries with similar levels of per capita income. We turn now to methods that allow for a more elaborate adjustment for differences in countries' economic contexts. Typically they require regression analysis, but as the two examples below illustrate, the extra work is not overly demanding and is well worth the additional insights it brings to the comparative analysis. The first problem addresses the relationship between coverage of the education system and the country's level of economic development. The second problem focuses on the relationship between teacher salaries and other income indicators in the country. Both examples show how comparative data can be used to inform policy development in the country of interest.

Problem 2

Suppose a formerly socialist country, X, approached an international organization for financial assistance to support expansion of its higher education system. The country has initiated and expanded market-friendly policies for a few years now, and these policies are expected to generate a growing demand for educated labor. Because it takes time to produce graduates, the government argues that investment to expand higher education is urgently needed now to prevent labor shortages from hampering future economic growth. Your task here is to evaluate the proposal, using the techniques of comparative analysis elaborated below to guide your evaluation.

10

245

Step 1   The first issue is to recognize that the usual rate-of-return approach is especially inappropriate as a guide to investment priorities in country X. Take a moment now to jot down a few reasons why you think it might be unsuitable.

Comment on limitations of the rate-of-return approach applied to country X:

_____

_____

_____

_____

Step 2   Given the limitations of rate-of-return analysis, we need some other basis to evaluate country X's proposal. Comparative analysis can offer some help in this regard. The basic idea is that we expect countries with market-friendly policy regimes to have enrollment ratios in higher education that are more or less consistent with the market demand for educated labor, which in turn depends on the size of industry in the economy, and more generally on the country's overall level of economic development.

To proceed with the analysis we need first to estimate two regression equations:

$$ind\_shr = f(pc\_gnp \text{ or } lnpc\_gnp)$$

$$hi\_enr = f(pc\_gnp \text{ or } lnpc\_gnp)$$

where *ind_shr* is the share of the workforce in industry, *hi_enr* is the enrollment ratio in higher education, *pc_gnp* is the per capita GNP, and *lnpc_gnp* is the natural logarithm of per capita GNP. The logarithmic transformation is preferred because per capita income would then be expressed on a relative rather than absolute scale, so that going from US$100 to US$200 is expected to have the same impact as going from US$1,000 to US$2,000.

The first equation is not essential for assessing the issue of immediate interest regarding the coverage of higher education in country X; it provides contextual information, however, and is included here for completeness' sake. Using the two equations we can evaluate country X's industrial structure and enrollment ratio in higher education in comparative perspective.

To estimate the equations we will use data on the 28 countries introduced earlier in this module. Tab over now to the worksheet titled "problem 2," where you will find a copy of the relevant data. As an example, the

10

first regression equation has been performed for you, and the coefficient estimates along with the relevant *t*-ratio and R^2 values are reported below as well as on the Excel sheet. Your task is to estimate the second regression. Enter the coefficient estimates and the corresponding *t*-ratio and R^2 values on the Excel sheet or in the equation below. Pause briefly here to understand your work so far and then go on to the next step.

$$(1) \qquad Ind\_shr = -24.0 + 6.24 \times lnpc\_gnp \qquad R^2 = 0.56$$
$$(t = 5.8)$$

$$hi\_enr = \underline{\hspace{1cm}} + \underline{\hspace{1cm}} \times lnpc\_gnp \qquad R^2 =$$

Step 3 Your task here is to use the two regression equations to simulate the share of the workforce in industry and the enrollment ratio in higher education for a country at X's current level of per capita GNP, and at X's future level of per capita GNP, given the country's projected rate of economic growth. For our purpose, the projected growth rate ranges from a lower case of 5 percent a year to an upper case of 7 percent a year over the next 10-year period. At these rates country X's per capita GNP in 10 years' time would range from US\$412 (= $250 \times e^{0.05 \times 10}$) and US\$503. Read on below for further instructions on how to proceed with the simulations.

Scroll down the worksheet now until you find a copy of table 10.B.2.9 (see below). The second column in the table contains actual data relating to country X's current situation. Based on equation (1) estimated above, a country with X's current per capita GNP of US\$250 would have 10.4 percent [$= -24.0 + 6.24 \times ln(250)$] of its workforce in industry, and a higher education enrollment rate of 1.3 percent [$= -41.8 + 7.80 \times ln(250)$]. Follow the same procedure to complete the simulation for the lower case

Table 10.B.2.9: Actual and Simulated Shares of Workforce in Industry and Higher Education Enrollment Ratios in Country X

Indicator	Country X's current situation		Country X's situation projected 10 years	
	Actual	Simulated	Lower case	Upper case
Economic growth rate (percentage per year)	n.a.	n.a.	5.0	7.0
Per capita GNP (US$)	250	250	412	503
Share of workforce in industry (percentage)	6.0	10.4		14.8
Higher education enrollment ratio (percentage)	6.0	1.3		6.7

n.a. Not applicable.

10

corresponding to a projected economic growth rate of 5 percent a year. The simulation for the upper case has been completed for you.

Step 4   Review the simulation results in table 10.B.2.9 and comment on whether they support a general expansion of higher education in country X. How would you refine the analysis to allow for possible differences in labor demand across fields of specialization within higher education? Had the comparative analysis thus far supported the government's proposal to expand higher education, what additional analytical work, if any, would you suggest to confirm that conclusion?

Comment on simulation results: _____

_____

_____

_____

Comment on additional analysis: _____

_____

_____

_____

Problem 3

Teacher salaries are a major cost in education. Policies affecting teacher pay are therefore a key concern in the sector, involving such questions as: Are teachers adequately paid relative to other workers? Is their pay high enough to motivate effective teaching? Although these and other questions concerning teacher employment and pay are best addressed through microeconomic analysis of the labor market for teachers, comparative analysis can offer some insights based on relatively simple data requirements, particularly as an entrée into the more in-depth analysis. Your task in this problem is to evaluate the directions for policy development regarding teacher pay in primary education in selected countries in our sample. Follow the steps below to accomplish your evaluation.

Step 1   For comparative analysis the data on teacher pay first must be standardized to the same unit of measure. The simplest procedure is to convert teacher pay denominated in the national currency into its equivalent in a common currency, such as the U.S. dollar, using the current exchange rate. The resulting data have limited use in comparative analysis, however, because wide differences in economic context make it diffi-

10

cult to interpret cross-country comparisons of teacher salaries in absolute terms. In Bangladesh, where the per capita GNP is US$220, a salary of, say, US$1,000 would make teachers a relatively expensive input, but the same salary in Brazil, where the per capita GNP is US$2,770, would make teachers a relatively cheap input there. To improve the basis for comparative analysis, a common approach is to express teacher salaries (and other financial indicators in education) as ratios of the per capita GNP.

Tab now to the worksheet titled "problem 3," where you will find data on teacher salaries and per capita GNP (*pc_gnp*) for our sample of 28 countries. To save time the data on teacher salaries in dollar units (*t_salaryd*) have been converted to per capita GNP units (*t_salary*). Table 10.B.3.10 shows selected data for C8 and C22, two countries in the sample. Comment briefly on these data, noting any implications regarding the difficulty of expanding enrollments in the two countries, and possible reasons why it is not a surprise that teacher salaries as a ratio of per capita GNP are higher in C22 than in C8.

Comment:

_____

_____

_____

_____

Step 2   Using the data for the entire 28-country sample, explore the relationship between teacher salaries and per capita GNP. As discussed in an earlier exercise, the latter variable is more meaningful in comparative analysis when measured on a logarithmic scale, so that an increase in per capita GNP from, say, US$500 to US$1,000 implies the same magnitude as an increase from US$1,000 to US$2,000, or indeed as any twofold increase.

In your worksheet, convert per capita GNP into logarithmic units, then plot a scatter graph with *ln* (per capita GNP) on the *x*-axis and primary school teacher salaries in per capita units on the *y*-axis. Comment on the general pattern in the relationship between the two variables, elaborating on the factors you think might account for the observed pattern.

Table 10.B.3.10: Primary School Teacher Salaries in Two Countries

Country	Per capita GNP (US$)	Teacher salaries as ratio of per capita GNP
C8	1,070	1.6
C22	410	4.0

10

Comment on relationship between teacher salaries and _ln_ (per capita GNP):

_____

_____

_____

_____

_____

Step 3   Your task here is to perform a more precise evaluation of the relationship between teacher salaries and per capita GNP based on regression analysis. Because the relationship has the appearance of a hyperbolic curve rather than a downward-sloping straight line, it is more appropriate to specify the following functional form for the regression equation than to specify a straight line:

(2) $$t\_salary = a + \frac{b}{lnpc\_gnp}$$

or equivalently,

(3) $$t\_salary = a + b \bullet ilnpc\_gnp$$

where _t_salary_ is the primary school teacher salary in per capita GNP units, _lnpc_gnp_ is the natural logarithm of per capita GNP, and _ilnpc_gnp_ is the inverse of _lnpc_gnp_ (that is, _1_ divided by _lnpc_gnp_).

Scroll down your worksheet to the working table for this step in the problem, where you will find the relevant data for the regression analysis. Create a new column in the table showing the values of _ilnpc_gnp_, then invoke Excel's regression command to estimate the desired equation. Enter your coefficient estimates in the blank spaces below.

$$t\_salary = \underline{\qquad} + \underline{\qquad} \times ilnpc\_gnp \qquad R^2 =$$

Step 4   Using the regression equation you have just estimated, simulate pt_salary_1, the value of _t_salary_ predicted by the above equation on the basis of each country's per capita GNP. Enter the results in the column colored yellow in the working table for step 4. Then compute for each country an index of the costliness of teacher salaries relative to international patterns of teacher pay ($index_1$), defined as the percentage deviation of actual teacher salaries from the regression-simulated salary:

$$index_1 = \frac{t\_salary - pt\_salary_1}{t\_salary} \times 100$$

10

The index thus measures the extent to which teacher salaries deviate from the level expected based on international patterns of teacher remuneration. Focusing on 6 of the 28 countries in our sample—C1, C7, C20, C21, C24, and C25—comment briefly on the results. If you prefer to use a graph for this purpose, scroll down your worksheet until you locate the graph for step 4, which identifies the six countries relative to the regression curve.

Comment on teacher salaries in the six countries in international perspective: _____

_____

_____

_____ __

_____

Step 5   To expand our understanding regarding teacher salaries and to explore possible avenues for policy development, the analysis thus far requires further elaboration. In particular it needs to be supplemented by an evaluation of teacher salaries in the context of domestic labor market conditions. The analysis would permit a distinction between two possible influences on teacher pay: a country's general labor market conditions, and the specific conditions relating to the market for teachers within the country. The distinction is important because of its implications for policy development regarding teacher pay. A detailed analysis requires data from labor market surveys, but such surveys typically take time to conduct and analyze. Comparative data are more easily gathered and analyzed and they can offer a helpful preliminary assessment, as this step in the problem is intended to show.

Scroll down your worksheet now to locate the working table for step 5. There you will find the data for this exercise: teacher salaries as well as the salaries of unskilled workers in industry, both variables being denominated in per capita GNP units. The latter variable is readily available and is used here mainly as a reference for standardizing the comparisons across countries. As before, we begin by plotting a graph to explore the relationship between the two variables, and then we formalize the work by estimating a regression equation of the following form:

$$t\_salary = c + d \cdot usk\_salary$$

where *t_salary* refers to average teacher salary, and *usk_salary* refers to the average salary of unskilled labor in industry. To save time these steps

10

have been accomplished for you. The relevant regression coefficients appear below.

$$(4) \qquad t\_salary = 0.29 + 1.51 \times usk\_salary$$
$$(t = 24.9)$$

Take a moment now to review the graph and regression results and comment briefly on them.

Comment on relationship between the salaries of teachers and unskilled labor:

_____

_____

_____

As before, we use the estimated regression equation to predict teacher salaries based on the salaries of unskilled labor. Labeling the result as pt_salary_2, we can compute an index of the costliness of teachers relative to the domestic labor market context ($index_2$), as follows:

$$(5) \qquad index_2 = \frac{t\_salary - pt\_salary_2}{t\_salary} \times 1,000$$

This index is similar to equation (4), except that it focuses on the domestic labor market. To save time the value of $index_2$ has been computed for you. Take a moment now to inspect the result, and then go on to the next step.

Step 6   Here we will consolidate all of the analyses accomplished thus far to evaluate their implications for policy development regarding teacher pay. As a prelude to analyzing the results for the full set of 28 countries, consider the results for the five countries shown in table 10.B.3.11. We focus on the two indexes computed in the preceding two steps. Recall that both indexes refer to the percentage of deviation in teacher pay in a country from some benchmark. For $index_1$ the benchmark is the pay expected on the basis of the relationship between teacher pay and per capita GNP, given the country's per capita GNP. For $index_2$ the benchmark is the pay expected on the basis of the relationship between teacher pay and that of unskilled labor, given the pay of the latter workers. As explained previously, $index_1$ may be interpreted as a measure of the general level of teacher pay, whereas $index_2$ may be viewed as a measure of teacher pay relative to domestic labor market conditions.

10

Table 10.B.3.11: Indexes of Relative Teacher Pay in Selected Countries

Country	$Index_1{}^a$	$Index_2{}^b$
C7	+41.9	−11.8
C20	−75.1	+36.6
C21	+31.2	+17.5
C24	+57.9	−3.7
C25	−61.5	+9.3

a. Teacher pay relative to international patterns.
b. Teacher pay relative to domestic context.

Review now the results in table 10.B.3.11. Try putting into words what they reveal about teacher pay in the various countries. As an example, consider C7. The value of $index_1$ is +41.9, which implies that teacher salaries are generally much higher than is consistent with international experience; $index_2$ on the other hand has a value of −11.8, which implies that in the domestic labor market, teachers' pay relates less favorably to the pay of unskilled workers than is expected on the basis of international experience. In combination, these results suggest that although teachers in C7 are relatively well paid compared with their peers in other countries, their standing in the domestic market may not be all that favorable. It may not be surprising in this context to encounter difficulties in teacher recruitment. Policy intervention within the education sector may be of limited effect because the problem is more generally one of overall economic policy.

Comment on the pattern of teacher salaries in C20, C21, C24, and C25, and on the implications for potential policy development in each setting. For this purpose you might find it helpful to use the plot of $index_1$ and $index_2$ in the Excel worksheet.

Comment: _____

_____

_____

_____

Comparing the Relationship between Schooling Inputs and Outcomes

The relationship between schooling inputs and outcomes is an issue of perennial interest in education. Outcomes may refer to the performance

10

of individual students or, more broadly, to the system's performance as reflected, for example, in the average level of student learning, the proportion of the eligible population benefiting from school services, the degree of equity in the distribution of learning opportunities across population groups, and so on. Because there are many ways to deploy resources and organize the education system, the relationship between schooling inputs and any of these outcomes depends on how well the system operates.

To evaluate the issue typically requires in-depth evaluation of alternative ways to deliver education services. Such studies often require expensive investment in data collection, and they invariably take time to complete. As a complement to the detailed studies, we can exploit cross-country analysis to evaluate an education system's efficiency. The approach has two main advantages over the detailed analyses: the requisite data are often easy to compile from published sources, and the analysis is usually simple to accomplish. As cautioned elsewhere, however, the lack of detail in the analysis has its drawbacks. An important limitation is that the results have only suggestive value, signaling the existence of potential problems of efficiency in an education system rather than offering a definitive diagnosis of such problems.

In the exercise below we focus on two dimensions of overall system performance: a quantity dimension as measured by the expected number of years of schooling for children who pass through the system; and a quality dimension as measured by the average score of students on international achievement tests. We will relate these outcome measures to the input of resources in the system. As an indicator of the latter variable we use public spending on education as a percentage of the GNP. This statistic obviously does not include all the resources invested in education because private spending on education can be substantial. The indicator is nonetheless relevant in policy analysis because it enables us to compare how effectively countries translate public spending on education into schooling outcomes, either directly or through the catalytic influence of public spending on the education sector as a whole.

Problem 4

You are asked in this problem to perform a comparative analysis of the relationship between public spending on education and the expected years of schooling of children who pass through the education system. Follow the steps below to accomplish the analysis.

Step 1   Tab over now to the worksheet titled "problem 4," where you will find the data for our 28 countries on the two variables, expected years of schooling (*expyrs*) and public spending on education as a percentage of the GNP (*ed_gnp*). Plot the relationship between these variables, with *expyrs* on the vertical axis and *ed_gnp* on the horizontal axis, and comment on the pattern in the graph. If you do not wish to plot the graph, use the one provided in the Excel worksheet to make your comments.

Comment on the plot of *expyrs* and *ed_gnp*:

_____

_____

_____

_____

Step 2   Your task here is to evaluate the relationship between *expyrs* and *ed_gnp* and other variables, using regression analysis. To save time two regressions have been completed for you and the results appear below. (For those wishing to perform the regressions, simply scroll down to the part of the worksheet marked "step 2," where the relevant data can be found.) The first regression equation uses only *ed_gnp* as a regressor, whereas the second includes an additional regressor, the natural logarithm of per capita GNP, *lnpc_gnp*. Review the results and comment briefly on them, noting other variables that might have been added to the model.

(6) $$expyrs = 8.04 + 0.25 \times ed\_gnp \qquad R^2 = 0.03$$
$$(t = 0.89)$$

(7) $$expyrs = -3.35 + 0.12 \times ed\_gnp + 1.73 \times lnpc\_gnp \qquad R^2 = 0.39$$
$$(t = 0.52) \qquad\qquad (t = 3.88)$$

Comment on regression results:

_____

_____

_____

_____

Step 3   Your task here is to compute an index of efficiency in coverage based on the data for the 28 countries. The purpose of computing the index is not simply to add precision to the analysis, but to combine it with a similar analysis on educational quality to shed light on quantity-quality tradeoffs in education. This will be done in a later problem. As

10

preparation you are asked in this step to compute the index of efficiency in coverage. The main purpose of the exercise is to clarify the underlying logic and mechanics of the calculation.

Scroll down now to the part of the worksheet marked "step 3" where, for convenience, you will find the plot of *expyrs* against *ed_gnp* again. Note the location of the following countries on the graph: C11, C5, C13, C8, C4, C1, and C17. All of these countries share the common distinction of having the highest *expyrs* in the sample, given their level of public spending on education. They therefore describe an empirical efficiency frontier that can be used as a benchmark to assess other countries' performance. To do this systematically we need first to fit a regression equation to the data to describe the frontier defined by the seven countries. The following equation provides an adequate fit for this purpose:

$$(8) \qquad \qquad expyrs_{frontier} = \frac{-20.75}{ed\_gnp} + 19.0$$

From this equation we can compute an index of inefficiency in coverage (*index*$_{cov}$) for each country, based on how far it is located from the efficiency frontier. Specifically, the index is defined as follows:

$$(9) \qquad \qquad index_{cov} = expyrs - \left(\frac{-20.75}{ed\_gnp} + 19.0 \right)$$

The term in parentheses comes from equation (5) above. Thus, *index*$_{cov}$ is interpreted as a country's shortfall in coverage relative to the best-performing countries with the same level of public spending on education.

Now compute *index*$_{cov}$ for the countries in the sample and enter your answer in the column colored yellow in the current worksheet (in the block marked "step 3").

Problem 5

In this problem you are asked to compare student learning outcomes across countries in the sample. The requisite data are available only for countries that participated in international studies on achievement. By combining these data with information on public spending on education we can compare countries' efficiency in transforming public resources into learning outcomes.

The procedures for this problem are essentially the same as those in the previous problem; to save time, all of the relevant graphs and computations have been completed for you. Tab over now to the worksheet titled "problem 5," where you will find the results corresponding to the following steps.

10

Step 1   Plot learning outcomes (*achieve*) against public spending on education as a share of GNP (*ed_gnp*).

Step 2   Identify countries on the efficiency frontier (here the countries are C2 and C17).

Step 3   Estimate the efficiency frontier by fitting the following function to the data for C2 and C17:

(10)
$$achieve_{frontier} = \frac{-95.07}{ed\_gnp} + 81.24$$

Step 4   Compute an index of pedagogical efficiency (*index_ach*) for each country, the index being defined as follows:

(11)
$$index_{ach} = achieve - \left(\frac{-95.07}{ed\_gnp} + 81.24 \right)$$

Review the results in the worksheet and comment briefly on them. You may write your comments in the spaces below or directly onto the Excel worksheet.

Comment on results: _____

_____

_____

_____

_____

Problem 6

In this problem you are asked to bring together analysis of the two dimensions of schooling outcomes considered above—educational coverage and student achievement. It requires you to consider the relationship between these variables from two perspectives: without adjusting for differences in public spending on education, and after adjusting for such differences. To save time the two graphs for this exercise have been completed for you. Your task is to examine them for their implications regarding the sample countries' performance in terms of coverage and learning outcomes.

Tab over now to the worksheet titled "problem 6," where you will find the two graphs. The first is simply a plot of *expyrs* (*x*-axis) against *achieve* (*y*-axis). There are four quadrants in the graph, marked off by the red lines corresponding to the sample averages of the two variables. The second graph is a plot of $index_{ach}$ (*x*-axis) against $index_{cov}$ (*y*-axis), defined in equations (9) and (11) above. Briefly, these indexes measure the extent to which a country falls short on coverage and learning outcome relative to

10

the best-performing country with a comparable level of public spending on education as a share of GNP. As in the other graph, the red lines denote the sample averages for the two indexes. Two blue lines also appear in the graph, representing zero deviation from the efficiency frontiers in coverage and learning outcome. Thus, the farther a country deviates from the blue lines, the more inefficient it is in transforming its public spending on education into one or both dimensions of education outcomes considered here.

Review these graphs simultaneously and compare the locations of countries that share the same quadrant in the first graph and note their positions in the second graph. Compare, for example, the following groups: C17 with C20, C21 with C18, and C4 with C13. As a matter of interest, compare also countries in different quadrants in the first figure—for example, C4 with C17, and C19 with C17. What conclusions emerge from these comparisons to inform policy dialogue? What implications do they hold regarding possible directions for further country-specific analysis and research? Answer these questions from the perspective of, say, countries C21, C20, C4, and C19.

Comment on policy conclusions and research directions:

_____

_____

_____

_____

_____

Part C: Compiling Country Profiles
from Comparative Analysis

Each of the various pieces of comparative analysis discussed so far offers useful information on some aspect of an education system's performance. We can consolidate many of the results to generate country profiles in comparative perspective. Such profiles are a concise means for signaling the main policy issues that warrant close attention in each country. They are thus a good instrument for developing policy dialogue strategies, as well as for identifying possible priorities for future analytical work in the sector.

For the purpose of this module we focus on a limited number of policy domains in the comparative analysis: overall system performance,

10

performance across subsectors in education, and performance within primary education. In actual practice, other domains obviously can be included, depending on the specific focus of the analysis.

Problem 1

Your task here is simply to review and manipulate the data that we will use to construct the profile of country X in comparative perspective. In table 10.C.1.12 consider the data for the country as well as the corresponding averages for its comparators. Notice that under each of the three policy domains we focus on specific aspects of policy choices or schooling outcomes (column 1), using well-defined indicators to represent their main features (column 2).

Step 1

Take a moment now to scan the rows in these columns in the table, noting the following logic in their presentation:
(a) The data focus first on aggregate public spending and general schooling outcomes measured in terms of coverage, student learning, and distribution of spending.
(b) They then shift to the structure of coverage and spending across levels of education.
(c) They zoom in on primary education, which in this example is the level of education of concern to policymakers.

Step 2

Retrieve the Excel file titled "Comparative_Policy_Analysis_Ex3" and check that you are in the worksheet named "problem 1." You should now have a copy of table 10.C.1.12 on your screen. For each indicator, complete the column colored yellow by dividing country X's indicator with the average for its comparators. The result is an easy way to standardize the comparisons. Review your results and comment briefly on them as appropriate.

Comment on results: _____

_____

_____

_____

_____

_____

10

Table 10.C.1.12: Country X's Educational Profile in Comparative Perspective

Policy domain	Definition of indicator	Data on indicator		
		Country X	Reference group	Ratio of X to reference group
Overall system performance				
Public spending	Public spending as a percentage of GNP	3.8	3.9	0.97
Coverage	Expected years of schooling[a]	9.7	7.9	1.22
Student learning	Average score on international tests	32.2	50.1	0.64
Inequity	Index of inequity in public spending[b]	0.44	0.34	1.29
Performance across subsectors				
Coverage by level of education				
Overall	Expected years of schooling[a]	9.7	7.9	1.22
Primary	Gross primary enrollment ratio	117.0	108.0	1.08
Secondary	Gross secondary enrollment ratio	42.2	39.4	1.07
Higher	Gross higher education enrollment ratio	11.1	7.2	1.56
Public spending by level of education				
Overall spending per student	Average spending per student at the three levels	1.24	1.15	1.08
Spending per primary student	Spending per primary pupil/per capita GNP	0.09	0.14	0.64
Spending per secondary student	Spending per secondary student/per capita GNP	0.29	0.29	1.00
Spending per higher education student	Spending per higher education student/per capita GNP	2.27	1.52	1.49
Primary education performance				
Student flow				
Waste	Percentage of public resources lost via repetition and dropout	36.2	22.1	1.64
Access rate to grade one	Percentage of relevant age group entering grade one	94.0	91.3	1.03
Survival rate within the cycle	Percentage of first graders reaching grade five	61.5	75.4	0.82
Transition rate to secondary cycle	Percentage of pupils leaving primary school who enter secondary school	75.1	64.1	1.17
Inputs for primary schooling				
Resource intensity per pupil	Public spending per pupil/per capita GNP	0.09	0.14	0.64
Intensity of teacher inputs	Ratio of pupils to teachers	51.4	34.1	1.51
Intensity of time input	Annual hours of instruction	825.0	986.0	0.84
Costliness of teachers	Average teacher salary as ratio of per capita GNP	4.3	3.1	1.39

a. Refers to the school-age population.

b. As measured by the Gini coefficient associated with the distribution of public spending on education across levels. The coefficient ranges in value from zero to one, with large numbers representing a high degree of inequality.

Problem 2

Using the data in table 10.C.1.12, comment on the following: (a) the current strengths and weaknesses of country X's education system, (b) policy issues warranting attention in developing a policy dialogue with the government of country X, and (c) priorities in a program of analytical work on education in the country. Follow the instructions below to develop your write-up.

Step 1

The mass of data in table 10.C.1.12 may be more convenient to view using the development diamond format first introduced in part A. Tab over now to the worksheet titled "problem 2," where you will find diamonds for each of the five sets of indicators in table 10.C.1.12. Take a moment to scan all five graphs and then briefly describe each of them in the CD-ROM.

Step 2

Using the above description as a basis, proceed now to identify possible directions for developing a policy dialogue strategy with the government. What information is missing from the current analysis that appears to warrant specific attention in future data collection efforts? What topics would seem justified to include in a forthcoming program of analytical work? What limitations might you alert readers to regarding the conclusions from country X's educational profile?

Annex: Data Issues in Comparative Policy Analysis in Education

Comparative analysis in education is relatively easy to accomplish. The data requirements are usually modest and the computations involved are typically uncomplicated. To evaluate investment priorities in education, for example, the preferred yardstick is social rates of return, but the paucity of estimates of the externalities to education makes it all but impossible to compute these rates. In such situations the comparative approach can offer some guidance. For example, if the enrollment ratio for a given level of education is substantially below that of other comparable countries, the comparison signals the *possibility* of underinvestment at that level of education. This possibility clearly needs to be confirmed through additional analysis, but the comparative analysis has already performed a valuable service simply by signaling the issue for further investigation.

10

The same reasons that make comparative analysis relatively easy to accomplish also account for its limitations. Cross-country or cross-region data are usually readily available, but they refer to averages that are likely to mask substantial variation within the country or region. Another problem arises from differences in the definition of the education indicators used in the analysis. Such differences often persist despite the best efforts of data-collecting agencies to standardize them. Education finance indicators are especially prone to error in this regard, in part because it is difficult to track the flow of funds in the education system. Even indicators relating to physical quantities are not free of the problem. Primary education, for example, can refer to five years of schooling in one country and to eight years in another, thus bringing into question the validity of straightforward comparisons of primary enrollment ratios in the two countries.

Although data flaws are admittedly an inescapable handicap in comparative analysis, they do not necessarily invalidate the results. Rather they call for caution both in how the data are used and in how conclusions are drawn from the analysis. Inaccuracies in education finance data, for example, imply that comparisons of consolidated indicators (for example, overall spending on education) are likely to be more reliable than comparisons of disaggregated indicators (for example, proportion of spending on pedagogical materials). In other words, the validity of comparative analysis deteriorates as the degree of disaggregation in the underlying data rises.

With regard to drawing conclusions from comparative analysis, two precautions are worth emphasizing. First, because comparisons reveal only relative performance it is invalid to conclude *on their basis alone* that countries automatically should aim to bring their lagging indicators into line with those of their comparators. Other countries' indicators do not automatically define optimal targets for the country of interest. This having been said, it is nonetheless worth recognizing that if the country's indicators deviate substantially from those of its comparators, the pattern does represent a warning bell that it would be wise to heed with further analysis in policy development. The second precaution stems from the fact that group averages tend to hide disparities within the group. Thus, to the extent that such disparities exist and matter for policy development, the analyses based on aggregate regional or country indicators obviously should be supplemented with analyses based on a more detailed breakdown of the data.

The government dominates employment in the formal labor market, which implies that wages are more likely to be influenced by administrative decisions than by market forces. Because wages have a tenuous link

10

to labor productivity, rate-of-return calculations based on such data are an unreliable guide to investment priorities in education. An additional problem is that even if wages do reflect labor productivity, rate-of-return calculations assume that the structure of wages will remain unchanged over time. If the wage structure changes in the course of economic development—as is likely in a rapidly changing transition economy—the results again would be unreliable for assessing priorities in the sector.

Endnotes

1. For simplicity of exposition this module uses cross-country data in the exercises.

2. Here the country group average is used to indicate general tendencies in the indicator of interest. If the distribution of the indicator is not skewed, the average serves as an adequate reference point for comparisons. If that is not the case, a more appropriate benchmark would be the median. This statistic is defined as the value of the indicator that would separate the observations into two subgroups of equal size, with the values of the indicator in one group exceeding the median, and the values in the other group lying below it.

3. The full set of results in the format of table 10.A.1.4 can be found in the Excel worksheet.

4. Computing the average across the three levels of education is perhaps the easiest method for defining an index of the overall intensity of public spending per pupil in the country of interest. Another way to define such an index is to take deviations in spending levels from the corresponding country group averages, calibrated in units of standard deviation, and then averaging the deviations across the three levels of education. A third method is to use factor analysis to develop an index reflecting the common element of intensity in spending per pupil across the three levels of schooling. The data for our 28-country sample indicate that all three methods yield indexes that are highly correlated, with all of the correlations exceeding 0.95. Given the simplicity of the first method, it is the only one we use here.

10

Appendix A: Regression Analysis

Regression analysis is a common tool for examining the relationship between two or more variables. It involves estimating an equation with the outcome variable of interest (for example, academic performance) defined as a function of the factors expected to influence it. The results are useful in policy work because they quantify the strength of the relationships involved, thereby providing a basis (along with cost considerations) for prioritizing policy interventions. This appendix gives a brief overview of the main concepts behind the technique and the statistical outputs typically associated with it—the regression coefficients, the R^2 statistic, and the t-statistic.[1] Steps for performing regression analysis in Excel are outlined on page 284.

The Simple Two-Variable Linear Model

Suppose we have data on the height and weight of a sample of eight men (table 1). An obvious way to describe the relationship between these variables is to plot them on a graph (figure 1). Casual observation of the plot suggests that taller men tend to be heavier. We could draw an upward-sloping line through the scatter plot, as is done in figure 1, to represent the positive relationship between height and weight.

Explanation of the Regression Equation and Its Coefficients

The line in figure 1 can be expressed as an equation. The general form of straight-line equation with two variables, X and Y, can be written as $Y = \alpha + \beta \cdot X$, where α is the intercept of the line and β is its slope. For any set of data, we can use regression analysis to estimate the values of α and β. The estimates—known as the regression coefficients—then allow us to specify the relationship between X and Y for the population represented by the data set.

Table 1: Data on Height and Weight for Eight Men

Observation	1	2	3	4	5	6	7	8	Mean	Standard deviation
Height (cm)	164	186	173	158	174	191	182	171	174.9	11.06
Weight (kg)	64.2	76.3	72.8	59.4	78.0	76.2	80.1	65.2	71.5	7.58

Figure 1: Plot of Height against Weight

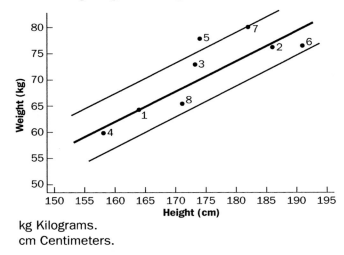

kg Kilograms.
cm Centimeters.

To see how the technique works, consider again our height and weight example. In figure 1 we have instinctively drawn the line going through the scatter plot, with observations on both sides of it, as the best way to represent the relationship between the two variables. The analytical equivalent of this operation is to minimize the square of the difference between the line and each of the observations; that is, minimize $S = \Sigma_j [W_j - (\hat{a} + \hat{b} \bullet H_j)]^2$, where $\hat{a}$ and $\hat{b}$ are the estimated values of α and β, respectively.

It can be shown that the values of $\hat{a}$ and $\hat{b}$ that minimize the expression are given as follows:

$$\hat{a} = \overline{W} - \hat{b} \bullet \overline{H}$$

$$\hat{b} = \frac{\Sigma_j (H_j - \overline{H}) \bullet (W_j - \overline{W})}{\Sigma_j (H_j - \overline{H})^2}$$

where $\overline{H}$ and $\overline{W}$ are, respectively, the mean of height and weight of the sample. Given our data set, $\hat{a} = -28.54$ and $\hat{b} = 0.572$, so our equation is estimated as:

$$W = -28.54 + 0.572 \times H$$

The value of $\hat{b}$ measures the estimated change in weight (W) corresponding to a one-unit change in height. The interpretation is easily seen by comparing the weights of two men whose heights are Z centimeters (cm) and $Z + 1$ cm, respectively. The weight of the shorter man would be $\hat{a} + (\hat{b} \times Z)$, whereas that of the taller man would be $\hat{a} + [\hat{b} \times (Z + 1)]$. Thus the difference in weight between them would simply be $\hat{b}$. In our data set, height is measured in centimeters and weight in kilograms, so $\hat{b}$ is expressed in kilograms per centimeter. The value of $\hat{b}$ in our example is 0.572, which implies that a 1-centimeter increase in height is associated with an estimated increase of 0.572 kilogram (kg) in weight.

Definition of the R^2 Statistic

The R^2 statistic is a standard output in regression analysis and reflects the overall tightness of the relationship between the dependent variable and its regressors (that is, the variables on the right-hand side of the equation). In our example, it would indicate how accurately height predicts a man's weight.

To understand what the statistic means, we need to examine its construction. Continuing with the height and weight example, for each man j in the sample, we observe that his weight W_j can be expressed as the sum of two components:

1. The average weight associated with men of the same height, as estimated by our regression equation
2. An error term equal to the difference between his actual height and the average predicted by the estimated equation.

We can express the decomposition more formally as follows:

$$\text{Actual weight} = \text{Estimated weight} + \text{Error term}$$

$$W_j = \hat{a} + \hat{b} \bullet H_j + e_j$$

To illustrate with a numerical example, consider the third man in our sample. On average, men as tall as he is (173 cm) weigh 70.42 kg ($= -28.54 + 0.572 \times 173$). His actual weight is 72.8 kg, which implies that he is over the average by 2.38 kg ($= 72.8 - 70.42$). Therefore, the man's actual weight is the average weight of men his height (70.42 kg) plus an error term (2.38).

Taking the variance on both sides of the equation, we have:

$$Var(W_j) = Var(\hat{a} + \hat{b} \bullet H_j) + Var(e_j) + 2Cov[(\hat{a} + \hat{b} \bullet H_j) \bullet e_j]$$

The covariance of H_j and e_j is nil by construction, on the assumption that H_j varies independently of e_j. We can then simplify the variance of W_j as follows:

$$Var(W_j) = Var(\hat{a} + \hat{b} \bullet H_j) + Var(e_j)$$

$$= \hat{b}^2 Var(H_j) + Var(e_j)$$

The first term on the right represents the variance accounted for by the explanatory variable (height in this example) while the second is simply the variance of the error term. Dividing both sides of the equation by Var (W_j), we obtain:

$$I = \frac{\hat{b}^2 Var(H_j)}{Var(W_j)} + \frac{Var(e_j)}{Var(W_j)}$$

The expression $\hat{b}^2 Var(H_j)/Var(W_j)$ can thus be interpreted as the proportion of variance in W explained by the variance in H. It appears routinely as the R^2 statistic in computer printouts of regression analysis. The values of Var(H_j) and Var(W_j) can be computed directly from the data, so once $\hat{b}$ has been estimated the value of R^2 is easy to compute. In our example, $R^2 = 0.696 (= 0.572^2 \times 11.06^2)/7.58^2$.

By definition R^2 is constrained to range from zero to one. A value of zero means that H has no influence on W, while a value of unity means that H predicts W with perfect accuracy (that is, all the observations in the sample would lie on a line in $H \times W$ space). Between these extremes the greater the value of R^2 the tighter the relationship between W and H.

Definition of the *t*-Statistic

Another standard output of regression analysis is the *t*-statistic associated with each of the coefficient estimates. To better understand what the statistic means, consider again our two-variable example. For each pair of men in the sample, we can compute b, the change in weight per unit of height, by dividing the difference in weight by the corresponding difference in height. We then will have as many values of b as there are pairs of men in the sample. As a random variable, b has a mean and a variance (as well as a standard deviation because it is simply the square root of the variance). Its mean is $\hat{b}$, the coefficient estimate that we computed earlier. The variance of b is given by:[2]

$$Var(b) = \frac{Var(e_j)}{\sum_j (H_j - \overline{H})^2}$$

$$= \frac{(1/n - 2) \times \sum_j [Y_j - (\hat{a} + \hat{b} \bullet H_j)]^2}{\sum_j (H_j - \overline{H})^2}$$

where n is the number of observations in the sample.

Assuming that b is normally distributed, we can compute the ratio between b and its standard deviation to obtain the t-statistic associated with it. The t-statistic follows a student's t-distribution with $(n - 2)$ degrees of freedom and is used in what is known as the "null hypothesis test" or t-test to evaluate the statistical significance of the b estimate.

Returning to our height and weight example, our estimate of b is positive, which suggests that an increase in height generally is associated with an increase in weight. The t-test is designed to tell us how much confidence we can place in the proposition that H (the regressor) affects W (the dependent variable) in the direction implied by the sign on b.

To understand the concept behind the t-test, consider figure 2, which shows the probability density function b, the ratio of differences in weight to differences in height, for all possible pairs of observations in the sample. The shaded part of the figure, which is defined by the area under the curve to the left of the y-axis, represents the probability of encountering a negative value of b, whereas its mean value, $\hat{b}$, is positive. The farther the y-axis is from $\hat{b}$ and the smaller the shaded area, the less often a negative value of b will be encountered, and the more confident we can be in rejecting the null hypothesis that H has no influence on W (that is, that the value of b is zero).

The distance of the y-axis from $\hat{b}$ (which is simply b itself because by definition the axis passes through the origin) bears a directional relationship to the area under the curve. The t-statistic, which is defined as the ratio of $\hat{b}$ to the standard deviation of b, therefore also relates directly to the area under the curve. The greater the value of the t-statistic, the smaller the probability of encountering values of b with a sign opposite to that of $\hat{b}$, and therefore the more confident we can be in rejecting the null hypothesis.

Figure 2: Distribution of Estimates of b

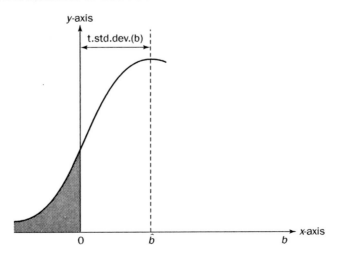

For any value of the *t*-statistic, we can look up the corresponding area under the curve in a statistical table of the *t*-distribution. To test the hypothesis, the confidence levels are set by common practice at 1, 5, and 10 percent, and the corresponding critical values of the *t*-statistic for samples with at least 30 observations are as follows:

$t = 1.63$ statistical confidence at the 10 percent level

$t = 1.96$ statistical confidence at the 5 percent level

$t = 2.70$ statistical confidence at the 1 percent level.[3]

Suppose the *t*-statistic for a coefficient estimate is 2.1. We say that the coefficient is statistically significant at the 5 percent level (because 2.1 exceeds 1.96 but is smaller than 2.70), which means that no more than 5 out of 100 observations from the distribution of b are expected to be opposite in sign to $\hat{b}$. We can be relatively confident, therefore, that the estimated coefficient is statistically different from zero.

Application of the Regression Results

After estimating our regression model, we can apply it in impact assessment and simulations. To continue with our height and weight example, we can use the estimated regression equation to project the weight of men who are 180 centimeters tall. The answer, 74.42 kg, is obtained by substituting 180 into our regression equation: $-28.54 + 0.572 \times 180 = 74.42$ kg.

We should stress that the estimated equation yields valid simulations or projections only in the range represented by the data on which they are based. Thus, the answer above would apply only to men and, among men, only to those from the same era or racial group as the eight men in the sample. To simulate the weight of women or of men from another century or racial group would require new regression estimates using data from the relevant populations.

A second point is that the simulation produces "midpoint estimates" that lie exactly on the estimated regression line. The actual weight of men of a given height is likely to vary around the regression line. The weight predicted from the regression equation is the mean of a distribution with the same dispersion as the error term in the regression model. This means that the predicted weight is a band around the regression line, with the point on the line being the midpoint of the predicted range. The closer the W is to 1, the smaller the variance of the error term and the narrower the band of the predicted weight.

Recall that the variance of the error term is given as follows:

$$\text{Var}(e_j) = \frac{\sum_j [Y_j - (\hat{a} + \hat{b} \bullet H_j)]^2}{n - 2}$$

Applying this formula to the data in our height and weight example, we obtain the variance of e as 20.3 (which implies a standard deviation of 4.51). We then can present our simulation of the weight of men who are 180 centimeters tall in terms of a range around the average, or midpoint estimate, of 72.42 kg. At one standard deviation from the average, the range would be (74.42 +/– 4.51) kg. Assuming a normal distribution in the error term, 68 percent of men who are 180 centimeters tall would fall in this weight range, whereas 16 percent would be heavier and 16 percent lighter.

Multivariate Linear Models

To enrich our two-variable model we can include other influences on weight—for example, gender, daily caloric intake, and amount of physical exercise. We can write the multivariate model as: Weight = f (Height, Gender, Caloric intake, Physical exercise).

Conceptually, the multivariate model is not much different from the simple two-variable model: both attempt to relate a given variable to factors that are thought to influence it. The estimation procedure and the regression output also are similar (although estimating the multivariate model is much more demanding and almost always requires the use of a computer). The output consists of coefficient estimates for each of the right-hand-side variables, the corresponding t-statistics, and the R^2 statistic. The regression coefficients have the same interpretation as those in the two-variable model, and the t-statistic is used in the same way to evaluate the confidence we can place in the influence of each regressor on the dependent variable. The R^2 statistic reflects the share of variance in the dependent variable jointly accounted for by the variance in all of the regressors in the model.

The multivariate model is richer and therefore more often encountered in policy work than is the simple two-variable model. Two aspects of multivariate regression analysis warrant further elaboration. The first aspect relates to the use of qualitative or categorical explanatory variables in the model. The second aspect arises in the context of interpreting or using the regression coefficient estimates under the "other things being equal" assumption. (Categorical dependent variables are more complicated and will be discussed in a later section.)

Categorical Explanatory Variables

There are two types of regressors: continuous variables, such as height in our simple model above, or class size or pupil-textbook ratio in an education context; and categorical or qualitative variables, such as gender, ethnic or language group, place of residence (urban or rural area), VAX of school attended (public or private sector), specific school attended (for example, Wyngate, Wood Acres, or Green Tree), and the teaching method to which a child has been exposed (method A or method B). We can use continuous variables in regression estimation as they appear in the data set, and interpret the coefficient estimate of such regressors as the change in the dependent variable associated with a unit change in the corresponding regressor. Categorical variables, on the other hand, typically need preparation before we apply them in the regression analysis, and we interpret their coefficient estimates in a slightly different way.

The most common practice is to define for each categorical variable a set of dummy variables to represent all but one of the possible states of the categorical variable. For gender, as an example, there are two possible states—male or female. We therefore include one dummy variable for gender in the regression. Suppose we call our dummy variable "GIRL" and define it as having a value of one for all of the girls in the sample and a value of zero for all of the boys. Its coefficient would be the average impact that being a girl has on the dependent variable, relative to the impact of being a boy. Thus, if the dependent variable is test scores, a coefficient of +1.4 with a t-statistic of 2.1 on GIRL implies that girls outperform boys by an average of 1.4 points, and the gap is statistically significant at the 5 percent confidence level. As an alternative we could name our dummy variable "BOY" and define it as having a value of one for all of the boys and zero for all of the girls. The coefficient then would be −1.4 with a t-statistic of 2.1, which implies that boys perform, on average, 1.4 points more poorly than do girls, and the gap is statistically significant at the 5 percent confidence level.

As another example, consider a qualitative variable with four possible categories: regions A, B, C, and D. We create three dummy variables for inclusion in the regression equation, and call them "REGION-A," "REGION-B," and "REGION-C," for example. We define each of them to take on a value of one for observations in the indicated region and a value of zero otherwise. "REGION-D" is the reference region because the dummy variable that might have been created for it is omitted from the regression. Assuming again that the dependent variable is test scores, a coefficient of –3.6 with a *t*-statistic of 2.4 on REGION-A implies that children in region A perform less well than those in region D, the reference region, by an average of 3.6 points, and the gap is statistically significant at the 5 percent confidence level.

If the coefficient estimate had been +1.5 with a *t*-statistic of 0.9, we could conclude instead that there is no significant difference in the test scores of children from the two regions. We also can use the coefficient estimates to compare test scores among children from regions A, B, and C relative to each other rather than to region D. For example, a coefficient estimate of 4.9 on REGION-B and 2.1 on REGION-C implies that children in region B outperform those in region C by an average of 2.8 points (= 4.9 – 2.1). We can test the statistical significance of this difference by calculating the relevant *t*-statistic using standard regression software.

Meaning of "Other Things Being Equal"

The coefficient estimates in multivariate regression equations typically are interpreted as the impact of a given variable on the outcome variable, "other things being equal." What does the phrase mean, and why is it important in policy analysis?

The question is best answered through an example. Returning to our height and weight regression, suppose our data set contains both men and women. The sample mean height and weight appear in table 2, and indicate that, on average, men in the sample weigh 15.4 kg (= 74.2 – 58.8) more than women.

We use the data to estimate an equation in which weight is expressed as a function of height and as the dummy variable "FEMALE," which is defined to take on the value of one for all of the women in the sample and zero for all of the men. Suppose we obtain the following results:

$$W = 27.51 + 0.59 \times H - 8.32 \times FEMALE \qquad R^2 = 0.78$$
$$(t = 3.2) \quad (t = 2.7)$$

The estimate of the height variable suggests that, on average, a 1-centimeter increase in height adds 0.59 kilogram to weight. It is more interesting for our purpose that the coefficient estimate of the dummy variable implies that women are, on average, 8.32 kilograms lighter in

Table 2: Mean Height and Weight in a Sample of Men and Women

Observation	Men	Women
Height (cm)	176	1€4
Weight (kg)	74.2	58.8

weight than men. Why does this figure differ from the earlier calculation based on the sample means alone? The answer is that, whereas the figure reflects the mean difference between men and women, *assuming they have the same height,* the earlier calculation based on sample means includes this difference as well as that associated with the fact that men are, on average, taller than women. The former result corresponds to the difference in weight, net of the difference in height between the two groups, and the latter corresponds to the gross difference associated with the differences in both gender and height.

To elaborate on the explanation, consider figure 3. Based on the estimated regression equation we can draw two lines representing the relationship between height and weight, one for each gender group. Both lines have the same slope (0.59), which is given by the coefficient estimate on the height variable in the regression. These parallel lines, however, differ in their intercepts by 8.32 kg, according to the coefficient estimate of "FEMALE." On the graph, M identifies the mean height and weight of men in the sample and F identifies those parameters for women. We can see that the gross difference of 15.4 kg in weight between the two groups consists of two components: one associated with gender alone, and one associated with the difference in height between the two genders. Given our regression results, the former component is estimated to be 8.32 kg. For the second component, we note that, on average, men are 12 cm taller (= 176 – 164), which implies that they would be heavier by 7.08 kg (= 12 × 0.59). The two components thus add up to the gross difference of 15.4 kg between men and women.

Figure 3: Relating Weight to Height among Men and Women

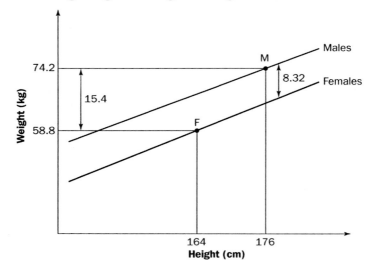

In that example the coefficient on the dummy variable represents the net impact on weight of being a woman, holding height constant. In an expanded model with regressors in addition to H and *FEMALE*, the coefficient would be interpreted as the impact of being a women, "other things being equal." The regression results therefore allow us to isolate the impact of individual factors on the outcome variable being analyzed. This feature of multivariate regression analysis is what makes it so useful in policy evaluation.

Extensions to the Classical Linear Model

The models discussed so far share two common features: they involve linear equations, and the regressors enter the equations additively. Although sometimes appropriate, these features may need to be modified as elaborated below.

Definition of Nonlinear Relationships

In education, as in other fields, the dependent variable in the regression equation may not respond proportionally to changes in the factors that influence it. The relationship between the variable and a particular regressor may exhibit the following patterns: below a certain threshold the dependent variable remains unchanged, regardless of changes in the regressor; beyond the threshold it increases at an increasing or diminishing rate in response to changes in the regressor. The marginal impact of the regressor on the dependent variable therefore varies according to its initial level. Under these circumstances a linear specification would misrepresent the actual relationship between the two variables and likely would distort the policy implications.

To show this point let's consider a regression to estimate the impact of teachers' years of formal schooling on student learning in lower secondary education. We probably can assume that illiterate teachers would be incompetent to teach the curriculum to their pupils, as would teachers with one, three, or five years of schooling. Indeed, up to some minimum threshold, increases in teachers' years of schooling are unlikely to affect student learning. In other words, below the threshold the two variables do not relate proportionally to each other.

Above the threshold the relationship is likely to be positive, with student learning responding in the same direction as changes in teachers' years of schooling. This positive response is unlikely to persist indefinitely, however, as teachers' years of schooling continue to increase. Past a certain point the teachers are overqualified—that is, they are equipped

Figure 4: Relation between Student Learning and Teacher's Years of Schooling

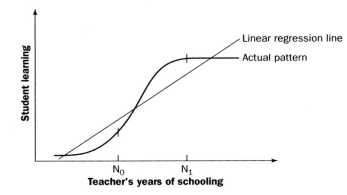

to teach a far more sophisticated curriculum than that for lower second-ary education. As teachers at this level, the holders of a doctorate degree, for example, probably would be only marginally more effective (if at all) than would the holders of a bachelor's degree. Thus, beyond the new threshold student learning again may not respond proportionately to increases in teachers' years of schooling.

If we specify a linear regression equation to represent the impact of teacher qualification on student learning, effectively we are estimating the straight line depicted in figure 4, although the true pattern is repre-sented by the curved line. Such regression estimates would yield mis-leading policy implications. For example, they might appear to justify the recruitment of teachers with more than N_1 years of schooling, although such teachers generally are not more than teachers with fewer years of schooling.

Specification of Nonlinear Relationships

Suppose our dependent variable Y is nonlinear in one of its regressors, X. In figure 5 the left panel shows two graphs corresponding to two types of nonlinear relationships: the top graph depicts a situation in which Y increases at a progressively greater rate as X increases; the bottom graph depicts a situation in which Y increases at a diminishing rate. In both sit-uations we can estimate the relationship by including a squared term in the regression equation, as follows:

$$Y = b_0 + b_1 X + b_2 X^2 + \sum_{j=3}^{n} b_j X_j$$

If X^2 has a positive coefficient it indicates increasing returns to scale, whereas a negative coefficient indicates the opposite returns. The mar-

Figure 5: Nonlinear Relationships in Regression Analysis

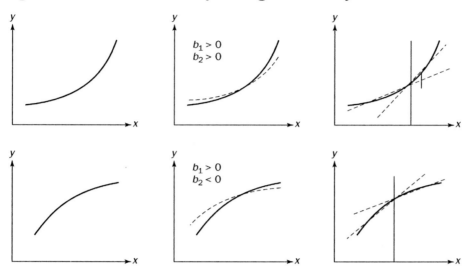

ginal impact of X on Y is expressed as $(b_1 + b_2X)$, so the impact depends on the value of X at which it is evaluated. In the middle panel of figure 5 the dotted curves depict simulations based on the regression estimates, whereas the solid curves depict the actual relationship between X and Y.

Another way to specify a nonlinear relationship is to transform X into a set of several variables, with each of them representing a segment of the curve. Thus, instead of the continuous quadratic form, we would specify a regression equation of the following form:

$$Y = c_0 + c_1 X_1 + c_2 X_2 + \sum_{j=3}^{n} c_j X_j$$

where X_1 takes on the value of X if $X < X^*$, and takes on the value of zero otherwise; and X_2 takes on the value of X if $X > X^*$, and takes on the value of zero otherwise. The specification essentially implies estimation of two lines whose intercepts and slopes differ according to the value of X (see the last panel in figure 5). The equation is no longer continuous in X, but the general pattern of diminishing or increasing returns is retained.

A third and even simpler way to specify a nonlinear relationship is to transform X into a set of dummy variables, again representing segments of the curve. Here, however, the impact of X is the same across all values of X within each segment. In figure 6, for example, there are three segments of X for which we define three dummy variables, X_1, X_2, and X_3. These variables each take on a value of one when X is in the indicated range and a value of zero otherwise. In the regression equation, one of the dummy variables, perhaps X_1, is omitted to serve as the reference

Figure 6: Specifying a Nonlinear Relationship between *X* and *Y* Using Dummy Variables

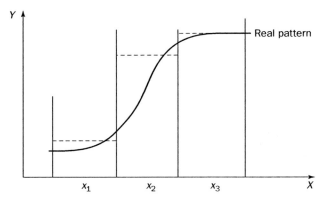

category. Under this specification, the coefficient estimate on X_2 represents the impact of an increase in X from the average in the X_1 range to the average in the X_2 range. This specification sometimes is useful in policy analysis because it allows us to match the dummy variable definitions to explicit options in policy design (for example, duration of in-service teacher training programs).

Interaction between Regressors

So far we have considered regression equations in which the left-hand-side variables are added to each other. This specification implies complete substitutability among the regressors in terms of their impact on the dependent variable. In reality, some of the regressors may be complements rather than substitutes. In the classroom, for example, chalk is a complement of the blackboard: one without the other renders either equally ineffective as an input in the education process.

In general an additive regression specification is inadequate when the impact of one regressor is sensitive to the level of another regressor. Education-based examples of interaction effects between regressors include the following:

- *Textbook availability and teacher training.* These inputs exert separate influences on student learning, but the impact of textbooks may be larger in classes taught by teachers with little or no training than in those taught by fully trained teachers.
- *Distance to school and gender.* Both of these factors influence the probability of school enrollment. However, distance often is a more powerful disincentive among girls than among boys.
- *Teaching method and student quality.* The effectiveness of a given method of teaching may depend on the initial scholastic ability of the children for which it is intended.

In all of the above examples, an additive regression model would fail to capture the possibility of interaction between the regressors. Documenting interaction effects is important because the results have implications for targeting policy interventions.

Specification of Interaction Effects

There are two ways to take account of interaction effects in regression analysis: by defining regressors whose coefficient estimates directly embody the interaction influence and by separately entering the two pertinent regressors with a new variable defined as their product.

To understand the first method, consider the example of distance to school and gender as correlates of the probability of enrolling in school. We expect that distance would lower the enrollment probabilities for all children, that the negative influence of distance would be greater for girls than for boys, and that reasons other than distance would be an added disincentive for girls to enroll. We can proceed with the regression specification as follows. First we define a dummy variable for gender, labeled "GIRL," which takes on a value of one for girls and zero for boys. Next, we define two distance variables, "DGIRL" and "DBOY." The former has a value equal to distance to school for girls and a value of zero for boys; the latter has the mirror definition, with a value equal to distance to school for boys and a value of zero for girls.

In a regression equation with all three variables as regressors (among others), their coefficient estimates have the following interpretation: the estimate on GIRL reflects the average gap in enrollment probability between boys and girls; and the estimates on DGIRL and DBOY reflect the impact of distance on the enrollment probability of girls and boys, respectively. If our hypothesis holds, we will find all three coefficients to be negative, with the coefficient on DGIRL exceeding that on DBOY in absolute terms.[4]

Regarding the second method, consider two variables, X_1 and X_2, that are perfect complements, as in the earlier chalk and blackboard example. In such cases we create a new variable, P, for inclusion on its own in the regression equation and define it as the product of X_1 and X_2. If the two factors are present, both X_1 and X_2 will equal one (assuming for simplicity of exposition that both are defined as dummy variables), and P will have a value of one. If either factor is absent, one of the two Xs will be zero, so that P also will be zero. The coefficient of P then will represent the impact of the combined presence of the two factors on the dependent variable.

Perfect complementarity or substitutability between variables is relatively rare in real life. For this reason we often use a regression specification in which the two variables concerned, X_1 and X_2, appear with P among the right-hand-side variables. The statistical significance of the three regressors reveals the nature of the interaction among them. If the coefficients on X_1 and X_2 are statistically significant but the coefficient on P is not, little interaction exists between the Xs; therefore they exert separate influences on the dependent variable. If the coefficient on P is statistically significant but the coefficients on the Xs are not, the two Xs are complete complements. Finally, if the coefficients on all three regressors are statistically significant, the Xs affect the dependent variable both separately and jointly; in other words, there are interaction effects among them.

More Sophisticated Models in Regression Analysis

Further refining the classical regression methods presented thus far sometimes is needed to address special features in the problem under analysis. Although it is beyond the scope of this appendix to explain the more sophisticated methods in detail, we elaborate below on circumstances that require their use. We focus on four situations commonly encountered in education: (a) the regression involves a qualitative (or categorical) dependent variable, or one that is truncated in its range; (b) the dependent variable reflects the culmination of a process over time; (c) there is selection bias in the sample; and (d) the sample contains nested observations with members in the subgroups sharing common experiences, as when they come from the same class or school or from the same family or village.

Qualitative or Truncated Dependent Variables

So far our discussion has assumed that the dependent variable is both continuous and restricted in range. Examples from education in which these assumptions are not met include the following:

- *Test scores.* The raw scores generally lie within a given range, which requires us to modify the linear specification. One option is to convert each score into a ratio between it and the maximum possible score. The ratio would then range between zero and one, and we would specify a regression function in which the dependent variable is restricted to this range.
- *Enrollment status.* At the level of individual observations, enrollment status is frequently a dichotomous variable: whether or not a child is enrolled, whether or not a student has passed an examination, whether or not he or she has been admitted to a certain school or a program of study, whether or not he or she must repeat the grade, and so on. In each of these cases the dependent variable has only one of two values, zero or one. (In more complicated models, the dependent

variable may be polythomous. For example, the problem may concern analysis of the probability that a student is streamed into one of four possible programs. In that case the model would involve even more complicated extensions to the classical model. A multilogit specification is one such extension.)

Common procedures for estimating the correlates of these dependent variables include the use of logistic regression functions. The general shape of such functions is represented by the curve in figure 7. The regression function would have the following form:

$$Y = \frac{1}{1 + e^{-(\alpha + \Sigma\beta_j X_j)}}$$

Logistic functions normally are estimated by maximum likelihood methods, which involve the principle of choosing coefficient estimates to maximize the sample's probability of occurrence. Computer software programs widely available now (for example, STATA, SPSS, and SAS) make the procedure relatively easy to implement.

Dependent Variables Culminating from Processes over Time

So far we have specified a single equation to represent the phenomenon under analysis, but in some situations a set of equations might be more appropriate. An example in education relates to analysis of the learning process in which a student's performance at one point in time is the product of past influences and a factor in influencing future performance.

Figure 8 illustrates this example. Suppose our goal is to analyze the correlates of streaming outcomes at time $t2$ ($STREAM_{t2}$). We model it as a function of a student's socioeconomic background (SES), the characteristics of the school he or she is attending (SCHOOL), and year-end test

Figure 7: Example of Logistic Functional Form

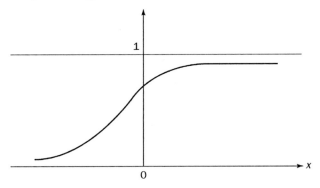

Figure 8: Example of Multiequation Regression Model

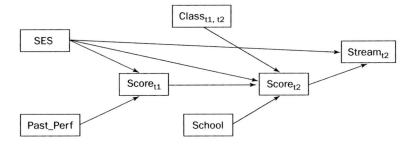

scores at time $t2$ (SCORE$_{t2}$). That third variable can be modeled as a function of SES, SCHOOL, and two other variables—test scores at time $t1$ (SCORE$_{t1}$), and the classroom environment to which the student has been exposed between $t1$ and $t2$ (CLASS$_{t1,t2}$). Finally, SCORE$_{t1}$ can be modeled as a function of SES and schooling performance prior to $t1$, (PAST_PERF). We thus can write a three-equation model as follows:

$$SCORE_{t1} = f_1 (SES, PAST\_PERF)$$

$$SCORE_{t2} = f_2 (SES, SCORE_{t1}, SCHOOL, CLASS_{t1,t2})$$

$$STREAM_{t2} = f_3 (SES, SCORE_{t2}, SCHOOL)$$

The purpose of estimating the three equations is to disentangle the direct and indirect influences of the various factors on streaming outcomes. In the example here, the model is sequential in that the events represented by the three dependent variables occur sequentially; implementing estimation procedures generally is straightforward. When the events of interest occur at the same time, simultaneous equation models (which generally are more difficult to implement) would be more appropriate.

Sample Selection Bias

To imagine the problem, suppose we are interested in analyzing the impact of education on the wages of women or on wage disparities between men and women. With straightforward application of the classical regression methods described earlier, sample selection may produce unreliable results. Unlike most adult males, not all women work outside the home. Those who do are likely to share such commonalities as a higher level of education, preference for outside work relative to household work, family circumstances (for example, single parenthood) that increase the need for outside income, and so on. The wage data therefore refer to a selected group within the female population. In this context, standard regression analysis most likely would yield biased results because it would have failed to control for the special characteristics of women who choose to work outside the home.

A similar sample selection problem occurs in education when we compare the effectiveness of public and private schools in adding value in student learning. This problem arises because the choice of school may be influenced by factors that account for differences in performance, including family background and income, and such unobserved variables as the student's personal motivation. The same sample selection problem exists when we compare academic success among students from two paraliel streams of study. Because selection into one or the other stream may depend on the factors affecting student performance within each stream, a straightforward regression analysis is likely to yield biased results.

In general, unless our interest is confined to the behavior of a particular segment of the population (for example, inhabitants of the southern region of the country only, pupils in public schools only, and so on), we need to modify the standard regression analysis in the presence of sample selection. A common technique involves estimating a two-equation (Heckman-type) model. The general idea is to establish in the first equation the correlates of the selection process, and then to use aspects from the analysis to specify the second equation in which the dependent variable is the phenomenon of interest. Software now available makes the estimation procedure relatively easy to implement.

Nested Observations

Suppose we are interested in estimating an education production function to gauge the likely impact of various policies on learning. Our task is therefore to relate outcomes observed at the level of individual pupils to policies that operate at the level of the school (such as the school-head's qualification or management practices) or the class (such as teacher qualification, class size, and so on). Typically for this purpose we would perform regression analysis using data on the performance of pupils drawn from a sufficiently wide variety of schooling environments. The data set has a nested structure in that subgroups of pupils in the sample come from the same class and school.

In such data sets we expect pupils belonging to the same class or school to share some commonality in their schooling experience, including both observed and unobserved factors. From an econometric perspective, the structure of the data implies that the error term in the regression equation will not be distributed evenly across observations in the sample. Thus it will violate the assumption of homoskedasticity in the classical regression model. With a heteroskedastic error term structure, the estimated regression coefficients are likely to be biased. Various approaches can be used to correct the problem. The technical details of these methods are demanding, but the procedures themselves—such as the Huber-White method and multilevel modeling—are relatively simple to implement using regression software packages currently available on the market.

Steps for Performing Regression Analysis in Excel

Step 1: Click on the "Tools" menu.

Step 2: Select "Add-ins..." option.

Step 3: Select "Analysis ToolPak" option. The window disappears and you are back in your spreadsheet.

Step 4: Click on "Tools" menu again.

Step 5: Click on the last item, "Data Analysis."

Step 6: You'll find a menu of data analysis options. Scroll down and choose "Regression."

Step 7: A simple menu-driven window will guide you through the regression analysis. Specify the

Y-Range [example: you must specify the range in this format: $D$10:$D$38].

X-Range [example: you must specify the range in this format: $E$10:$E$38].

[Click on] "Labels" option.

[Click on] "Confidence Intervals at 95%" option.

Output Range: [example: $A$45]

(the exact cell where you would like the *Regression Summary Output* to be displayed on your screen).

Step 8: Your analysis appears in a block beginning in the output range cell that you have specified. Notice the R^2, the coefficients of the intercept, and your chosen variable(s).

Endnotes

1. Readers may consult standard textbooks on statistics and econometrics for more detailed discussion of regression analysis; for example, E. Berndt, 1991, *The Practice of Econometrics: Classic and Contemporary* (Reading, Mass.: Addison-Wesley); A. S. Bryk, and S. W. Raudenbush, 1992, *Hierarchical Linear Models:*

Application and Data Analysis Methods (London: Sage Publications); C. Dougherty, 1992, *Introduction to Econometrics* (New York: Oxford University Press); W. Greene, 1993, *Econometric Analysis*, 2nd ed. (New York: Macmillan); W. E. Griffiths, R. C. Hill, and G. G. Judge, 1993, *Learning and Practicing Econometrics* (New York: John Wiley & Sons); P. Kennedy, 1992, *A Guide to Econometrics*, 3rd ed. (Cambridge, Mass.: MIT University Press); G. S. Maddala, 1977, *Econometrics* (New York: McGraw-Hill); and T. H. Wonnacott, and R. J. Wonnacott, 1981, *Regression: A Second Course in Statistics* (New York: John Wiley & Sons).

2. It can be shown that the variance of $\hat{b}$ can be approximated by the following expression:

$$\frac{(1 - R)^2 \bullet \text{Var}(W_j)}{\text{Var}(H_j)}$$

Thus, the larger the value of R^2, the smaller the variance of $\hat{b}$.

3. For smaller samples, the critical values of the t-statistic are different and must be looked up individually in the statistical table of the t-distribution. For a given confidence level, the critical t-statistic is that which corresponds to $n - 2$ degrees of freedom (n being the number of observations in the sample). In our height and weight example, the coefficient estimate on H has a t-statistic of 3.7, which implies that the coefficient is statistically different from zero at the 1 percent confidence level.

4. Another way to specify the interaction between distance and gender is to include in the regression equation the following regressors: GIRL, DGIRL, and DISTANCE. Define the first two variables as discussed above, and define DISTANCE as the distance from home to school for both boys and girls. The impact of distance on boys' enrollment probability would be given by the coefficient on DISTANCE, whereas that for girls would be given by the sum of the coefficients on DISTANCE and DGIRL. The coefficient on DGIRL therefore would refer to the difference in the impacts of distance on the enrollment probabilities of boys and girls. Its statistical significance tells us directly whether the adverse impact of distance to school differs between boys and girls. In the specification discussed in the text, the t-statistics for the coefficient estimates on DGIRL and DBOY tell us only whether distance affects enrollment probabilities for boys and girls; they do not test whether the coefficients are statistically different from each other.

Appendix B: Instructions for Drawing Graphs in Excel (Version 5.0)

1. Click on the **Chartwizard Tool**. The mouse pointer changes to a crosshair.
2. Place the mouse point in the cell in which you want the top-left corner of the chart to be located and drag until the rectangle is the size and shape you want the chart to be.
3. A box will prompt you to supply the following information:
   - Step 1: Select the range of worksheet cells that contain the data you want to plot, including any worksheet column or row labels that you want to appear on the chart; choose **Next**.
   - Step 2: Select a chart type; choose **Next**.
   - Step 3: Select the format of the chart type; choose **Next**.
   - Step 4: A box will prompt with the sample chart; choose **Next**.
   - Step 5: Type in the chart and axis titles; choose **Finish**.

Appendix C: Instructions for Performing Array Formulas in Excel

Arrays are calculating tools that are used to build formulas to produce multiple results or to operate on groups of values rather than on single values. An array formula acts on two or more sets of values.

Array formulas differ from single-value formulas in that they can produce more than one result from a group of operands. Because array formulas can produce multiple results, they can be used to reduce the amount of time spent on entering repetitive formulas. The easiest way to learn about array formulas is to look at an example. Suppose you want to compute the total value of your holdings in a number of different stocks. You can compute the total value in two steps by using single-value formulas as follows:

	A	B	C	D
1		Acme	Apex	Telo
2	Shares	500	300	150
3	Price	$10	$15	$50
4	Value	$5,000	$4,500	$7,500
5				
6	Total	$17,000		

1. Compute the value of each stock by entering three formulas: = B2 • B3, = C2 • C3, and = D2 • D3 in cells B4, C4, and D4, respectively. These formulas produce three single values: $5,000, $4,500, and $7,500.
2. Sum the three single values by entering the formula = sum(B4:D4) to produce the total value of $17,000.

Instead of having to enter four single-value formulas, you can compute the total value of $17,000 with one array formula, like this:

1. Select B6 as an output range.
2. Type = sum(B2:D2 • B3:D3) to compute the array of stock values and to sum these values in the array.
3. Press **Ctrl-Shift-Enter** to lock in an array formula. Excel then places a set of braces ({ }) around the formula to indicate that it is an array formula. Don't type the braces yourself; if you do, Excel interprets your entry as a label.
4. Total $17,000 will show in cell B6.

Index

Printed in the United States
26811LVS00002B/47-306